SHORT-TERM PSYCHODYNAMIC PSYCHOTHERAPY

AN ANALYSIS OF THE KEY PRINCIPLES

SHORT-TERM PSYCHODYNAMIC PSYCHOTHERAPY

AN ANALYSIS OF THE KEY PRINCIPLES

by

Penny Rawson

KARNAC

LONDON   NEW YORK

First published in 2002 by
H. Karnac (Books) Ltd.
6 Pembroke Buildings, London NW10 6RE
A subsidiary of Other Press LLC, New York

British Library Cataloguing in Publication Data

A C.I.P. for this book is available from the British Library

ISBN 1 85575 293 X

10 9 8 7 6 5 4 3 2 1

Edited, designed, and typeset by The Studio Publishing Services Ltd, Exeter

www.karnacbooks.com

TABLE OF CONTENTS

INDEX OF APPENDIX AND TABLES

INDEX OF ILLUSTRATIONS

Acknowledgements

I would like to gratefully acknowledge the help received without which this book would not have been written. I would especially like to thank Fr. Tom More for his reading and re-reading and for his encouragement and support. Thanks are also due to colleagues who have allowed their work to be analysed or offered comment, in particular B. Nolan, C. Swan, G. Dargert, A. Mann and Dr. Frances Lannon. Thanks are due to Sally Beard who tidied up and kept track of the typing side of the work and others who also contributed to the typing. There is one person who could be said to have inspired the whole initiative and who merits a special place in these acknowledgements and that is Louis Marteau.

I am very grateful to the clients who permitted their work in therapy to be used, many of whom took the time and trouble to write their own version of the experience to aid the analysis.

Some of the case work has been changed in order to protect confidentiality and some of the material excluded altogether for the same reason. All names used in the case material are fictitious and any resemblance to any individual is therefore chance.

About the author

Dr. Penny Rawson has published articles in various journals and *Short-Term Psychodynamic Psychotherapy* is her first book.

She is the Director of FASTPACE, a consultancy specialising in brief psychodynamic therapy, training and supervision. She has served on a number of national committees including the British Association of Counselling and Psychotherapy's (BACP) Accreditation and Standards and Ethics.

She has worked as a therapist for many years managing services in Higher Education, as Director of a youth counselling service and as Partner of one of the first Employee Assistance Programmes (EAP) in Britain.

To my parents and Basil

Introduction

This book concentrates on short term psychodynamic psychotherapy. It aims to discover and analyse the key principles involved. It aims to enrich the understanding of an approach to therapy that is already of benefit to many in our community but that could reach very many others if it were better known and understood. There is currently a gap in awareness and knowledge about the approach. The focal and short term psychodynamic model is not being advocated as *the* method of therapy but as *a* method of therapy. It is not the only method of brief therapy that is being practised today but it is the only approach that is to be studied here. My concern here is not for example, about Cognitive Analytical Therapy as advocated by Anthony Ryle or Solution Focused Therapy as expounded by Steve de Shazer, which are two of the better known contemporary brief therapies. It is not my intention, to be arguing the case for the efficacy of this model over and against other models of therapy, whether brief or longer term, it is simply to respond to the question: What is short term psychodynamic therapy? This is a question that I have very often been asked and in order to answer this question in a way that the model could be accepted as an authentic method of

1

practice, it needed to be more than simply the way my colleagues and I practised. It needed to be rooted within a tradition and be seen to link with the work of other professionals acknowledged as experts in the field. It needed to be examined in sufficient detail to reveal its constituent parts. I decided to undertake such an examination using my own casework and that of colleagues as the starting point.

I began with the following questions. Were there common elements to be found in each case? Were these principles thought to be important by earlier exponents of the method? Who were the earlier exponents? In order to discover this and to be able to locate the approach within the appropriate professional context, I searched the literature for key proponents of this brief approach. When I began this research there were few substantive works on brief therapy. However others, too, have clearly thought this area of knowledge deserved greater recognition and a number of new volumes have been published during the time span of this study, each addressing different aspects of the brief therapy work. A Dictionary of Counselling by Feltham and Dryden published three years after my research for the book began also has a definition of brief therapy. (1993, p. 22). However, I am not beginning the book with such a definition, since I want the reader to join me in the journey of discovery.

Narrowing the focus of the book

The main task was to tease out in detail what is meant by short term psychodynamic therapy as revealed through the selected cases, the key proponents and the literature. Clearly as Lincoln observes "texts are always partial and incomplete" and I acknowledge this freely (1995, p. 280). This text is limited and aims to examine in detail only one area of therapy within the wider therapeutic community and within brief approaches: The focus of this book is: What is short term psychodynamic therapy? In the process of this discovery it is hoped that shortening factors are to be highlighted. The intention is to remain concentrated on this task and to include other material only in so far as it contributes to the primary focus.

The aim:

In deriving and analysing the key principles involved and providing an accessible exposition of the model I hope that more counsellors and therapists will:

a) become aware of the existence of focal and short term psychodynamic psychotherapy;
b) become aware of its salient features;
c) be encouraged to explore its use within their own practices.

I also hope that, as therapists become more aware of its existence, potential clients in the community will:

a) be able to have more choice in their selection of counselling/therapy approaches;
b) be helped out of their pain, and to a greater freedom, more quickly.

I believe that this book will fill a gap presently existing in the field. It is not so much a discovery or a rediscovery but in parallel with the approach of the psychodynamic therapist, a looking at the present, in the form of my cases and the current literature; at the past in terms of the literature, the developments and the approach; and the future in the shape of a clear exposition of the key principles involved.

.Since I am both the author and the investigator who is examining and commenting upon the casework, much of which is from my own client group, I think that it is important to give the reader some idea of my own stance and position. Therefore Chapter 1 includes a personal and contextual perspective as to my professional background in the field and expands upon how I came to write this book.

CHAPTER ONE

Why this book? A personal and contextual perspective

What is focal and short term psychotherapy? This is a question that I am frequently asked by professional counsellors, therapists and lay people and this is what inspired me to write this book.

I am asked the question because it is an approach that I practise and believe in. It is an approach that I teach and write about and have appeared on TV to talk about in Carlton TV's programme "What Therapy"—November 1990 and again in March 1995.

"So, what is it?" I know that the approach I have come to practise is called focal and short-term psychotherapy—but how to explain it to other professionals. How do they not know of its existence? Very many people are practising a brief approach—but often due to external pressures. These are often caused by economic factors. GPs may restrict their counsellors to six sessions per client, and colleges and employee assistance schemes often restrict therapists to six or eight sessions or less. The Tavistock Clinic has an Adolescent Unit where sessions are restricted to four. All of these do so for economic reasons, i.e. scarcity of counsellors/therapists in relation to the client demand.

Many counsellors/psychotherapists working in such situations, who practise a brief approach by compulsion, believe that they are doing a disservice to their clients. I reflect on a conference on brief therapy I attended in November 1988, where some 40 counsellors/ therapists attended and only my colleague and myself appeared to have prior knowledge of the method and to be practising it *by choice* rather than by constraint.

At a recent training course I ran for counsellors in GP practices I encountered a sense of guilt in the participants who believed that clients were being given "short shrift" by the brief approach. There was also a general ignorance as to the historical place of focal therapy in the development of psychotherapy or its inherent features. Many were practising elements of the approach unknowingly and reluctantly and thereby were, potentially, also undermining its efficacy. The fact that the FHSA (Family Health Service Association) funded the course I ran recently no doubt reflects an economic factor—and a hope that more clients would be helped to move on quickly and therefore more cheaply.

The feedback at the end of the course included the following comments.

"The course gave short-term work much more validity and helped me to focus much more on it specifically".

"Helpful towards working more flexibly".

"Especially helpful in helping me to shift with the focus in six sessions".

"Made me think hard about short-term work as a treatment of choice".

A treatment of choice

I wish to stress that my choice of and interest in this method is a choice—it is not due to economic or social constraints. I choose the approach since I believe that very many people can be helped to resolve the issues that are causing them pain or difficulty in a shorter time, when facilitated by a therapist skilled in the focal and short-term approach. I see it as a treatment of choice, as shown in the following extract from an article (Rawson, 1992) wrote to refute John Rowan's statement about short changing clients.

WHY THIS BOOK?   7

"FOCAL AND SHORT-TERM THERAPY—A TREATMENT OF CHOICE"

I read, with interest, Stephen Palmer's interview of Professor Windy Dryden with reference to brief short-term psychotherapy (February 1992). Professor Dryden quotes John Rowan as saying:

> "We are short-changing individuals who come for counselling if we don't encourage them to see that counselling is an opportunity for them to reflect on themselves in the context of their entire life. We can't do that," says John, "if we are only offering brief psychotherapy."

I would like to ask who's short-changing whom?

I believe the principles of brief and focal psychotherapy make it clear that we are not short-changing clients by offering them this type of counselling/therapy. Brief and focal therapy is a treatment of choice—not simply a method to use because financial or resource restraints so dictate as Professor Dryden implies.

I have been spurred to write this in the hope that many potential clients may benefit as more counsellors become aware of the value of the focal and brief approach.

In my experience a large number of individuals approach counselling/therapy with the assumption, encouraged by popular opinion and their therapist that their problem will take a very long time to resolve. This may be the case if, for example, their presenting "depression" has been with them for several years. Some will have been receiving medication for many years and will anyway be sceptical as to whether a counsellor can help. It is my contention and experience that very many people can be helped significantly in less than 10 sessions. Many in as few as 2–6. By significantly, I mean reach a point:

1. Where they understand the roots of their depression often from a traumatic experience in childhood;
2. Where they have discharged the emotions relating to that; and
3. Are in a position to say: "I feel I can cope with my life now—I'll know how to deal with similar events if they occur."

I believe the majority of people approach counselling/therapy because they are "unhappy". There is usually something they wish to change and they hope to feel better. Many more people would approach counselling/therapy if they had confidence that they could be helped in a few (2–10) sessions. These they could afford—

whereas the idea of ongoing therapy for six months or years may prevent them even considering therapy. Many more could be helped in this way if they were aware of the focal and short-term method." (1992, p. 106).

My professional background

I learned the brief approach at the Dympna Centre under the tutelage of Louis Marteau. The Centre specialized in therapy for members of religious orders and clergy. The therapists, who trained and worked there, were truly ecumenical and came from all branches of the Judeo–Christian tradition.

The training approach was one of applied practice under intense supervision, with videoed role plays and intensive teaching. I attended these 2½-hour sessions weekly from 1975–1984.

In parallel with my experience at the Dympna Centre, I undertook full-time training at the Westminster Pastoral Centre (WPF) in Westminster and then Kensington. There the long-term analytic approach was advocated within a Jungian framework.

The Dympna Centre model was an eight-session focused model with the option for further eight-session contracts if required. Louis Marteau would describe the approach taught as "psychodynamic using the newer therapies".

It was this process of parallel training, in long- (WPF) and short-term (Dympna Centre), that aroused my curiosity about the more brief method. The clients I saw in both settings seemed similar, in one setting they completed seemingly successfully in eight sessions, in the other 1 year or more was not unusual. Indeed, as part of the training we were required to see clients for 40 sessions at least or we were not permitted to go on to the next stage of training. Is this an ethical requirement? I now feel in a stronger position to quote the BAC Code of Ethics to refute such a requirement. Surely this puts the needs of the student or therapist before the needs of the client? Equally, in looking at the brief approach and whilst I wholly support the brief method, I do so within the framework of what the client needs. I therefore staunchly support the concept of flexibility with regard to the length of counselling contracts. This is to be judged in relation to client need.

The Dympna training was more in the style of an apprenticeship than a formal academic course. I learned there the foundations of my practice in therapy, although I gained no paper qualifications from the Dympna Centre. There I learned something more valuable—a very special quality of "care" and respect for the individual that underpinned the whole philosophy of the Centre. I gained the necessary pieces of paper and valuable breadth to my training at the Richmond Fellowship and the Westminster Pastoral Foundation.

Economic factors

I earlier referred to pressure for brevity in the interest of economy. Other aspects of the economics of brief therapy is the effect on the therapist and on the client.

For therapists working in private practice the constant turnover of clients may seem daunting. To acquire an ongoing case load of several clients over months or years is a more secure source of income than seeing many people for a few sessions. I believe all therapists must keep the focus of client need to the fore in making judgments about the duration of therapy. In this way they can be sure of an ethical approach.

Since there is such widespread ignorance about the method of short-term focal therapy despite its history going back to Freud and being progressively developed by his later colleagues, could the economic angle be significant here? One aspect of focal therapy's history is the aspect of rediscovery. Could it be that it is convenient to lose it from an economic viewpoint?

I believe it is not insignificant that Louis Marteau at the Dympna Centre is a priest and therefore not primarily earning a living from his work in establishing and directing the Dympna Centre. Could this have freed him to be open to the brief approach? A sentiment that rings in my ears from the years of training there is helping the client through and out of their pain as quickly as possible! This reflects a different sort of economy.

My own view is that, in fact, the brief therapist's clients would not be in short supply if they but knew about this method. From the client's perspective, the fewer sessions required to move them on is surely economically a good option. If a therapist can offer help to the required end in a limited number of sessions, many clients would choose this over and against a more open-ended contract. A brief contract can be budgeted for and managed. The ongoing open-ended one may mean some clients never start because they simply cannot afford it.

I am not alone in making such observations with regard to the economics. Wolberg (1965) makes the challenge strongly.

Early on in my career I decided that I would never wish to earn my living solely by private practice. I would always prefer to finance this practice from other sources, so that such economic factors would not be allowed to intrude on any client decisions. In practice I have been fortunate in being mostly in paid employment where I have been paid regardless of client numbers. I believe this may have been significant in freeing me to develop the brief approach in my work.

A refinement of the methods

I referred earlier to the eight-session model I was taught at the Dympna Centre. Over the 12 years I was practising full-time as a Senior College Counsellor at Thames Valley University (formerly Ealing College of Higher Education) I became much more flexible in my approach and counselling/therapy contracts became on average much more brief, often being one or two sessions and the mean being around four to six.

Over the years I have also become more flexible in the application of skills and techniques borrowed from traditions other than the psychodynamic in which my earlier training was rooted. I believe that I now have an integrated approach to client work fusing many different strands together. Whilst I believe this to be helpful to the client, it is less easy to unravel in order to clarify what the key principles are.

Assumptions

Before moving on to set the parameters of the study and to define terms which begins the work of the exploration and takes place in the next chapter, I have outlined below some of the assumptions which I bring to the work and which colour the practice from which the case studies are drawn.

An assumption that is made in this therapy practice is that most human beings can develop and function well in all areas of their lives without requiring a therapeutic intervention to achieve this. It is only when this normal development becomes blocked that the therapist is required. For example, bereavement is something that most people have to cope with in the course of their lives. The majority are able to come to terms with their loss without having recourse to a therapist. If however the grieving process is more than normally debilitating, or is still in process several years after the loss, then it would indicate that there is a need for professional help.

This basic assumption that people can "cope alone" enables the short-term and focal therapist to "focus" on the issue that needs to be addressed with the client and then to allow the client to "cope alone". The expectation is that there is a problem to be tackled, dealt with and the therapeutic alliance ended at that point. The intention is that the therapist will help the client towards a new under-standing and to change. The client then is expected to continue the development subsequent to change in his/her life. The changed behaviour will produce changed consequences which in themselves will reinforce the new insights and behaviour. This does not necessarily require a therapist's intervention or support. This assumption does not intend to imply a superficial or present-day problem oriented approach. It assumes a psychodynamic approach which is referred to in the next chapter under definitions.

Another assumption made in the therapist's practice is that people are mind, body and spirit. Therefore every aspect of the individual's response to life and its stresses are considered important. This includes spiritual aspirations and beliefs.

The client has to be able to form a relationship, at least with the therapist for any success to occur in the therapy. If no rapport can be established no therapeutic alliance can take place and this would be a counter indicator for this type of therapy.

In focal therapy client motivation is a crucial and critical factor. This needs to be established in the initial or intake session. There is often resistance to therapy since change is usually a painful process. This does not necessarily mean that the client is not motivated to change. What needs to be established is that the client is there from choice—not because anyone has compelled them to make an appointment.

The client needs also to be clear as to what the process of therapy is. So clarification of the assumptions of the client should be explored. In this way misconceptions can be corrected and the client is then free to commit themselves to a clear therapy contract. This process is to further ensure client motivation.

Outline of the book

In order to provide the reader with a sense of what follows, I have provided below an outline of each chapter.

Chapter 1 introduces the book. It outlines my own development in the field and current professional status that enables me to speak with some authority in the area. It explains how I came to be interested in the method of Focal and Short-term Therapy and points to the gap in knowledge about short-term therapy: that is about what it is and that it can be a treatment of choice. It summarizes my aim to contribute to the body of knowledge available to help fill the existing gap about short-term psychodynamic psychotherapy. This book is written with the professional therapist in mind although it may also interest the layperson.

Chapter 2 defines the parameters and terminology to be used in the book. Both my casework and the analysis are therefore to be seen as working within these.

Chapter 3 explains how I am going about the study and how the approach that I am adopting is rooted in and developed from recognized approaches to research in this relatively new professional field of counselling. It outlines the several cycles of analysis undertaken.

Chapter 4 gives a summary of the initial findings in terms of the literature search and themes from my cases, colleagues' cases, colleagues' comments and the literature. These themes form the basis for the subsequent in-depth analysis (see Chapter 5). Within the reviews a clear line of development evolved and has been included as part of Chapter 4 since it may be of interest to the reader to be able to locate the subject of short-term therapy in context.

Chapter 5, Part I presents the findings from the in depth analysis of the selected themes. Each theme is examined separately forming sub-sections of Chapter 5, i.e. 5 (i)–(vii).

Chapter 5, Part II summarizes the findings from the in-depth analysis and draws preliminary conclusions.

Chapter 6 provides some client comments on their experience of the therapy process in relation to three of the research cases. It also provides a complete case which demonstrates aspects of the brief approach.

Chapter 7 locates the conclusions of my analysis within the wider context of the latest thinking in the field.

Chapter 8 examines my conclusions in relation to a number of statements from the literature of, so called, "universal elements" in brief therapy.

Chapter 9 presents the key principles of brief psychodynamic psychotherapy succinctly within the conceptual framework. It outlines the reflections leading to the final conjecture as to what it is about the key principles that contributes to the shortening process.

Having explained how I came to embark on this book, declared my own stance on the subject and outlined the subject matter, the next chapter sets the parameters for the study.

CHAPTER TWO

Setting the parameters

Terminology and definitions

B efore I move onto the expansion of my chosen methodology for the study, it seems appropriate to clarify some of the terminology with definitions. This is as important for the knowledgeable practitioner as it is for the lay person. The field of psychotherapy is not an exact science where there are clear definitions agreed as a basis for development of argument.

I am therefore declaring the definitions, which will set the parameters for my arguments. Firstly, I am making no distinction here between the terms "psychotherapy" and "counselling". I therefore use the words counselling/therapy/psychotherapy interchangeably. In terms of counselling, I refer to psychodynamic counselling that is, according to Feltham and Dryden, a method of counselling that draws on the psychoanalytic tradition and expects to employ "concepts of the unconscious" such as "resistance and transference" and uses techniques such as "free association" dreams and "interpretation" (1993, p. 147).

What is psychotherapy?

The definition I have selected for psychotherapy, is consistent with my own understanding of therapy. The following extract written by Louis Marteau in Campbell's "A Dictionary of Pastoral Care" will give the reader clarity as to how I intend to use the term:

Psychotherapy

A psychological method of treatment which aims at bringing about changes in the patient through direct, mainly verbal communications.

Psychotherapy has as its basis a psycho-dynamic approach to the situation, in that the individual's past life, especially childhood, is seen to have an emotional influence on present adult relationships. This influence may arise from emotional traumas which were experienced in childhood and remain not only unresolved, but have also been banished from memory (1987, p. 228).

The definition goes on to refer to three aspects inherent in psychotherapy, these are *insight, emotional discharge* and *behaviour modification*. That is insight into the cause of the present problem, *emotional discharge* of feelings related to this past painful event and a *change in behaviour* from acquired adaptive patterns in the present in order to move on more freely. The reader may have noted that these points are inherent in my own understanding of the process of therapy as expressed earlier in the extract from the article—Short-term Therapy—a Treatment of Choice.

How many sessions in short-term psychotherapy?

What is understood by short-term in the context of focal and short-term therapy? This is one of the areas of exploration and analysis in this book and firmer conclusions will be made in the context of the discussion subsequent to the analysis. However, to give the reader some idea as to the starting point I will outline the existing broad spectrum that is referred to in the context of brief therapy. Short-term in the literature can be any number of sessions from one to perhaps 40–50.

What does strategic mean?

What is understood by the term "strategic" in relation to the psychotherapy under discussion?

The term strategic which will be examined in the context of the focus in Chapter 5 is to be understood as follows: "strategy designed to disorganize the enemy's internal economy" (1964, p. 1273). Although this definition is more usual in a military setting and focal therapists in no way see the client as the enemy, it is true to say that the malfunctioning internal economy is the focus of sessions. The aim is to facilitate change by dealing satisfactorily with the strategic focal issue that is holding up development.

Nomenclature of short-term therapy

The literature reveals a number of different titles for brief psychodynamic therapy. It is not always clear whether it is the form or the name of the approach that is different. In the selected reviews we find references to many titles and to some leading figures who work within these terms.

Often a number of therapists work within the compass of several titles of brief therapy. Rogawski (1982) refers to Gillman, McGuire, Natterson and Grotjohn in the sixties and Balint, Morrill and Cary, Malan and Davanloo in the seventies who all work within the terms *Intensive Brief Therapy* and *Short-Term Dynamic Psychotherapy*. The former term is one that Bauer and Kobos (1984) tend to associate with Malan. Migone (1985) observes that Malan, by the 1980s, follows and supports Davanloo's approach under the latter title. Rogawski (1982) also refers to *Short-Term Anxiety Provoking Psychotherapy* which is the name Sifneos gives to his approach. Bauer and Kobos (1984) associate Alexander and French with this term too. *Focal Therapy* is another title, this one coined by Balint according to Migone (1985). Budman and Stone (1983) add two more titles to the list *Brief Dynamic Psychotherapy* and *Time Limited Psychotherapy*. They cite several therapists who worked within the latter two terms in the early 1980s:- Strupp and Binder, Lazarus and Leibovich. Further titles appear by the mid 1980s to the time of writing in the 1990s. Luborski (1991) for example talks of *Short-term support expressive psychoanalytic psychotherapy* J. Pollack, Flegenheimer and A. Winston (1985) refer to *Brief Adaptive Psychotherapy*. Budman and Gurman (1988) use the term *Interpersonal Developmental Existential in their model of Brief Time Sensitive Therapy*. I refer to *Focal and Short-Term Psychotherapy and Client Education*, Rawson

(1990) and one of the latest names to be introduced is M. Alpert's (1992) *Accelerated Empathy*.

To summarize then, the approach as seen from the literature is referred to under the following names:

Intensive brief psychotherapy: IBP
Individual dynamic psychotherapy: IDP
Short-term dynamic psychotherapy: STDP
Short-term psychodynamic psychotherapy: STPP
Short-term anxiety provoking psychotherapy: STAPP
Brief dynamic therapy: BDT
Time limited dynamic psychotherapy: TLDP
Focal psychotherapy: FP
Strategic psychotherapy: SP
Short-term support expressive psychoanalytic psychotherapy: SE
Interpersonal developmental existential: IDE
Brief time sensitive therapy: BTST
Brief adaptive psychotherapy: BAP
Focal and short-term psychotherapy and client education: FASTPACE
Accelerated empathy: AE

In this book I will use the terms short-term or brief therapy as generic terms. This will apply unless the subject under discussion requires a more specific reference to a particular title. Having set the parameters, the next chapter spells out how I went about discovering the key elements in brief therapy in a systematic way.

CHAPTER THREE

Theoretical framework and methodology

I f my conclusions in this book are to carry real weight in the therapeutic community then they must be seen to evolve from a rigorous study that can withstand academic scrutiny. This chapter therefore is primarily aimed at those who wish to reassure themselves in this way. It outlines the methodology and theoretical framework used to direct the analysis of the literature and selected case studies. It sets the scene for the cycles of analysis that follow and which systematically build up a picture of what makes short term therapy short. I hope that the reader who prefers to get straight to the discoveries will feel free to move swiftly to the next chapter, but for those who want to know how I came to these particular cycles of analysis I continue here.

In this study I seek to derive and analyse the key principles in short-term psychodynamic therapy as it emerges from the selected case work and the literature. To achieve this, a pluralistic approach, within a qualitative framework, has been adopted.

In thinking about my approach, I was interested in the concept of parallel process in relation to the projected exploration and to therapy. In my practice (where the approach is psychodynamic using the newer therapies) I look, with the client, at the present as the starting point, the past and how it influences the present and where this new insight and clarity may lead to for the future. I approach the client with an open mind, although I bring my knowledge and experience the prime objective is to be "with" the client. As Jung writes:

> I must confess that I have so often been deceived in this matter that in any concrete case I am at pains to avoid all theoretical presuppositions about the structure of the neurosis and about what the patient can and ought to do. As far as possible I let pure experience decide the therapeutic aims. This may perhaps seem strange, because it is commonly supposed that the therapist has an aim. But in psychotherapy it seems to me positively advisable for the doctor not to have too fixed an aim. He can hardly know better than the nature and will to live of the patient (1993, p. 40).

It is this openness that I wished to reflect in this study. It is my intention to analyse selected cases from my casework practice with the same approach that I might apply within the therapy itself. That is, although I bring my subjective experience, my attempt is to remain an objective/subjective participant, I seek patterns, themes and inconsistencies to begin to make sense of and give new meaning to the situation presented. Thus in approaching the analysis of cases in the first instance I wished to avoid all theoretical preoccupations. Clearly I could not ignore my previous knowledge but by immersing myself in the case material I aimed to arrive at key issues derived from and grounded in the material. McLeod, a leading figure in the relatively new subject area of counselling research methodology, refers to this process of immersion in the data as "inductive analysis". He suggests that the researcher should "bracket off" his or her assumptions about the phenomena being studied (1994, p. 72). At the same time he highlights the concept of reflexivity: "the idea that the researcher is his or her primary instrument and as a result must be aware of the fantasies, expectations and needs that his or her participation introduces into the research process" (1994, p. 78).

I planned to undertake the literature search only *after* I had largely completed the cases that were to be used for the analysis. I did this in order to be as little influenced by early writers as possible at this stage of collecting my data and at the first cycle of analysis.

This idea of *not* reviewing the literature before undertaking the study is inherent in the grounded theory approach. It is hoped that in an effective analysis new categories will emerge. In approaching the analysis and looking for ways to categorize and make connections between the categories emerging from the data, grounded theory seemed relevant. However, it did not sufficiently provide for the inclusion of the subjective awareness that I wanted to acknowledge in that much of the case work is my own. I needed to move beyond this. Dey refers to the "restrictive confines of grounded theory" (1993, p. 7). He sees qualitative analysis as a circular process as follows in his Fig 3.1: (1993, p. 31).

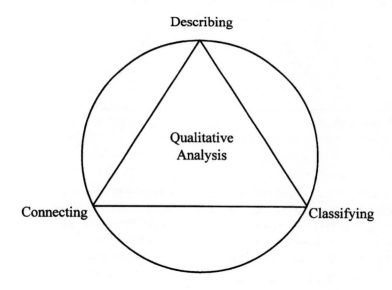

Fig. 3.1.

New paradigm research

I refer to this first stage of the analysis as naïve enquiry and in the subjective/objective approach I am supported by the new paradigm research advocated by Rowan and Reason:

"new paradigm research is an approach to enquiry which *is* a systematic, rigorous search for truth, but which does not kill off all it touches: we are looking for a way of inquiry which can be loosely called *objectively subjective* [See Figure 1 reprinted from Rowan and Reason (1981, p. xiii)]. The new paradigm is a synthesis of naïve enquiry and orthodox research." (1981, p. xiii)

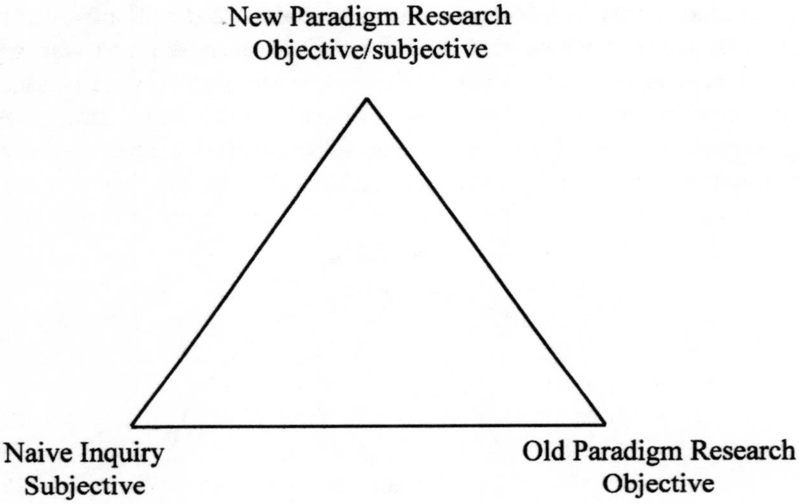

.New Paradigm Research
Objective/subjective

Naive Inquiry   Old Paradigm Research
Subjective   Objective

Fig. 1.

One of my objectives was to undertake a study in the form of naturalistic enquiry, that is studying "real-world" phenomena in as unobtrusive a manner as possible with a sense of openness regarding whatever emerges. Other "aliases for the term naturalistic" have been identified by Wolcott as: "post positivistic, ethnographic, phenomenological, subjective, case study, qualitative, hermeneutic, humanistic" (1990, p. 10).

Case studies and prototypes—seeking a conceptual model

It was with this concept of unobtrusiveness in mind that I decided to use my own casework as data.

The concept of using cases as a foundation for study is examined by Bromley who sees the case study approach as quasi judicial. Bromley points out that "case law provides rules, generalizations and categories which gradually systematize the knowledge (facts and theories) gained from intensive study of individual cases" (1986, p. 2). I intended to make just such an intensive study of several individual cases and from these to derive rules and categories. Bromley observes that "natural history and common law" support the view that "systematisation, classification and general rules can be developed without the aid of statistics" (1986, p. 275). The approach adopted here is qualitative and cases are studied "in the context of a developing framework of ideas" and Bromley's "models" or "prototypes" developed (1986, p. 277). His prototypical case emerges as individual cases are compared and contrasted within a category. McLeod observes that each case may be regarded as "exemplars of what is possible" and this uniqueness must be borne in mind also (1994, p. 116).

Bromley insists that "case studies are not an inferior sort of scientific method. On the contrary they are possibly *the* basic method of science" (1986, p. 289). It is to be "seen as a strong form of hypothetico–deductive theorizing, not as a weak form of statistical inference. We do not infer things 'from' a case-study, we impose a construction, a pattern of meaning 'onto' the case" (1986, p. 290). However, I prefer to see a pattern of meaning derived from and grounded in the evidence presented by the data rather than imposed upon it. Bromley states: "The business of identifying the key features of cases and of developing a robust system for classifying (grouping) cases gives rise to "case law" (1986, p. 281). "A case study is heuristic"—it leads to "the development of a new theory" (1986, p. 289). The idea of replication assumes that the same results will be found within each case, which are seen as single experiments. The analysis therefore is "cross-experiment" in its design and logic. This is in line with Yin's view also. He argues that "where several cases are examined each one is to be regarded as a separate experiment". He considers *"multiple cases as one would consider multiple experiments*, that is, to follow a 'replication' logic. ... Thus, if one has access only to three cases ... If similar results are obtained from all three cases, replication is said to have taken place" (1994, p. 45).

In this study it is the themes that have emerged which have merited detailed examination and the examples from casework and the literature used to achieve this. The notes therefore as Yin suggests remain substantially as "notes". Yin actively discourages the rewriting of case notes since such "effort should be directed at the case study report itself, not at the notes" (1994, p. 96).

Yin sees case studies as the preferred strategy "when the focus is on a contemporary phenomenon within some real-life context" (1994, p. 1). He suggests that a "pluralistic" strategy is appropriate for "exploratory, descriptive or explanatory" case studies (1994, p. 3). As McLeod observes "it is extremely difficult to construct a theory that will allow the interactions between the phenomena to be understood" (1994, p. 150). He charts a number of methods of researching process variables using for example, accurate empathy scale, working alliance inventory, client and therapist vocal quality, the Vanderbilt psychology process scale but also observes a "lack of emphasis on the development of relevant theory" (1994, p. 150). As the reader will observe this pluralistic strategy has proved important in this study of therapy.

New paradigm research and the inclusion of subjectivity

The grounded theory approach, although thoroughly qualitative, arguably falls on the side of the "old paradigm" at the objective level—the new paradigm offers the inclusion of a greater degree of the reflexive aspect. Mitroff argues that it allows for the "exercise of expert judgement in the face of incomplete evidence" and that "the presence of bias forces the scientist to acknowledge the operation of bias and attempt to control for it" (1981, p. 38). The personal perspective that I have given in the first chapter "comes clean" about my professional stance as Lincoln describes the process and hence my bias which the process of triangulation already referred to attempts to control (1995, p. 280). The client commentaries also act to control the bias and gives the opportunity for differing perceptions of the same shared experience. With regard to Mitroff's concept of expert opinion the personal perspective in Chapter 1 also gives some indication of my credentials in this field.

Thus I approached the study on my own casework as the starting point, planning to use a phenomenological approach and in accord with Rowan using "subjective and first-person experience as a source of knowledge" (1981, p. 87).

A relational research—ethical issues

Having decided to use my own case work as data and being aware that the subsequent cases would be potential material for the study, I endeavoured not to let this intrude upon the therapeutic process. Nonetheless I am aware that there was still an impact. From the date of beginning the study my notes of cases that were typical, unusual or theoretically interesting and potential candidates for the analysis were written up with greater care. I saw any intrusion of research interest as a disservice to the client—my primary task was to *be there* for them with all my attention. Thus I consciously endeavoured to exclude the therapist/observer from the sessions. The success of this is at times apparent in the scantiness of some of the case notes. At times when I was most immersed in the casework I was not able to retrospectively note down the full scale of the client/therapist interaction. This I see as inevitable where the relationship forms part of the process and I will return to this dilemma later. This aforementioned difficulty may have lessened the quality of data for research purposes, but is necessary as an ethical approach in that the client remains the focus of the therapeutic work. This points to a conflict between research and clinical needs and as Lincoln suggests this conflict "between rigor in relation to the data and ethics ... signals that the new research is a relational research—a research grounded in the recognition and valuing connectedness between the researcher and the researched, and between knowledge elites and the societies and communities in which they live and labour" (1995, p. 286).

Casework research and triangulation

As I progressed both with the cases selected and with the study of methodological approaches to counselling research I realized the need to check the accuracy of the data collected. To this end, at the conclusion of the therapy, when I requested permission to use our therapy work for research purposes I also requested any thoughts/ comments that the client would like to give. With the first cases selected this had not been automatic. With case B, for example, I had shown and discussed the write up with her, but had no written or verbal recording of her comments other than that incorporated in the write up. With the later cases there is a client commentary. In case J, one of the earlier cases, we interpreted her poem as a concluding comment on the outcome of our work together. The gathering of data by different routes is known as the practice of triangulation and so asking the client for their version or commentary serves the purpose of validation.

Another aspect of triangulation was to obtain an external view as to the key categories emerging from the cases. To this end I asked two past colleagues as external observers to examine one particular case to see what key issues they discovered.

The analysis of two other colleagues' cases was a further stage in strengthening the validity of the findings.

The process of the research took on a cyclical aspect and finally involved several cycles, each one being seen to strengthen the validation process (see the end of the chapter).

In search of detailed understanding

Rowan and Reason highlight another aspect of the cyclical approach required of new paradigm research. They refer to the "encounter" and "making sense" moments of the research cycle. Their Table 10.4 (see below) summarizes the approach that is compatible with my way of analysing the case analysis and that of the literature. They suggest that an ability to "unfocus" is required "to allow a kind of communion to emerge ... The whole trick is to suspend thinking and to stay aware of your experience in the ever flowing present" (1981, p. 122).

Table 10.4 (1981, p. 122).

FROM	TO	REFERENCE
Focused attention	Free floating attention	Freud (1925)
Ordinary listening	Listening with the 3rd ear	Reik (1948)
Clear cut contrasts	Intuitive sensing	Rogers (1968)
Scatteredness	Mindfulness	Schuster (1979)
Mystery-mastery	Consciousness	Torbert (1972)
Avoidance	Awareness	Enwright (1970)

Reason and Rowan see existentialism "as an appropriate mode of enquiry" and they draw on Hainer (1968): "Existentialism begins with experience, phenomena and existence as these are perceived. Concepts arise out of the uniquely human process of perceiving, pattern (Gestalt) forming, of symbolising, of comparing and of conceptualising, which are not explicitly conscious" (1981, p. 126).

This approach of knowing from the inside and of attempting to systematically make the implicit explicit can be termed hermeneutic. It is imperative in this process not to impose a theory onto the phenomenon, but rather to allow meaning to be derived from the phenomenon.

The classification is a conceptual process which attempts to group basic themes. However the intention of the discovery process is geared more to a "detailed understanding" rather than abstract classification. Greenberg states: "We need measures that differentiate clinically relevant features that distinguish change in specified contexts" (1994, p. 125). In this study the context is focal and short-term psychotherapy. Greenberg continues "We need to observe these phenomena and develop coding schemes that will describe and define different features of the phenomena. It is only through the description and study of what is ... agreed on as actually occurring in therapy that we will advance our understanding of how change takes place" (1994, p. 125).

In this approach I align myself with the "fourth generation" researchers referred to by Orlinsky and Russell, where getting "back to the phenomena" and "revelling" in pluralism is seen to be an activity that is quintessentially scientific (1994, p. 204).

In this regard too, Greenberg exhorts us to regain the curiosity of wonder in psychotherapy "rather than deaden it within a restricting methodological straight jacket" (1994, p. 114).

McCall calls for a "truly phenomenological approach, one that construes experience in the hermeneutic manner, allowing reality as given to speak for itself, and that searches always in direct experience for the deeper meaning and the inter-relationships which are characteristic of the things themselves. The hermeneutic method follows closely Husserl's injunction to go back to the things themselves ("*Zu den Sachen Selbst*") and Heidegger's warning to "let Being be" (*Seingelassenheit*) not forcing it into any pre-fabricated paradigms, but allowing it to speak for itself. Hermeneutics is a method of *uncovering* (*unverborgen*), of remaining *with* the experience until it reveals its hidden inner truth (*aletheia*)" (1983, p. 113).

In analysing the data I planned to see what key issues emerged from the data. As Marshall states for her content analysis she does not so much look for "a word, a sentence, or a section ... the units are really fairly obvious you get chunks of meaning which come out of the data itself" (1981, p. 397). She goes on to say that she lets "the categories build up all the time as I put things together that go together". This is part of the immersion process and Marshall stresses the importance of the fact that it is "*my* translation, what I have found and interpreted from the data" (1981, p. 399).

Calloway observes that the approach is perhaps to be perceived as a more feminine approach to scientific enquiry. She suggests that it resides somewhat uncomfortably within the: "academic framework of our disciplines, the categories of our research, the distinctions and nuances even, have evolved within a male tradition of language and intellectual style" (1981, p. 471).

McLeod tells us that "there is no one right way to do counselling research" (1994, p. vii). He defines research as: "*a systematic process of critical inquiry leading to valid propositions and conclusions that are communicated to interested others*" (1994, p. 4). McLeod points out that "Readers of counselling research need to bear in mind that different studies may be expressed in quite different languages and voices" (1994, p. 9).

Narrowing the focus

In approaching the study I was determined to adopt a focused approach. Whilst the first consideration is to discover what constitutes short-term focal therapy, the second aspect is to discover what makes it short. What is it about the key components that is of significance? In this examination I will take for granted such basics as the widely accepted "core conditions" of Carl Rogers introduced in the 1950s in bringing about positive personality change in clients. My concern is to remain focused on the above questions.

In this analysis the microscope is on one particular branch of brief psychotherapy—that of focal and short-term psychodynamic psychotherapy. The intention here being to "*do less, more thoroughly*" as Wolcott describes the process (1990, p. 62).

Fieldwork

The content of the client group and an aspect of bias

This study is based on reflections from a therapy practice with a particular client group. This group is a college student group. The age range of the client group varies between 18 and 60 years. The group therefore has reached a recognizable higher education level. As a student group they are familiar with analysing and examining concepts in detail. They are used to verbalizing concepts. It can be assumed that they are basically functional—that is are able to see to their daily needs and in general are capable of attending class and to some degree, at least, are able to relate to their fellow students.

Casework used in this study

My own casework forms the major focus in this study. A factor to consider was the time scale for this study. I allocated a year for a substantial number of the cases to be completed. As soon as I decided to embark on this I began to record all my casework that offered potential for analysis with greater clarity than I would have been accustomed to do just for my practice notes. I wanted to make the process as naturalistic as possible and decided to request the client's permission only after we had completed our work together. I chose not to record sessions or video sessions, since both features would have been a change from my normal practice. Each client came to the counselling service in the normal manner and were booked in with the first available session, that is with any of the counselling team, as was customary.

I chose cases that were complete and in my view completed to a satisfactory level of success. This criteria seemed the best way to discern the key components of the process. Whilst unfinished work or disrupted work could have been included I saw this as deflecting from the true focus of this study i.e. to discover what short-term focal therapy is. I envisaged that such cases, if available, would merit a discrete research project, ideally as a follow up to this research, where others could endorse—or refute—my conclusions.

I considered each case as a separate "experiment" to be analysed and replicated. Each session constituted a part of the process. The notes that were recorded were the basic data which would be analysed. In this way I perceived the notes as akin to the results recorded after a science laboratory experiment. I use this metaphor to move away from the expectations of the notes of the case being seen as a literary exercise. They were sufficient to enable key components of the process to emerge.

Eight cases were selected. These were the first eight completed cases regardless of age or sex.

Validity

As referred to earlier, the analysis involved several cycles in order to enhance methodological validity which are listed at the end of the chapter. In examining the findings in a positively analytical way the interrelatedness and similarities from each cycle also become significant. In the third cycle, as part of the validating process, I asked two independent persons to undertake a further analysis of one selected case. Both individuals have an academic background and are familiar with the process of analysis. CS in addition has training and experience in counselling. BN has a background in logic and philosophy and was formerly Professor of Metaphysics at the International College, Donnybrook, Dublin. The case selected was case J. They were asked to examine the case and to draw out the key themes or categories that struck them from the case. Their findings were very similar to each others and to my own and to the categories highlighted. If their results had been very different either from each others or from my own I would then have felt it necessary to undertake a further process of verification before moving onto the next stage. Since they proved to be sufficiently similar to my own analysis I believed it appropriate to continue onto the next stage.

In the fourth cycle of analysis, in order to provide a comparative source of cases, my colleagues working within the same practice provided two cases. A further case was provided by a practitioner working outside this practice, but also in the brief approach. The use of colleagues" cases was part of the validation process. Both are very experienced with some 15/20 years experience.

A bias, that has to be stated here, is my own link with both colleagues since in the year in question both were in supervision with me. Both also had other supervision for different reasons elsewhere. The outside assessors I referred to were also known to me as friends and former colleagues, so a bias must be owned here also. I have already referred to the subjective aspect involved in using my own casework and declared my own position and stance in Chapter 1.

The cases of my colleagues were analysed, as a comparative sample group, against my key themes. In keeping with the earlier analysis this was sufficiently open to allow new themes to emerge.

The further cycles of research which strengthen and deepen the process of analysis have been referred to earlier and are shown at the end of the chapter.

Further ethical issues

I was very conscious of the dangers of the research "influencing" my work with clients. The danger, particularly of following up lines of work with the client that might be theoretically interesting, rather than be with the client in their particular situation. I hope that my awareness of the dangers prevented this from happening.

Confidentiality in the writing up process is an issue I have concerns about. Although I have in each case the client's permission to use the case material I wished to be cautious in my use of the material to prevent clients from being identified by interested others. As Bond observes, this is likely if the therapist is talking about their own clients from a particular context (1994, p. 138).

In Client "I"'s case I believe the public nature of the situation made it permissible to print the whole of the material. In some of the other cases I have changed the final write up to avoid identifying the person, I have nonetheless preserved the content.

I considered excluding all case material except for the one complete Case "I". Here, though, I decided that I would be understating the extent of the fieldwork. This was a very substantial element in the whole process, constituting a considerable amount of time. The inclusion of the case material also allows the reader to verify the conclusions and emerging categories for themselves.

I have adopted the approach of quoting from the case material, where it seems useful, in order to illustrate a point. I have not, therefore, included the full case notes within the book, but rather used them as resource material.

Three of the clients were kind enough to take the time and trouble to reflect on their experience in therapy and to write up a commentary for me to use. The commitment which they demonstrated in doing this indicated to me that they were very clear as to the public nature of the research and therefore I have also printed in full client commentaries Client M, Client C and Client "I". These present the reader with a clear way of making an assessment as to my own findings measured against another's view, albeit a participant observer's.

The cycles of analysis

The cycles of analysis referred to are shown below to guide the reader through the pages that follow:

1. Case work Cases: B: C: D: F: I: J: K: M.
2. My analysis of my case work.
3. Two objective colleagues' analysis of one case—Case J.
4. Analysis of colleagues' casework GD1, GD2, AM1.
5. Analysis of my casework in relation to the additional themes from colleagues work.
6. Analysis of literature.
7. Analysis of my casework and colleagues' casework against the key themes from literature.
8. Reflection on themes.
9. Selection of themes for further analysis.
10. In depth exploration of each theme through my case work, colleagues' case work and the literary sources to provide a thorough description of each theme.
11. Location of my findings within the latest thinking in the field and in the research context.
12. Conclusions.

The next chapter reports the findings from the initial cycles of the analysis.

CHAPTER FOUR

Findings from the initial cycles of analysis

T his chapter reports the findings from the first phase of the analysis. It is organized as follows:

Section A. Summary of fieldwork

Section B. The empirical data
i) Key themes from the analysis of my selected cases
ii) Key themes from a combination of my own cases and those of colleagues

Section C. The data emerging from the literary sources
i) Key proponents
ii) The developmental context of brief psychodynamic therapy
iii) The key themes emerging from the literature

Section D: Empirical data: key themes from analysis of the cases against themes from literature

Section E. Reflections on the initial findings

Section F. A reflective process to select key themes for further analysis

Section A. Summary of fieldwork

The first stage was to undertake case work that would become the focus of detailed analysis. Eleven cases were examined in total, eight from my own college practice, two from a colleague within the same college and one case from another therapist (AM) in private practice. The rationale for the way that the case material has been used and presented has been discussed in the last chapter. In summary Case "*I*" is to be seen in full in Chapter 6 and extracts from the other cases are used in the detailed examination of the key themes. Three commentaries written by the clients also appear in full in Chapter 6, Clients M, C and "*I*".

To help set the scene for the reader the main focus and the number of sessions for each case is presented below.

My research cases

Case B: 11 sessions, relationship issues arising from relationship with parents.

Case C: 6 sessions, anxiety.

Case E: 6 sessions, difficulty in forming relationships "I feel unconnected with some people".

Case F: 5 sessions, depression: "I've been depressed since I was nine years old."

Case *I*: 12 sessions, child abuse.

Case J: 4 Sessions, abortion.

Case K: 2 sessions, learning to say: "no" and how to express her need to give and receive affection within the family.

Case M: 10 sessions, suicidal inclinations.

Cases from colleagues AM and GD

Case AM1: 4 sessions, effects of a pregnancy and a miscarriage and echoes from the past for both partners.

Case GD1: 4 sessions, anxiety: "like skimming over the surface".

Case GD2: 9 sessions, afraid of losing friends because of behaviour when drunk i.e. when violent, incoherent and angry.

Section B. Empirical data

B (i) Key themes emerging from the analysis of cases

1ST CYCLE OF ANALYSIS: NAÏVE ENQUIRY RE AUTHOR'S EIGHT CASES

Using the theoretical framework outlined in the previous chapter eight cases from my regular client group were systematically analysed. This process was undertaken prior to the literature review. As outlined in the methodology I wished to approach the empirical part of the exploration with as open a mind as possible in order not to be too influenced by the findings of other researchers. This naïve enquiry was, therefore, undertaken soon after completion of the casework.

The reader is reminded that the themes result from the first cycles of analysis and are to be the subject of further in-depth analysis at a later point. They are therefore presented here without comment.

Empirical data re the key themes that emerged are presented in Table I and are summarized below.

Table I
Key themes from case studies

	B 1	C 2	E 3	F 4	I 5	J 6	K 7	M 8
Importance of first session	x	x	x	x	x	x	x	x
Importance of being "in tune" sensitivity	x	x	x			x		x
Flexibility of technique	x	x	x	x	x	x	x	x
Brevity 2–12 sessions Limited contract	x	x	x	x	x	x	x	x
Renegotiation of focus/contract	x		x					
Checking out with client	x	x	x		x	x	x	
Use of challenge	x	x			x			x
Teaching	x	x	x	x	x	x	x	x

In eight out of eight cases the following elements emerge: the therapist's teaching role, the flexibility of the therapist, the limited contract and the importance of the first session.

Six cases reveal the aspect of checking out with the client, five that of the importance of therapist sensitivity and four the use of challenge.

The renegotiation of the focus is referred to within two of the cases.

2ND CYCLE OF ANALYSIS: NAÏVE ENQUIRY: TWO INDEPENDENT REVIEWERS RE CASE J

As outlined in the methodology, in order to provide a level of objectivity to this process, independent assessors were asked to review one of the cases—Case J—to see what themes they selected. Both independently arrived at similar themes to the above. Additionally both commented on the seeming successful outcome of this case. Although the book is not a study on efficacy it is reassuring that the success of the case was commented upon spontaneously by both outside reviewers. Their comments can be seen as attesting to the "truthfulness" of my own selection of key themes. As Lynch states that if: "there was a convergence of opinion between the counsellor, client and another observer [the fact] that the counselling had been effective would seem to possess a reasonable degree of truthfulness" (1996, p. 147). In view of the convergence of opinion with regard to the key themes I moved to the next cycle as outlined in Chapter 3.

B (ii) Key themes from a combination of my own cases and that of colleagues

3RD CYCLE OF ANALYSIS: NAÏVE ENQUIRY RE THREE CASES PROVIDED BY TWO COLLEAGUES

In order to provide a comparative sample group of other practitioners work, colleagues' casework was analysed against my key themes. Two colleagues provided three cases in total for this analysis. The analysis was approached in an open way to allow for new themes also to emerge.

The analysis draws out clearly the factors found in analysing my own cases and also adds two further categories: This empirical data is summarized below and may be seen in Table II.

The following themes were identified in each case:

- the importance of the first sessions;
- the importance of being in tune;
- the flexibility of the therapist;
- the helpfulness of the brevity of time available; and
- the teaching role of the therapist.

The following were identified in two out of the three cases:

- checking out with client re focus; and
- the use of immediacy in response (challenge).

Two new categories emerged in each of the colleagues cases:

- the importance of therapist experience; and
- the intensity of the brief therapy process.

4TH CYCLE OF ANALYSIS: NAÏVE ENQUIRY RE COLLEAGUES' NEW CATEGORIES

A further cycle of analysis was then undertaken with regard to my own casework in relation to the new themes and evidence of these two new categories were found in each case.

Table II
Analysis of colleagues' case studies against my own categories

	GD2	GD1	AM1
Importance of first session	x	x	x
Importance of being "in tune" sensitivity	x	x	x
Flexibility of technique	x	x	x
Brevity 2–10 sessions Limited contract	x	x	x
Renegotiation of focus/contract	x		
Checking out with client	x		x
Use of challenge		x	
Teaching	x	x	x

Section C. Data emerging from the literary sources

C (i) 5th cycle of analysis: key proponents

The literature was examined with the objective of drawing out key proponents and key themes in relation to the brief approach. These themes, in conjunction with those emerging from the casework, were subsequently the subject of more detailed analysis in relation to the works of the key proponents and reflection on the casework.

Whilst substantive works on the area of brief therapy are few, articles are many and there exist a number of reviews of the literature. These have been undertaken by a number of eminent specialists in the field of therapy. In view of this I decided, rather than undertake a further review, I would examine the reviews and the substantive early works that are listed with their authors' status in the Appendix. These span the period 1963–1986. From these I have drawn out the key writers and proponents of Short-Term Therapy. To summarize, the authors seen to be the main contributors in the development of Short-Term Psychodynamic Psychotherapy are: Freud, Ferenzi, Rank, Alexander, French, Malan, Balint, Sifneos, Wolberg, Mann and Davanloo (see Table III).

Table III

Proponents of short-term psychotherapy consistently referred to in the literature

	Freud	Ferenczi	Rank	Alexander	Alexander & French	French	Malan	Balint	Sifneos	Mann	Davanloo	Wolberg
Malan, 1976	√	√	√	√	√	√	√	√	√	√	√	√
Marmor, 1980	√	√	√	√			√	√	√	√	√	√
Rogawski, 1982	√	√	√	√	√		√	√	√	√	√	√
Kovacs, 1982												
Budman & Stone, 1983	√	√	√	√	√		√	√	√	√	√	√
Bauer & Kobos, 1984	√	√	√	√	√	√	√	√	√		√	√
Sifneos, 1984	√	√	√	√	√		√		√	√	√	
Migone, 1985	√	√	√	√	√		√	√	√	√	√	√
Reich & Neenan, 1986		√	√		√		√		√		√	

C (ii) The developmental context of brief psychodynamic therapy

In examining the contribution of these writers to find key themes, the development of the psychodynamic brief approach also emerged and although it is not the focus of this study, it is included here in outline, to give the reader a sense of the history. This is in order to give a contextual perspective to the particular brief approach to therapy that is to be studied, that is, psychodynamic short-term therapy. However in doing this the reader should note that some of the data presented here may reappear in later chapters albeit with a different perspective.

(The reader is reminded that since this section forms part of the findings section it is appropriate that some quotes are not direct sources but those selected by the reviewers as being of importance. The style of writing in this section is also appropriate to the presentation of data in the findings section.)

THE DEVELOPMENT OF FOCAL AND SHORT-TERM THERAPY

The history of focal and short-term therapy begins with Sigmund Freud (1856–1939), who was an Austrian physician and is generally regarded as the founder of psychoanalysis. Although he is not usually thought of in connection with short-term therapy, Freud is referred to, consistently, in the reviews as one of the earliest short-term therapists. Freud's treatment of Sandor Ferenczi (also an analyst) is cited as an example. It was brief and undertaken in two blocks. Both were periods of 3 weeks with a 2-year gap. It would appear that Freud was leading the way to the use of interruptions in therapy. A concept that will be discussed further in Chapter 5. Whilst Freud did not lay great stress on the use of time limits, he did acknowledge their usefulness. He is better known, however, for his long-term analytical approach. It is his discovery of "transference" that forms one of the key elements in psychoanalysis, that is, feelings put onto the therapist by the client, that really belong to another figure in the client's life. The other key issue is the importance of childhood events on the present. It is the discovery of the painful childhood experience and the working through of emotions relating to this, that are seen as the substance of analysis. The expected outcome is that new patterns of behaviour can be learned, once the blocked emotions of the past can be understood and released.

The methods employed, by the analysts, to achieve this include hypnosis and dreams and a passivity on the part of the analyst who follows the patient where he/she leads. The development of analysis tended towards a longer and longer process. This, then, encouraged the client to develop a dependency on the therapist and a disinclination to conclude the therapy. On the analyst's part there was a tendency to want to trace every hurt of the past. Malan described this later, as a kind of "therapeutic perfectionism," which also led to prolonging the therapy (1963, p. 9).

Rogawski takes us to the next stage of the development of brief therapy as he examines the influence of Sandor Ferenczi whom he sees as one of the pioneers of brief therapy. Marmor observes that Ferenczi was particularly concerned about the passivity required by psychoanalysis which he said caused "stagnation of the analysis" (1979, p. 150). In an attempt to shorten analysis, Ferenczi began to experiment in 1918 with what he described as "active therapy". He experimented with various types of activity, some successful and some less so. One of his methods was to stand as surrogate parent for his patients, as a reparative measure. In this role he included hugging and kissing and non-erotic fondling of his patients. After Freud intervened, predicting that this would lead to difficulties Ferenczi then ceased this particular technique but continued to experiment.

Bauer and Kobos describe Ferenczi and Rank as analysts within Freud's "inner circle" (1995, p. 16).

Otto Rank (1834–1939), who was an Austrian psychiatrist working on the active therapy model in the early 1900s, joined forces with Sandor Ferenczi in 1925 to produce "The Development of Psychoanalysis".

Marmor attributes to Otto Rank an important place in the development of brief therapy. He describes him as perhaps, "the most important theoretical precursor of the brief psychotherapy movement" (1980, p. 5). Rogawski points out however that the analytical establishment of the time rejected his ideas.

In psychoanalysis, at that time, the emphasis was on the oedipal period. Rank stressed the idea of birth trauma and the pre-oedipal relationship in personality development. Rank also emphasized the concepts of termination and separation as key issues in brief therapy and linked this up with his ideas about birth trauma. He is the first therapist to deliberately utilize the concept of time limits as a way of facilitating the work on separation.

Another pioneering aspect of Rank's contribution to focal short-term therapy, is the stress on motivation. He saw this as essential for successful therapy. He laid great stress on the "will" and of the need for the therapist to mobilize the client's will in order to shorten therapy. This became known as "will therapy".

Bauer and Kobos (1984) attribute to both Rank and Ferenczi an important role in the history of short-term therapy. They focus on these therapists' use of the transference. Both Rank and Ferenczi emphasized the use of the here and now in the interpretations of the transference, whilst still not ignoring its relationship to past material. This was a new emphasis in therapy. Rank and Ferenczi refer to the reliving of maladaptive patterns, in relation to the therapist and to the "acting out" within the analytic treatment.

Marmor gives Franz Alexander—working at the Chicago Institute of Psychoanalysis along with French, a key place in the development of brief therapy. In his view: "Alexander more than any other modern psychoanalyst is responsible for leading the way toward the application of psychoanalytic principles to short-term dynamic psychotherapy" (1979, p. 9). Bauer and Kobos too, see Alexander as an "innovator" and a psychoanalyst who had a broad experience with training in Europe and experience as a "member of the Berlin Institute of Psychoanalysis in the early thirties" (1995, p. 34).

Franz Alexander builds on the ideas of Ferenczi and Rank and develops a process which he later refers to as the "corrective emotional experience!" Marmor quotes Alexander (1946): "Because the therapist's attitude is different from that of the authoritative person of the past, he gives the patient the opportunity to face again and again, under more favourable circumstances, those emotional situations which were formerly unbearable and to deal with them in a manner different from the old!" (1979, p. 9). Here Alexander is referring to the actual experience of the client in the therapeutic relationship.

Alexander laid great emphasis on flexibility of the therapist. In this he was being, according to Marmor, quite "revolutionary" at that time by daring to deviate from the standard analytic method. Alexander maintained that the therapist should adapt the technique to the needs of the patient. He himself experimented with time scales, the use of the couch and the chair, the control and manipulation of the transference, and drug therapy, thus demonstrating both flexibility and activity.

Alexander was very concerned about the tendency for clients to regress in the course of therapy. To prevent this, he recommended the use of gaps in the treatment, referred to as interruptions. This was referred to earlier in a case of Freud's. Both saw this as a way to prevent overdependence and to foster autonomy. It also controlled the transference and prepared the client and the therapist for termination. Alexander stated, that the regressive tendency should be checked from the very start of therapy. Besides Marmor's, five of the major reviews give Alexander and French a central place in the development of short-term psychotherapy. Budman and Stone draw attention to their seminal work on brief treatment "Psychoanalytic Therapy" (1983, p. 930). Bauer and Kobos (1984) suggest that Alexander and French provided the foundation for other developing systems of short-term and anxiety provoking psychotherapy. Rogawski declares, that it is by advocating the new idea of flexibility that Alexander and French have, "more than any other analysts ... laid the ground work for the development of Short-Term Dynamic Psychotherapy" (1982, p. 337).

Marmor observes that, just as Rank's ideas were attacked by his contemporaries, so Alexander's ideas were attacked by most classical psychoanalysts of the day. Now however, many of his ideas are incorporated into the normal working methods of psychoanalysts.

POST 1960s—THE RADICAL VIEW

Key figures emerge consistently from post-1960s literature. They fall within the radical spectrum, in terms of expecting real change to occur in the client in the course of therapy.

They are: Malan, Balint, Mann, Sifneos, Wolberg and Davanloo.

Malan is referred to by all of the reviews as a key proponent of brief therapy and owing to two of his substantive volumes on the subject, is one of the better known. He places himself at the radical end of the spectrum of the approach. That is, he aims for extensive change in clients treated in the brief approach.

In his own review of 1976 he observes, that there has been a change in thinking about brief therapy since the 1960s. Formerly, it had been seen only as a palliative form of treatment. This is known as the conservative view. Now, that is post-1960s, Malan stresses, brief therapy is seen as suitable for patients with acute current conflicts or long-standing disorders. Successful outcomes and permanent change are anticipated. This is known as the radical view.

All of these proponents of brief therapy remain key figures into the 1980s and 1990s.

Their approach is rooted in psychoanalytic tradition and relies heavily on transference and its interpretation, especially in relation to childhood. Issues about separation and loss of the therapist and motivation for insight are also key features.

Malan (1976) also stresses the use of transference in short-term therapy. He refers in particular to the triangle of insight as an inherent part of the process of brief therapy. That is the relationship between what is happening with client and therapist and how this relates to the past traumatic relationships and what is happening in the present day relationships of the client. He describes Brief Psychotherapy as a technique, involving the effective utilization of the transference manifestations, to complete the triangle of insight. His aim in Intensive Brief Psychotherapy is to uncover, re-experience and work through repressed emotional conflict.

Bauer and Kobos (1984) on the other hand highlight Malan's stress on the therapeutic alliance, that is, the client and therapist agreement as to what they are working on: the agreed focal area.

REDISCOVERY—A RECURRING THEME IN THE HISTORY OF SHORT-TERM PSYCHOTHERAPY

As the development of brief therapy is examined aspects of brief therapy that were experimented with in the 1920s are seen to be discovered again and again by different proponents. We see Mann in the 1970s, for example, basing his whole approach on time limits, following Rank using time limits in the 1920s and Malan in the 1960s. Even the concept of shortening therapy, is itself a rediscovery. As Malan observes, there seemed to be a tendency for the early work of analysts to be brief and successful and then gradually the length of the work seemed to inflate. Malan said, "It's as if the ontogeny of individual analysts recapitulates the phylogeny of psychoanalysis itself. The only possible explanation seems to lie in changes in the therapist's enthusiasm!" (1963, p. 13).

Again, there is an aspect of rediscovery when we see the work and discoveries of Balint and Malan in the 1960s at the Tavistock Clinic in England being duplicated by Sifneos at Massachusetts General Hospital in Boston working quite independently. It was not until they met at a conference that they were aware of each other's work. Their discoveries and work were in parallel and are described by Malan as "rediscoveries," of the radical brief therapy technique used by Alexander and French in the mid 1940s.

Equally, I myself, having become increasingly interested in the brief method, launched The Association of Short-Term and Strategic Psychotherapists, as an original and independent idea in 1989, only to find, at a later date, that Sifneos had recommended just such an association some years earlier in 1984.

This concept of "rediscovery" in relation to brief psychotherapy recurs and is a feature of its history.

Malan observes that the concept of a focal area is a rediscovery. In, *A Study of Brief Psychiatry* he points out that Alexander and French, in 1946, had stressed the need for a limited aim and later in 1958 refer to the "focal conflict"; Finesinger also stresses this in his "goal directed planning" and "focusing of material"; Deutsch too, restricted the area of work in his "goal limited adjustment" (1963, p. 29). These, Malan sees as simply other ways of describing the importance of concentrating on a focal area. The method of keeping the client to the main focus was described by Balint as Focal Therapy. Malan and Migone acknowledge Balint as the first therapist to coin the phrase, Focal Psychotherapy. Balint et al. (1972) stresses this aspect of having a focal area to explore as the key differentiating feature of Short-Term Focal Psychotherapy.

In emphasizing the need of focusing on a circumscribed problem area, Malan states that therapists must give up trying to solve all areas of a person's life. Balint and Malan and the other radical short-term therapists, however, do expect to help even longstanding problems, by working with the limited focus.

Dr Michael Balint led a team of psychoanalysts in exploring Brief Therapy and initiated the project which was "nicknamed the Workshop". His team included Malan who wrote up the work. "The Workshop consisted of members of the staff of the Tavistock Clinic and the Cassel Hospital" (1963, p. 39). The aim was to "investigate brief psychotherapy" and this was to be "by therapists with a fairly complete knowledge and experience of the technique of psychoanalysis" (1963, p. 3).

Balint stressed the aspect of actively involving the client from the beginning and of the therapist and client following the same aim. This feature, of agreeing the aim for therapy, was greatly stressed by Sifneos who sees psychotherapy as a joint venture. Sifneos describes his active approach to therapy as "Anxiety Provoking Psychotherapy" (1968, p. xiv). He also expects activity on the part of both client and therapist. He stresses early interpretation of resistance, challenging and making links with the past, in the transference. In his selection process he will ensure that the client is motivated, not just to undertake therapy, but to seek change and insight. Marmor draws attention to Sifneos's use of the terms "willingness" and "willingness to change" as criteria for patient selections (Sifneos et al., 1980). This has echoes of Rank's "will therapy" in the 1940s.

Sifneos's anxiety provoking psychotherapy requires great flex-ibility on the part of the therapist, observes Rogawski. Techniques must be adapted to each patient's individual need. Flexibility is referred to with respect both to the length of and frequency of sessions.

Sifneos stresses the importance of focusing on a circumscribed problem area. Indeed, he states that the ability to delineate a focal area is one of the conditions for patient selection for this brief method.

The idea of a focal area within Brief Therapy was universally agreed by 1976.

Sifneos (1984) highlights the didactic component of the short-term approach. He refers to the use of rewards and re-enforcements in order to help the patient utilize what they have learned, internalizing the therapist.

Wolberg in New York, at the Postgraduate Centre for Mental Health is widely seen as one of the pioneering psychoanalysts taking up the torch of Brief Therapy (Marmor, 1980; Rogawski, 1982; Malan, 1976).

He is referred to as one of the writers holding radical views on Short-Term Psychotherapy. Wolberg also advocates a flexible use of skills and uses behavioural and cognitive approaches in Brief Therapy. These techniques include hypnosis, homework and ego building activities.

He emphasizes this idea of flexibility further when he says: "If the therapist is flexible, sensitive, empathic and understands the basic process of psychotherapy, and if he is aware of his neurotic impulses as they are mobilized in his relationship with his patient, he should be able to bring the average patient to a sufficient understanding of his problem within the span of a Short-Term approach!" (1965, p. 156).

Mann, of the Division of Psychiatry, Boston University School of Medicine, Boston, Massachusetts (1973), takes the concept of time limits as the fundamental aspect of short-term therapy. He sees it as the prime factor for success. He suggests that, the pending end tends to highlight issues of dependence/independence, activity versus passivity and self esteem verses loss of self esteem and unresolved or delayed grief. In Mann's view it is the expedient management of termination that allows the therapist to be internalized. Mann's method became known as Time Limited Psychotherapy and is a 12-session model. Rogawski observes that this idea of time limits is but a rediscovery (1982).

DEVELOPMENT IN THE 1980s TO THE MID 1990s

Davanloo is referred to as a prominent figure in the development of short-term psychotherapy (Marmor, 1980; Budman and Stone, 1983). Habib Davanloo (M.D.) is "Associate Professor of Psychiatry, McGill University and Director, Institute for Teaching and Research in Short-Term Dynamic Psychotherapy, The Montreal General Hospital, Canada" (1992, p. 393). Bauer and Kobos emphasize his work with confronting and interpreting the transference. They also observe that Davanloo reiterates the idea of client and therapist agreeing a focal area to be worked on. It is of great significance that Malan, although a leading figure in Focal Short-Term Therapy in the late 1960s and 1970s, now follows and supports Davanloo's approach according to Migone (1985). The approach is now called Intensive Short-Term Psychodynamic Psychotherapy.

Davanloo (1980) introduces the view that the first session is of paramount importance. He pays meticulous attention to the patient's responses, and challenges everything. For Davanloo it is also important that there is a high degree of involvement of both client and therapist. His goal is that the symptoms complained about will disappear or that the maladaptive behaviour is given up. If there is cognitive and emotional insight into the neurosis that caused the difficulties, this too is seen by him as successful. This is clearly well within the radical end of the spectrum.

The development in the later 1980s–1990s, which has taken place since the start of this study will be addressed in Chapters 7–9. There, my own conclusions will be located within the latest thinking of the day.

C (iii) The key themes emerging from the literature.
6th cycle of analysis

Using the theoretical framework described earlier the reviews were examined again. This cycle of analysis aimed to find the key themes emerging from the literature. These then would be subject to further analysis in conjunction with the themes from the cases and with reference to the works of the key proponents mentioned above. The findings therefore are presented below without comment at this stage.

In summary the most common theme emerging, in the brief psychodynamic approach, is activity, seen by all nine reviewers as a key component.

Seven, of the nine reviewers, refer to flexibility and the importance of working with a focal area.

Only five of the reviewers stress the experience of the therapist and motivation in the client.

Three of them underline the therapeutic alliance and therapy as a learning experience.

Only two of the reviewers, allude to the importance of the first session and only two to the fact that aspects of the brief approach are rediscoveries. (See Tables IV and V, p. 48 and p. 49.)

Table IV
Main ideas emerging as common elements in short-term psychotherapy from the reviews in the Appendix

	Malan	Marmor	Rogawski	Kovacs	Budman & Stone	Bauer & Kobos	Sifneos	Migone	Reich & Neenan
	1976	1980	1982	1982	1983	1984	1984	1985	1986
Psycho-analytic tradition	x	x	x		x	x	x	x	x
Transference issues	x	x	x	x		x	x	x	x
Brevity	x	x	x	x	x	x	x		
Time limits	x	x	x			x	x	x	x
Interruptions		x	x	x	x	x		x	x
Activity	x	x	x	x	x	x	x	x	x
Focus	x		x		x	x	x	x	x
Flexibility	x	x		x	x	x	x		x
Name			x		x	x		x	
Selection criteria	x		x		x		x	x	x
Importance of the first session				x		x			
Therapeutic alliance	x						x		x
Rediscovery	x		x						
Learning process	x				x		x		
Motivation	x	x				x	x		x
Experience of the therapist		x	x		x	x		x	
Evaluation							x		
Outcome	x		x	x		x	x	x	x

Table V
Ideas/themes introduced by some of reviewers

	Malan	Marmor	Rogawski	Kovacs	Budman & Stone	Bauer & Kobos	Sifneos	Migone	Reich & Neenan
	1976	1980	1982	1982	1983	1984	1984	1985	1986
Learning process	x				x		x		
Importance of first session				x		x			
Development theory				x	x	x			
Association of short-term therapists							x		
Calling for an integration of the short-term therapies					x				x
Rediscovery of the method	x		x						

Section D. Empirical data

D (i) Analysis of selected cases against themes from literature to find key themes: 7th cycle of analysis

The next cycle of analysis was to examine the cases against the key themes drawn from the reviews (see Table VI, p. 50).

Once again it is not the intention here to explore the issues raised since deeper analysis takes place later. The intention is simply to show the results of the initial cycles of the analysis which lead to the themes which become the focus of the study.

Every case revealed evidence of:

- psychoanalytic roots;
- the importance of having a focus;
- therapeutic alliance;
- motivation; and
- the experience required of the therapist.

Table VI
Analysis of cases against key themes drawn from authors' reviews

	B 1	C 2	E 3	F 4	I 5	J 6	K 7	M 8
Psychoanalytic tradition	x	x	x	x	x	x	x	x
Transference issues	x	x			x			
Brevity (2–16 sessions)	x	x	x	x	x	x	x	x
Time limits interruption	x	x	x	x x	x	x	x	x x
Activity	x	x	x	x	x	x		x
Focus	x	x	x	x	x	x	x	x
Flexibility	x	x	x	x	x	x	x	x
Importance of first session	x	x	x	x	x	x	x	x
Therapeutic alliance	x	x	x	x	x	x	x	x
Motivation	x	x	x	x	x	x	x	x
Experience of the therapist— by implication	x	x	x	x	x	x	x	x
Outcomes— client written comments	x	x x	x	x x	x x	x x	x	x x

- Seven cases showed evidence of activity.
- Transference issues were evident in three of the cases.
- The use of interruptions in the contract appeared in two of the cases.

The next stage of the process was to reflect on the findings and to select the themes for further analysis.

Section E. Reflections on the initial findings

E (i) In looking at the literature the themes that emerged were all evident in both my cases and those of my colleagues and yet had not surfaced immediately. Equally themes that emerged in my cases were not uppermost in the literature. This is precisely the value of work such as this. It is an opportunity to look afresh at the approach and to visit new themes and revisit well documented ones.

E (ii) In the first cycles of analysis, which I have referred to as naïve enquiry there is less emphasis on focus than in the literature, although I have highlighted the aspect of renegotiating and checking out the focus which makes the assumption that it is important. Also, in the later analysis of cases against the themes in literature the importance of focus is apparent in every case. My interpretation of this is that I take this aspect so much for granted in the approach that it did not emerge as readily as other facets. It was indeed a factor given great emphasis in my training in this brief approach.

The same reasons could apply for the absence at this stage (though evident in the later cycle of analysis) of reference to a number of the themes that emerge from the literature. For example in this first cycle there is no mention of the psychodynamic roots, which I take for granted, given the nature of my professional background and yet evidence is clear when I returned to the cases to look for it.

These findings supported the grounded theory approach that I adopted and were the very reason I had wanted to examine the cases before studying the literature. I had hoped that a fresh look could reveal a new perspective.

E (iii) In the comments of the two external observers the only different observations related to the successfulness of the case in question. This perhaps reflects their outside and uninhibited perspective for the analysis.

E (iv) In examining colleagues' cases, which inevitably has a more outside perspective, I observed the intensity and importance of the experience of the therapist in each of the colleagues cases. I was struck particularly in GD1 by the skilful adaptability of the therapist in staying in tune with his client and using different therapeutic tools appropriately to move the client on. This will be discussed further in the more detailed analysis to come.

E (v) In returning to my own cases, to see if these factors found in colleagues' cases are present, it is clear that they are. In being able to find evidence of these in this cycle I am assuming that I have taken a more outside perspective. It is clearly more difficult for me to make comment on my own experience as a therapist, but it is easy to recall the intensity of an experience that I have been part of. In colleagues' cases a quality of "being" emerged, which I could observe more easily and objectively from outside. This related to both the therapeutic alliance and the aspect of intensity. I could then see and recall this also in my own work. The intensity is in a sense a bi-product of the therapeutic work and what is happening within this relationship.

Section F. A reflective process to select themes for further analysis

F (i) Emergent themes

In order to focus the next phase of the analysis I decided to conflate some of the emergent themes.

A good starting point was to set the parameters of what is understood by *"short-term"*. This category took into account also the idea of *limited contract* and *interruptions*.

Since I have limited this study to the exploration of psychodynamic short-term therapy the next logical theme seemed to be *"psychodynamic roots"*. This heading incorporates the idea of *transference* and also of *rediscovery*. The *teaching aspect* is also addressed here.

"Activity" which was addressed by all the reviewers and is seen in all the cases, *"flexibility"* that appears in every case and some of the reviews were chosen for their commonality. Both of these include the idea of the *experience of the therapist*.

"Focus" was included in most of the reviews and all the cases so again there was commonality in this. It included the idea of *checking out* and *renegotiating*. I often use the term *focal and short-term therapy*, in order to describe the approach, so this too, led to the choice of this heading. *Experience* and *use of challenge* are included under this heading.

The heading *"therapeutic alliance"* included by some of the reviewers appeared in all the cases and takes in *motivation, being in tune, challenge, intensity* and *teaching*.

One theme that was consistently seen in the empirical work, but curiously only mentioned by two of the reviewers, is the *"importance of the first session"*. These findings in the empirical work pointed to a new emphasis within the approach and clearly merited further analysis and so this theme is included as a key theme for the next stage of exploration.

F (ii) Themes within themes

Each of the themes is interlinked with the others and it is somewhat artificial to attempt to separate them, but this is necessary to gain a fuller understanding of the approach. In order to avoid too much repetition I have limited the number of themes to focus the next stage of analysis. Thus some of the themes that emerged, in particular from the cases, have not been allocated discreet headings. For example *"teaching" on the part of the therapist* and it being *"a learning experience", on the part of the client*, might have combined to become a theme in itself. Equally *"intensity"*, the *"experience of the therapist"* and the importance of being *"in tune"* or *"sensitivity"* as I sometimes refer to this aspect of the relationship, could also have each become discreet themes. I decided however that these important themes that emerged consistently from the empirical work, and yet received little emphasis from the literature, were to be held in mind as the other themes were examined in greater detail. They in fact are so important that they permeate every other aspect of the therapeutic work and therefore I expect in the next stage of analysis to see examples of this last mentioned group evidenced within the examination of the other themes.

F (iii) Key themes for further analysis in Chapter 5

The themes that have been selected for further examination are summarized below. They are derived, as seen above, from the earlier cycles of analysis of the selected cases, which include my own and those of my colleagues and of the literature.

(1) What is understood by short-term.
(2) Psychodynamic roots.
(3) Flexibility.
(4) Activity.
(5) Focus.
(6) Therapeutic alliance.
(7) Importance of the first session.

Each of these themes will be examined by returning to the literature and the selected casework for further detailed analysis. The aim is to come to a clearer picture as to what constitutes short-term psychotherapy and what makes it short.

Part One: analysis of the emergent key themes: Findings from in-depth cycle of analysis

T he last chapter showed the findings from the cycles of analysis leading to the selection of key themes. In the first part of this chapter the findings from the in-depth cycle of analysis are reported. Each of the key themes listed below is examined in turn to elaborate clearly what is understood by each of these from the case work, key proponents and literature. Although some inchoate conclusions emerge spontaneously these are in no way comprehensive since that is not the purpose of this section.

Although in the early cycles of analysis, the casework was examined before turning to the literature, in this section I have chosen to outline the work of the key proponents and the findings from the literature first. This is to emphasize that the clinical team's empirical work stands on and within a tradition and at times moves on and beyond the confines of that same tradition in keeping with a dynamic process.

The second part of this chapter gives a summary of the findings from the analysis of key themes and preliminary conclusions which will be examined further in later chapters.

In giving references from case work I draw on appropriate examples from the work of my colleagues, i.e. Clients AM1, GD1 and GD2 and from my own cases B, C, E, F, J, K, M. In the following exposition I make no further reference as to whether they are my own cases or those of the colleagues, but simply cite the example that most clearly illustrates the point.

In writing up the findings from this analysis I have attempted not to repeat the same extract although one case example often illustrated aspects of several of the key themes and so the case appears more than once. I have also given just sufficient detail, of the case, to illustrate the particular aspect of the key theme under scrutiny in order to keep focused on the purpose of this study. I therefore do not expand on other aspects of more general therapeutic interest, nor do I attempt to give alternative ways of interpreting the evidence since, in keeping with a positively analytical approach and the theoretical framework chosen, this is my interpretation. The focused and brief nature of the examples from the casework are also in the interests of confidentiality, as discussed under ethical issues in the methodology section.

Refocusing

Before moving on to this report of the in-depth analysis of the key themes, it is appropriate to refocus with the reader as to the purpose of the study and hence of this cycle of analysis.

It has already been noted in the first chapter and introduction, that psychodynamic psychotherapy is widely considered to be a lengthy process: *Lengthy* being seen as a period from 1 year to several years of one or more sessions a week. The process is thus available to the few who may access it via the National Health route or privately, being of sufficient means to be able to afford the high fees for this extended period. This puts therapy beyond the reach of many who could benefit from it. Therefore, the question arises— could there be a way in which therapy could be brought within the reach of more people? This is not only a matter of finance, where perhaps the government could fund therapy for all, but is a matter of time and resources being available. More important still is the need for people to be free and out of emotional pain sooner rather than later. One way forward is to explore the shortening of the therapy process. In this way people's expenditure of time and money and the endurance of aspects of suffering could be limited. If effective therapy can be shortened it would then, by virtue of economic factors, come within the reach of many more people.

In order to explore the shortening process we need to see what short-term therapy is. It is with both these objectives in mind that the exploration was begun. These same objectives form the focus of the further in-depth stage of analysis.

The key themes

The preceding cycles of analysis have revealed the key early proponents and a number of key themes. Within this chapter each key theme is examined separately and in detail in the following order.

5.1.1.   What is understood by short-term
5.1.2.   Psychodynamic roots
5.1.3.   Flexibility
5.1.4.   Activity
5.1.5.   Focus
5.1.6.   Therapeutic alliance
5.1.7.   Importance of the first session

When analysing the key themes in relation to the literary sources and the key proponents, I was especially alert to references to some other important themes that emerged consistently from the clinical work and which permeated it. I was interested to see if these other themes could be found and whether my discoveries bring a new dimension of short-term work into the foreground. These themes that I shall refer to as *subsidiary themes* are as follows:

● the teaching aspect of the therapeutic work;
● teaching the clients to be their own therapists;
● the intensity of the short-term therapy experience;
● the experience required of the therapist; and
● the sensitivity of the therapist in order to be in tune with the client.

The aim is to come to a conclusion as to what constitutes short-term psychodynamic psychotherapy, within the parameters out-lined in an earlier chapter and what makes it short.

The idea of shortening therapy is not a new one, as the section on the development of short-term therapy shows, it dates back to Freud—but how short is short? This is the question to be addressed first.

5.1.1. What is understood by the phrase "short-term"

Although "short-term psychotherapy" is a phrase that is often used in the literature on psychotherapy the definition of "short-term" is not consistent. It may be seen in one context to mean one session or three or four sessions, in another context 12 and in another 24, or even a period of 2 years or more.

I therefore examined the literature with regard to the length of brief or short-term therapy to see if there was a mean number of sessions or whether there were clear parameters beyond which brief therapy was no longer considered brief. This then was compared with the results of the analysis of the empirical work, to see how, in the 21st century, we define brief.

Brief whether intentional or not

A number of research studies exist on the duration of therapy and in the light of these, Reich and Neenan conclude that short-term refers to "therapies lasting 15 or fewer sessions" (1986, p. 63). They refer us to a number of studies on the duration of therapy in support of this. These examine how many sessions clients attend, in therapies that are intended to be open ended and with no initial set termination date. It was found for example, in an extensive study by Garfield covering patient data over 22 years "from 1948–1970 ... that the median number of visits in most settings was 5 to 6", although "Langsley found that psychiatrists in private practice saw patients for longer periods averaging between 12 to 13 visits" (1986, p. 62).

Rogawski also observes, in view of the studies by Butcher and Koss in 1978 and Lorion in 1974 that "most psychotherapies prove to be brief whether they are initially so planned or not" (1982, p. 332). These studies found that a high percentage terminate after six to eight sessions despite having contracted, not for brief therapy but simply for therapy.

Malan points out that, in defining how short is short in brief psychotherapy one should take account of satisfactory results. He looks to case studies of 10–50 sessions with positive outcomes by Alexander and French, Rogers and Dymond. He observes "frequent" case studies of one to four sessions. However, when Malan refers to frequent he is talking about "Alexander and French, 5 cases; Saul (1951), one case; Rothenberg (1955), 3 cases; Knight (1937), 3 cases; Berliner (1941), one case" (1963, p. 34).

Setting time limits

Whilst Mann (1973) is often cited as the forerunner of deliberately setting a time limit, limits were set many years earlier by Ferenczi in 1918 and by Rank in 1947. Malan also points to others preceding Mann who set limits. These include Seitz (1953) "setting a time limit from the very beginning" and Phillips and Johnston (1954) who, within a child guidance practice, applied a limited time and in 16 cases reports a greater proportion of "improvement", "mutually agreed termination", and a lower proportion of "premature withdrawal", than in 14 cases where the limit was not set (1963, p. 35).

Malan observes that external factors limit the time available for therapy on the part of both client and therapist. He speaks of a case of 40 sessions and another of 20 but refers to an "unrealistic" limit of eight sessions for the Paranoid Engineer (1963, p. 209). He does not elaborate as to why he believes the latter figure is unrealistic. One could speculate as to why this was but that would deviate from the present task that of coming to a norm for the term "brief". It may be that Malan did not believe eight sessions to be a viable length for successful treatment. I would take issue with him if he held to the latter point since one can point to many successes with a median of four sessions. The four-session clinic operated by the Tavistock Clinic in the 1990s for example.

Malan himself, although setting a time limit of 20 sessions or a maximum of 40, would expect a satisfactory outcome by a specified date rather than an exact number of sessions.

Sifneos sees "long-term psychotherapy as therapy of one or two years duration" and therefore suggests that 1 year could be seen as a parameter of therapies that might be described as brief (1987, p. 202).

Davanloo's parameter is 40 but he tends to average between 15–25 sessions (1980). He observes that often improvement occurs between the 5th and 8th session.

Time limit as common denominator in brief therapies

Migone points to the setting of the time limit as being a "crucial factor in the STDP ... rather than a ... specific technique". He points out that time limitation is, in fact, "the common denominator of all the techniques of brief therapy, whether rigidly fixed at 12 sessions, as in Mann's technique, or with a maximum of 40, as in that of other therapists" (1985, p. 62).

In this it would appear that Migone does not conceive of brief therapy as being less than 12 sessions. Here again, I would observe that cited above are many instances of brief therapy being less than 12 sessions and that even one session can bring about significant change.

Therapist expectation

Alexander maintains that we should be careful not to encourage procrastination by saying "Do not bother about time or worry about the duration of treatment ... (he) believes this is the worst kind of attitude one can convey to a patient ... Instead, one should say that we wish to complete treatment as fast as possible" (1965, p. 91).

Alexander attests to an early statement made by Freud that "treatments often reach a point where the patient's will to be cured is outweighed by his wish to be treated" (1965, p. 91).

Freud himself refers to the usefulness of a time limit: "I determined—but not until trustworthy signs had led me to judge that the right moment had come—that the treatment must be brought to an end at particular fixed date, no matter how far it had advanced. I was resolved to keep to the date". Freud observes almost with surprise that: "All the information, too, which enabled me to understand his infantile neurosis is derived from this last period of the work, during which resistance temporarily disappeared and the patient gave an impression of lucidity which is usually attainable only in hypnosis" (1991, p. 238). Freud's brief cases with Bruno Walter and Gustav Mahler of less than six sessions are frequently referred to by the reviewers (Migone, 1985; Marmor, 1979; Rogawski, 1982). These examples and comments of Freud make him an unexpected early proponent of the brief approach.

Wolberg also stresses the need to expect therapy to be short-term, estimating up to 20 sessions as short-term. He says, "The best strategy, in my opinion, is to assume that every patient, irrespective of diagnosis, will respond to short-term treatment unless he proves himself to be refractory to it" (1965, p. 140).

Sifneos cites an incident showing the influence of attitude on the length of therapy. One of the therapists who wished to learn short-term work but who had a great deal of experience with long-term work was assigned a patient by Sifneos. However, he had requested that he be supervised by his own long-term supervisor. That patient took 1 year, although therapist and supervisor considered they were making good progress.

The patient when asked about the therapy later said: "I don't know why he was so much interested in my great grandfather's death" (1987, p. 74). Sifneos says: "from then on Dr Fishman—a member of our research team—and I supervised all STAPP with our residents" (ibid).

Interruptions in therapy

There are other aspects that merit consideration in relation to the question how long is brief therapy. For example, Bauer and Kobos (1984) refer to the use of interruptions in therapy as a way of limiting sessions—a method advocated by Alexander and French in the 1940s. Some interruptions are due to circumstances like holiday breaks or illnesses, but interruptions may be planned to capitalize on the good therapeutic effects. The gaps can allow time for the client to digest the insights that have been gained in the sessions with the therapist, or can be used as a time to practice new ways of responding to situations. It enhances client independence.

Spaced sessions

Budman and Stone (1983) refer to the spacing of sessions which can be similarly useful as demonstrated by Selvini-Palazzoli and her colleagues (1978), for example, who see clients monthly for a year or more. This provides an ongoing support structure through the therapeutic contact and encourages independent work on the part of the client in the time between sessions.

Follow-up sessions

Budman and Stone (1983) draw to our attention the fact that many patients who have received therapy return for more after termination, the level is shown to be about 60% in one study undertaken by Patterson and colleagues.

To make full use of this information it would be necessary to have detailed studies of why people reappear. Is their situation at the same point as when they first presented, or is the starting point beyond where they left off? My own practice shows that in the main clients have moved on and return in order to move on still further, often saying, *"It helped before so I thought I could look at this now."*

Certainly, also within my case work, clients have returned apparently entirely back at square one. For some, challenging this proved the client had no motivation to change. For others the task was to explore the reason for the return to the original symptom, often with successful outcomes.

Alexander, Marmor and Malan allow follow up sessions—whilst others such as Mann believe this to negate the impact of a fixed and clear termination date. My own view is that a flexible approach is required and each client's case should be dealt with on an individual basis.

Rites of passage

Kovacs refers to the phenomenon of clients returning for further therapy as "rites of passage" and sees therapists as a kind of new, secular priesthood. He suggests: "We will find many of our patients become life-long companions, appearing and reappearing in our offices every 5 to 10 years ... We do not cure, we only facilitate important rites of passage" (1982, p. 159).

Other aspects of brief therapy are the modification of length of sessions:- ½ hour session twice a week; 10 minute sessions; unscheduled single encounters such as "sidewalk consults" or emergency phone calls as Sperry (1987) calls some of the brief encounters; or one very long session of several hours as recommended by Dr James Thompson at the British Psychological Society's annual conference 1996. In general, however, the therapists cited maintain traditional 50 minute or 1 hour sessions.

Flexibility

Flexibility is, in my view, required of therapists in their application of the time limit. The desired end must be borne in mind. Brodaty (1983) observes that Pumpian-Mindlin (1953) ended "when appropriate"; Alexander and French (1946) required "sufficient therapeutic gain" before termination; Wolberg finished when the patient was "satisfied" (1965, p. 110).

I suggest that the two approaches of flexibility and setting a limit can be fused together so as to enhance the process. If, for example, a fixed contract is near completion and in reviewing the agreed focal area it is clear that another issue needs exploration it may be appropriate to renegotiate the contract and to continue for a definite period to cover the unfinished business. Another example is where progress is slow and the client simply feels unready to go and yet is working. If the difficulty is about ending, then perhaps a contract to explore endings may be necessary. This might be for four sessions.

Sifneos points out also that whilst some therapists do set limits they are rather flexible about it. He includes here "Davanloo, Gillieron, Guyotat and Brusset, in Montreal, Lausanne, Lyon and Paris" (1987, p. 73). Sifneos himself recommends working over a short period of time but leaving the termination date open. He states, however, "that usually STAPP patients achieve a resolution of their difficulties in a 2 to 6 month period" (1984, p. 475).

The approach adopted by my colleagues and myself is a flexible one. The expectation is that the contract will be short and that improvement can occur in that period. Often the statement will be made *"We will start with four sessions and review at that time"*. In practice, some clients need only one or two sessions. Others may initially contract for 8 or 12 sessions. Each case is dealt with on an entirely individual basis. Flexibility is given with regard to spacing sessions, interruptions, follow-up sessions or shorter sessions. Each situation is looked at individually but within the general framework of brevity.

Experience factor

All the therapists within this study are very experienced and therefore perhaps able to work rapidly with clients. Malan (1979) believes that experience is an important element in the shortening of therapy. He allowed his experienced therapists 20 sessions at the Tavistock Clinic and 30 sessions for the less experienced.

Wolberg points out that there is not time to make mistakes in a brief contract and suggests that: "The short-term approach requires the wisdom born of experience" (1965, p. 128).

Clinical benefits of time limits

The setting of time limits has many benefits clinically. Rogawski (1982) points out the increase in optimism the time limit can give clients. That is, that improvement may be possible in a short time. A time limit provides a structure—a clear beginning, middle and end. It limits the client's opportunity to surrender responsibility to the therapist and highlights the aspects of separation and individuation.

I would wish to counter the latter point. Some patients find that they can depend more on the therapist because they are aware of the brief time span involved and so a deeply intense therapeutic alliance can be achieved very quickly.

The time limit enables the client's reaction to termination to be carefully monitored and managed. It also, Rogawski suggests, "helps patients to integrate the new insights as a step towards achieving self-reliance and independence" (1982, p. 341).

Dynamics of the deadline

I refer to the clinical benefits of the time limit as the "dynamics of the deadline". The existence of a definite end-point helps to concentrate the mind and energies of the client and the therapist. Clients themselves can see the benefit of the limit, as one of my research clients, Client M commented:

> *"I thought that the idea of having a fixed number of sessions was very good. It made me realize that if I did want to be helped I had to start talking and not waste the counsellor's time. Spacing out the sessions with the gap*

of 2 weeks was good too. It made me less dependent and gave me more time to think."

The sessions had been spaced towards the end of the contract for the reasons stated by Client M.

Another aspect of the "dynamics of the deadline" was demonstrated by Client C.

The following extract from Case C shows how the "deadline effect" put pressure on C to really make use of the last two sessions of the contract to seemingly good effect, as her concluding words show. She was due to leave the country 6 weeks after commencing therapy so she had her own personal time limit which increased the impact of the clinical deadline effect. Although I had not, at that time, known that she was going abroad we had agreed to six sessions at the start of therapy. It was in the penultimate session that she finally revealed her worst fears. She admitted later that it was the knowledge that there was only one more session that put pressure on her to speak out. She says:

"I quickly felt that the time was running out and I never seemed to get to the point."

When she is under stress she tend to begin to feel pressures and tension in her body. This is especially so when she talks about home.

She eventually described her fears in the penultimate session as follows:

"The feeling is like a flat round pulsating crimson shape in my stomach. There is a second feeling too in my chest, this is like a soft dark cloud that invades and envelopes me so that I can't breathe."

She drew this all-embracing feeling presenting a picture of being submerged by the *"cloud"*. She described the feeling as *"being out of control and afraid"*. She finally admitted to a terrifying fear of becoming mad or having a brain tumour or AIDS.

Usually these feelings coincide, she said, with situations where *"I feel rejected or out of control"*.

"C" had expended a lot of emotional energy in talking about these issues and was feeling quite drained and yet relieved to have finally managed to express these fears. She also began to see these in perspective and to see how they relate to the real situation and what the "trigger situations" are that lead to these fears she understands to be neurotic. She seemed to have a new insight that feelings are after all expressible.

The next and last session was one of integration of the insights gained over the previous weeks. We worked together with pen and paper in diagrammatic form.

We began with her fears expressed in the previous session—there seemed to be a theme of "loss" underlying these. We looked back over her life as she acknowledged the loss of her first home—a place she had been happy and peaceful, a school where she *"fitted in—they were like me"*. She looked at the loss she feared behind her fears of AIDS or a tumour—that is children/marriage, life—and as we looked at all the losses of the past she realized that in the present she is facing the loss of a really good friend who is going abroad and looked at the reality of partings and losses.

We moved into an intellectual discussion on existential issues briefly—this seemed to symbolize a shift from client/counsellor—to a more "equal" relationship—appropriate as a client ends the contract.

We reflected on "C's" capacity for intense feelings and her high intellect and what this can mean in terms of looking for peer support and in experiencing pain. We ended however (and here "C" led the way, energetically and enthusiastically) by reaching an understanding that if she experiences pain in depth, so too can she experience love and the fullness of life intensely and positively. "C" felt that this was the right place to end, she had not wanted to stay with all this understanding of the pain on its own. She rightly reminded me of the other side of this. I was reminded of Casement's idea of the client supervising the counsellor and saw this as a good example of "unconscious supervision" (1985, p. 186). There had been a moment earlier in the session that felt like an "end"—but "C" had felt uncomfortable with ending there and questioned this negativity—was she here too within the transference questioning "mother" and mother's negativity? We then worked together towards a tremendous sense of her capacity to enjoy life and to be positive to a point where, after these intensive last two sessions, she felt able to say:

"I am free".

Summary

To conclude, the parameters of what is described as short-term in the literature to the mid 1980s is from 1 session to 40 sessions, most therapists stating that they work to around 15–25 in practice. Thus there is no clear consensus.

Budman and Stone conclude that the difficulty in coming to some agreement as to the duration of short-term therapy is such that another way of resolving the problem is required. They turn to a description coined by Budman and Gurman who concluded that the only commonality was the "rationing of time" and so the terms "time sensitive" or "cost–effective therapy" might be more useful (1983, p. 940).

In my case material, the sessions range from one to 12. Within the 11 cases studied the average is 6.6 sessions and the median being four–six sessions. This was compared with an overview of 150 cases over 1 year in the same practice when the average number of sessions was four as mentioned earlier.

This is slightly more brief than in the research studies referred to earlier. These were studies of all kinds of therapy not specifically short-term. In these studies it was found that the average client terminates at between five and eight sessions regardless of the intention of the therapist (Garfield, 1978; Lorion, 1974; Butcher and Koss, 1978).

My cases indicate that we are returning perhaps to the briefer sessions described by Freud in the 1920s, i.e. one–five sessions. However, rather than allowing therapy to get longer and longer with experience my team have maintained the brief approach within the parameters one–12 sessions, the more usual number being somewhere between four–six sessions as an intentional and agreed time span.

Integration and development

It would seem that we therapists, participating in this project, in the late 1990s have found ways of integrating and developing concepts of practice to shorten therapy further than those working from the 1940s to 1980s.

In the following sections that examine the themes for the constituent parts of brief therapy, it is anticipated that the ways of shortening therapy will also become more clear.

To begin the process of looking in detail at the constituent parts of short-term therapy the next section 5.1.2 focuses on the psychodynamic roots of the particular approach to brief therapy which is the subject of this book.

5.1.2. Psychodynamic roots

This book is focusing on the brief therapy approach evolving from the psychodynamic tradition, which owes its heritage to psychoanalysis. It is therefore important to examine more closely whether this psychoanalytic heritage is evidenced within brief therapy from the empirical work and in the writings of the key proponents.

The developmental history of brief therapy, evolving from psychoanalysis, which has been outlined in the last chapter, attests to this in relation to the work of the key proponents. The history shows that this brief approach is firmly rooted in the psychodynamic tradition. It further shows that by the 1960s therapists who practised the brief approach had moved from the "conservative" view with regard to its efficacy to what is known as the "radical" view. That is, from the expectation that the effects could only be limited and superficial, to recognizing that significant and real change can result from brief psychodynamic therapy.

In this section, therefore, I do not intend to duplicate the developmental history which places the key proponents within this psychotherapeutic framework, but to focus more on the findings to the following questions related to the psychodynamic influence. This is with reference to the key proponents of brief therapy and in particular with reference to the examination of the cases to see how the empirical work demonstrates aspects of its psychodynamic heritage. Are there examples of transference, that is of the past influencing the present in the transference of feelings that relate to past people or events onto the present? Is there evidence of patterns of behaviour stemming from the past, resistance, the therapeutic alliance and the working through of the problem to a satisfactory resolution? Is there also evidence of radical change? Is there evidence of the use of dreamwork, interpretation and the satisfactory emotional discharge to allow new ways of behaving to be evolved?

Transference

In addressing the above questions I shall begin with the concept of transference. Transference is the core concept that informs the psychodynamic therapeutic process. This stems from Freud's seminal ideas. Transference refers to the inappropriate transferring of feelings from past childhood relationships onto figures in the present time and in particular within the therapeutic relationship onto the therapist. This forms the transference neurosis. Freud realized, in closely examining the evolving relationship, attitudes and feelings within the therapeutic relationship, that conflicting patterns of behaviour could be examined and modified. In making the modifications within the therapy situation, the client is also helped to modify the same patterns in the external relationships.

Transference is also considered important by the proponents of brief therapy in order for it to be effective. As all the reviewers point out Freud led the way in this regard, his brief casework with Mahler, Bruno Walter and Ferenczi being frequently cited as seen earlier. Within the context of brief psychotherapy Strupp and Binder (1983), Balint et al. (1972), Davanloo (1980), Malan (1979), Mann (1973) and Sifneos (1979) all reinforce the need for interpreting the transference and resistance. However, the transference is used in different ways, by the different proponents of brief therapy, in order to find ways of shortening the process. For example Franz Alexander, one of the earliest proponents of the brief method, suggested that excessive encouragement of the transference was a cause of lengthening therapy. He recommended a greater emphasis on current relationships to modify this. He also recommended interrupting sessions as a way of reducing the development of the transference neurosis. Bauer and Mills highlight Alexander's emphasis on working with the transference "patterns" of behaviour rather than moving into the "regressive transference neurosis". This they regarded as a "modification of the traditional dynamic work to fit the needs of the brief format" (1989, p. 339).

Davanloo adopts a different approach to transference, aimed at diffusing it. He challenges the first indication of transference reaction. Thus in the face of "avoidance and passivity" on the part of the client, he recommends the therapist to "confront the patient with this in the transference and further link it with significant people in his current life ... persistently confronting the patient with how he really feels" (1980, p. 76).

Bauer and Mills, conclude that in short-term therapy:

> confronting transference reactions to STDP should generally be limited to times when such feelings and/or behaviours are a resistance to the therapeutic focus or when working with transference feelings can yield more effective learning. Transference manifestations should be confronted as they are manifest in the immediate therapy in order to maximize the impact of the work. Finally, transference feelings should be dealt with quickly and energetically in STDP, not only for the sake of time but also as a means for preventing the development of a more difficult and regressive transference (1989, p. 342).

Sifneos (1979) highlights the importance of examining the transference within the therapeutic relationship, so that the feelings and emotions that reflect the past situation can be examined in detail in the present therapy situation. The therapist can help the client to make links with the past from their present reactions to situations and see how such links can lead to inappropriate reactions. From this can develop a corrective experience on two counts. Firstly that the therapist's different reaction to thoughts and feelings expressed brings about what Alexander and Selesnick call a "corrective emotional experience" (1967, p. 323). Secondly the therapist by "modelling" an alternative response challenges the cognitive structures that the client has built up regarding past experiences. This can bring about insight and the realization that the client has a choice in relation to the behaviour.

This "corrective emotional experience" and the influence of the past on the present can be seen in the extracts from Cases C and B seen below.

> In Case C past relationships were having a negative influence on how C felt about herself. Case C came to the therapy saying, *"How can I be more confident and why don't I like myself?"* She then began to talk about how home relationships impact on her and led the way into exploring her relationship with Mother whom she sees as a *"machine"* and as someone who never had time for her. Her younger sister had a lot of attention following an assault incident the year before C left home and she felt she had to cope and be *"good"* all the

time because of the younger sibling needing all the *"care"*. When she finished her *"A"* levels, she was very depressed and stayed in bed all the time—her parents did rally round then. Since then she left home and country and now when she goes home, finds any questions by her mother about her well-being as *"intrusive"* and yet she longs for Mother to really listen to her and talk to her.

She found a real refuge in a grandmother, her father's mother. Mother is always negative about gran, her dad and her. C is like both Dad and Gran. Gran values people and gives her time to C, listening to all she's concerned with. Gran also has a high regard for music and poetry *"she'd like my boyfriend"*. Mother would say: *"Yuck to poetry and music"*.

I reflected softly that: *"Gran sounds really nice"* and in the pause that followed, C gave in to tears of frustration and sadness of *"Why can't Mother like me and the things I value?"* She so wants Mother's approval. The only way she achieved this is to be *"strong"* and to be *"good at work"* and by both of these, she tended to get into trouble at school with her peer group and hence was very alone and lonely at school.

Since the last session, she has allowed herself to experience the sadness we opened up last session and has shared her *"weakness"* with a friend, whose warm and loving response helped her to feel *"strong"* in her weakness. Later on she was able to share in-depth feelings about her parents with her boyfriend also.

The transference patterns are seen to be at work as the past is explored in relation to its effect on the present especially in her difficulty in receiving affection from her friends and in letting them see her as she is i.e. with feelings. The "corrective experience" is evident as I model a different *"mother"* for the client who having opened up with me began to open up to others as she had not previously been able to do.

Case B gives another example of where patterns of behaviour and past events are still producing adverse effects in the present.

Case B approached the counselling service indirectly. She was doing a research project on the counselling service and wished to consult me about it. Her demeanour indicated to me that she was avoiding addressing her own need in the research project she was doing for the sake of others. I suspected that she was also testing out the situation for herself. She was clearly holding herself in check lest tears should flow and when I let her know I had noticed and gently asked if she had just come about the project or could I help she gladly booked some sessions. There was a "challenge" in the gentle offer of counselling and my wondering whether it was typical of her to subjugate her own needs for others which is what she seemed to be doing with the project? Although we had not technically embarked on the counselling relationship at that moment I suggest that it illustrates Davanloo's point about challenging avoidance as soon as it occurs within the transference. I maintain that the transference is present from the very first moment of the encounter.

She said that she would like to *"look at family issues and her relationship with mother"* since she herself could see that these past events were still affecting her present life adversely.

In Session 1 she painfully recalled a number of events from her younger years. I helped Client B to explore the events she recounted, focusing in particular on an event when as a 7 year old she'd offered to pay for some toys and Dad became upset by this. When she went to his study to apologize, he turned his back and said *"Go to hell"*. To the little girl of 7, for a church-going person such as her father to say this was the ultimate rejection—*"nothing could have been more terrible"*.

As the session unfolded it became clear that rejection was and is a common theme throughout her life.

At school she didn't fit in—she was *"the one at the big house"*—her friends tended to be the other ones who didn't fit whom she could *"help"*.

Her fiancé is not approved of by her parents and she endured 2 years of non-communication with them because of the relationship. They want *"better for her"*.

At the time things went so badly for her last year she was *"helping"* her landlady look after her children since the landlord was dying of cancer. Also her fiance's Nan died around that time. This lady used to really care for B—giving her little things—usually useless or worthless materially but given with love, which were cherished by B. When her own Nan died soon after, although not close or even liked, she cracked up: this was also connected with her boyfriend with the fact that her boyfriend needed her less. She was afraid that if he didn't need her she would lose the relationship. A friend was very supportive and took her away with her to a retreat house— where it was very peaceful and therapeutic. She cried *"buckets"*. This friend invited her to join her and another girl in a flat. They gave her a small room and on moving in the situation seemed difficult and disappointing: she felt excluded and the familiar feeling of rejection.

The other important time she recalled was at 18 when she was *"thrown out"* of the house, she could not understand them, *"they said they grieved for me"*—all she felt was rejection and loneliness.

The aspect of past events impacting on the present is inherent in the psychoanalytic approach. It is by dealing effectively with the past that the therapist helps the client to move forward in the present. Already in Session 1 there is a transference element within the relationship. The therapist as an authority figure, or parental figure, is able to model a new response within a familiar pattern, a "corrective experience" as referred to above.

She desperately longs for her parents' love and approval and feels lonely and rejected without it. Approval or support makes her dissolve into tears—at one point in the session she said *"I expect you disagree ..."* I said: *"No, feelings are okay, there's no right or wrong."* And the tears welled.

Client B worked throughout the contract to understand and move on from the enmeshments of the past and the transference issues, concluding in session 11 with a clear affirmation of her selfhood. Client B will be returned to in more detail in the section on activity (5.1.4).

Interpretation

Interpretation is another psychoanalytic concept used in the brief approach. Interpretation is used to help something unconscious become conscious. Interpretation is demonstrated via the use of dreamwork in Client GD1's case. The dream work and interpretation takes the client back to the past.

The presenting problem was that GD1 had *"lost his zest for life"*. He felt as if he were *"just going through the motions"*. He had no feelings at all except a vague background feeling of anxiety. T (Therapist) asked him when he first noticed these feelings or lack of feelings. He told T they began 3 months before coming to England but he had no idea why this should be. T asked if anything else unusual was going on at the same time. He said it was peculiar but that was the time he also found a new girlfriend and he should have been feeling really good. There were no problems with this relationship. He and the girl were good friends and they had resolved to *"keep things light"*. Even if the relationship didn't survive his stay in England, he was confident they could continue to be good friends. He said his anxious feeling was like *"skimming over the surface"* of something. T wondered what was going on under the surface.

T asked if he ever had dreams. He said that he did and told T that the father of his girlfriend invited him to go sailing. He thought this was really weird because he had finished with the girl 4 years previously.

T interpreted this by suggesting that GD1 had unfinished business with his old girlfriend. He felt taken aback by this comment but said he had had no other girlfriends until just before his trip to England. He had been so badly hurt by her unfaithfulness that he resolved to keep things light ever afterwards. T pointed out the connection between his comment about "skimming over the surface" and the sailing metaphor of the dream and suggested he was avoiding the deep water of the feelings about his rejection from his first girlfriend. The dream was reminding him of feelings he thought he had left behind.

GD1 said he found the session very interesting and was clearly quite thoughtful about the idea that his present emotional state could have something to do with events 4 years before. The account continues in the therapist's own words.

GD1's time in England was limited. We had agreed to meet on another four occasions on a weekly basis to see if we could find out what was going on "under the surface", in the expectation that this knowledge might help to restore his feelings and interest in life.

By the time of our second meeting, he had given some thought to the idea of something being under the surface. He described this in a pictorial way, so I asked him to draw it. He felt as though the figure (himself) drawn in a box had acquired a little bit more room to move as a result of the last session. Clearly there was also some way to go.

He was very keen to explore further and offered me a second dream: In the dream he was talking to a man in England who spoke about his girlfriend. Gradually he realized that the man was actually talking about his own girlfriend, whom he had left 4 years ago.

We agreed that this dream seemed to reinforce the idea that came up in the previous session with the image of the girlfriend's father. The girlfriend and his feeling about her actually needed to be dealt with.

He skipped the next and penultimate session. I was not greatly surprised by this. He had worked hard and uncovered a lot of material very quickly and needed time to assimilate his experience.

On our final meeting, he explained his absence by saying he wanted to *"stay strong"*. He told me he now realized that his problems had come about *"because I kept my thoughts and my feelings separate"*. He had telephoned his girlfriend overseas and told her this. He now felt a lot closer to her. He also wanted to share this insight with his two close male friends.

The girlfriend had told him that one of these friends had also spoken of feeling a distance from him. This news made him feel closer to his friend and hopeful that he could share his newly discovered feelings and insights with him.

In reflecting on issues which were explored in an agreed 5-week contract, the therapist states:

> *"I felt that in our five-week contract we succeeded in looking beyond his present symptom of "just going through the motions" of life. We identified the point where he was blocked, i.e. the unfinished issues around the break-up of his last relationship. We went on to explore the feelings around this and he allowed some of the emotion to be expressed. This led to a feeling of release which enabled him to contact his present girlfriend and to regain a feeling of vitality and connectedness with her by acknowledging his deeper feelings."*

This is also an indication of the successful working through of the core problem to change the client's present and existing relationships. A clear example of brief work at the radical end of the spectrum.

Resistance

Resistance, too, is one of the key features of psychoanalytic therapy. Freud refers to this as one of its "cornerstones".

In the following case Freud used a time limit to overcome his client's resistance to getting better. "Under the inexorable pressure of this fixed limit his resistance and his fixation to the illness gave way, and now in a disproportionately short time the analysis produced all the material which made it possible to clear up his inhibitions and remove his symptoms" (1979, p. 238).

Davanloo has developed a technique in dealing with resistance called "head on collision"; especially for those with resistance against emotional closeness (Davanloo, 1992).

Davanloo is a leading proponent of brief therapy and many follow his lead in dealing with the resistance. Konzelmann (1995), demonstrates how this approach is used in a number of case examples. I however find the therapist interventions harsh and the "breaking through" of the defences needlessly painful for the client. The terms "breaking through" and "breaking down" the defences is frequently used with reference to Davanloo's "head on collision" (Schubmehl, 1995; Konzelmann, 1995). The process involves challenging and putting pressure on the defences. The purpose is as Kalpin describes it:

> (1) Acquainting the patient with his or her defences and mobilising the complex transference feelings and anxiety; (2) Getting rid of a key defence (e.g. defiance or ambivalence) when it is prominent and threatens to destroy any potential for success; (3) allowing the mobilized complex transference feelings which are at threshold level to break through to consciousness, thus triggering an unlocking of the unconscious" (1993, p. 19).

In my own cases below and those of my colleagues, the defences rather than being seen as "broken through" are rather worked through, melted or circumvented. This is through a *teaching* approach combined with other factors which may be seen in the case examples below and will be returned to in later sections, e.g. therapeutic alliance and focus. The different approach to dealing with the resistance may be an important factor here in shortening therapy since my cases prove to be considerably shorter than those of Davanloo's. The average number of sessions in my cases is 6.6 with the parameter of 12, as against Davanloo's 15–25 with a parameter of 40.

Shefler (1988) mentions that in short-term dynamic psychotherapy resistances are "bypassed" rather than worked through or interpreted. In support of this argument Shefler then goes on to cite Mann whose use of empathy and support reduces resistance and Davanloo who attacks the patient's defences initially and then supports and interprets. Malan avoids resistance and relates to patients' material with selective neglect. I see this as a misinterpretation on the part of Shefler. These therapists are equally dealing with and acknowledging the resistance.

Melting the resistance

In my own approach to resistance I may well challenge or support, often however I use the technique of *teaching*. This is to be seen in Cases F and M.

Case F

> F was referred for counselling/therapy by the nurse. She had seen me once before for one session when she looked at homesickness. She also saw another counsellor for three times in the previous year.
>
> She stated that she was depressed and indeed that:
>
> *"I've always been depressed—well, since I was 9 years old"*.
>
> One of the themes emerging from the research so far is the significance and importance of the first session in brief therapy and a subsequent section will look at this more closely.
>
> In Case F we see that in the first few sentences when she explained why she'd come to see the therapist she actually gives the key to the focal issue of the contract *"I've ... been depressed ... since I was 9 years old"*.
>
> Here the *general focus* and the catalyst bringing her to the therapy was the "depression". The clear *specific focus* of the therapy was quickly established as the events taking place when she was "9 years old". The brief therapist will focus in on this, teasing out the events at the time.

The subject of focus will also be covered in greater detail in a later section.

F was very resistant to counselling, yet neither did she want to remain on pills. She had omitted to take the antidepressant the doctor had given her, for the last week.

TEACHING ASPECT

In order to establish a rapport and attempt to move towards a "therapeutic alliance", I explained how counselling might be relevant to her. It was already significant that she was able to pin-point a date at which she became depressed.

In demonstrating why I thought this was significant, I asked her what had happened when she was nine. It transpired that her Nan had died after a spell of gradually going senile. This disrupted the whole family—F said:

"it fell apart" and *"it was never the same again"*.

Thus in this first session the therapy itself was begun. As she unfolded the events of her life when she was nine there were very clear links for me to her present feelings of depression and anxiety.

F's biggest current fear is about nuclear war, irrational all absorbing and depressing fear. We explored what a war would/could mean. She saw it as something that

"would destroy everything"—*"nothing would be the same again"*.

The sessions were taking place at a time when Saddam Hussein had invaded Kuwait. The whole world was watching and waiting and the United Nations had come together to oppose this act of aggression. Thus there was reality in her fears. This element needed to be acknowledged. However, it was apparent that her fear of war had pre-dated any of the recent world conflicts.

At this stage she herself could see no link between her fears of the war and the events in her family around the time she was nine and was quite resistant to this kind of exploration. She reported another fact in relation to her "depression", that for her October and November are always bad times and so are May and June. This information led me to move into *teaching* mode again as I talked to her about the effect of anniversaries, about body memory and about grief and about the process of therapy and how we could search for causes of her "depression", if she wanted to.

As we talked she found herself getting back in touch with some of the emotion connected to the disturbing events of that time. (Her Nan becoming senile and *"the family falling apart"* and her present fear of war and *"nothing ever being the same again."*)

This getting in touch with the pain gave F sufficient confidence in me and in the process of therapy to lower her resistance and to request a therapy contract.

This case provides us with a clear example of resistance and demonstrates how the therapist challenges this and establishes a therapeutic alliance within which F's fears can be explored.

In this focal approach expounded by the author, education is a key factor and here it is seen as the method used to challenge and overcome the resistance. Whilst this helped to some degree the breakthrough in the resistance came because of the homework that the client undertook. It also began the working through process which is another psychoanalytic process referred to below. F's homework was to create a chronology of events from when she was 9 years old. When she looked at her own list of dates she clearly saw that the key events in her past were echoing in her present. Until her personal discovery of the key dates of these events, which verified for her the importance of the past on the present, she was very resistant to the process of therapy. Subsequently she was able to work through to insight and change very rapidly and within the brief contract.

F will be returned to in more detail under the activity section 5.1.4 where the good effect of homework will be looked at in greater detail.

Case M

In Case M's first session she makes the connection between the present prevailing problem and the past. Throughout the therapy the past issues are explored, i.e. her schooling and difficulties as a child in relationship with Dad and how this affects her present life as a student.

This aspect will be returned to in more detail in the section on focus. Here, however, I wish to concentrate on a slightly different slant on resistance seen with M. She demonstrates resistance under the guise of concern about confidentiality. She talks about the feeling of *"disloyalty"* in talking about family matters to an outsider.

I again use *teaching* as a way of dealing with the resistance. I explained about confidentiality and about the process of therapy including the freedom to be expected from resolving past issues. Also the potential of lightening her load by sharing her worries in a safe context. M's resistance "melts" rather than is broken through and the process of exploration begins.

The outcome of the exploration is that by the last session:

> M felt that she could now *"handle the home situation better"*—had made a decision to get *"a good enough degree"*—had become more realistic in her expectations about marriage. She had trusted me enough to share a number of deep issues including violence. Clearly, however, there were still some painful areas she did not feel able to get to talk about. Perhaps at a later date she will.

The unravelling and exploring of the past painful events served to free her from repeating maladaptive problems in the present situation. The cathartic aspect of getting in touch with the pain also released her to get on with her life.

M told me that she felt angry when I interpreted (another psychoanalytic tool) that since she was *"gagged"* at home it is not surprising she finds it so hard to talk to me in the sessions. She's aware when she gets angry and she is able to move on from this.

She told me that after the last session when she told me very deep secrets, she felt *"initially drained for a few days and then much better"*.

Working through

Working through is seen by Shefler to be a "problematic concept in STDP associated with the extended duration of psychoanalysis and psychotherapy and related resistances". Shefler says it is "not applicable in STDP" but concedes that this can occur "within the focus" as well as after termination of treatment (1988, p. 201).

Shefler sums up what is expected of the psychoanalytic technique in the words of Sandler et al.: "It is perhaps worth commenting that psychoanalytic writers uniformly maintain that, although working through is an essential part of the psychoanalytic process, interpretation of unconscious mental content and of transference repetitions, together with the gaining of insight, are equally vital to it. Thus, any technique which does not make use of all these elements would not be regarded as psychoanalytic" (1988, p. 203).

I believe, however, that working through can be rapid, as in the examples above, although this does not always occur within the set number of sessions. It can, as Shefler admits, be completed, or further aspects of working through can occur after termination. This is entirely within the remit of short-term and focal therapy. This is because this approach allows for the client to become their own therapist and therefore to take the ongoing development or working on patterns and habits of behaviour as part of the ongoing process to health. It is a necessary part of the process, but the therapist does not have to be on hand to enable this. It is the internalized therapist that will monitor this development. The idea of homework can facilitate this process as demonstrated in F above.

Summary

In this section I have focused on the more obvious links with psychoanalysis. In looking at the empirical work we have seen themes that relate to the psychoanalytic framework recurring in each of the case examples. There have been examples of the past influencing the present, the transference of feelings that relate to past people or events onto the present. That is the transference repetitions referred to by Sifneos (1979) and Malan (1976). We have seen the evolving patterns, resistance, the therapeutic alliance and the working through of the problem to a satisfactory resolution. There have been examples of the therapist modelling a different response, to challenge the cognitive structures that the client has established, in relation to the past. There have been examples of resistance challenged but worked around in an educative way, coaxing the client by explaining the pros and cons of working with the therapy process. This differs from Davanloo's more confrontational approach. It highlights both the *sensitivity* of the therapist and the *teaching* element that are underlying themes that I have referred to earlier.

With Malan I conclude that this form of therapy is a "technique of brief psychotherapy based on that of psychoanalysis" (1976, p. 281). I also fully endorse Malan's view that it "deals fearlessly with most of the same issues" (p. 280). Malan suggests that the opposition caused when this brief approach proposed by Alexander was due to the way he wrote it up as "a modification of psychoanalytic technique, rather than simply the flexible application of basic psychoanalytic principles to brief psychotherapy" (p. 351). "Anyone who reads their case histories can see the clinical ... evidence ... for the use of all the basic psychoanalytic principles, especially interpretation of the transference and transference/parent link, in a radical technique of brief therapy leading to a radical outcome" (p. 351).

This section of Chapter 5 has shown that psychodynamic therapy, which has tended to be thought of as a long-term process, can also be short-term. In the next section we continue the examination of the component parts of brief therapy. This is in order to see the ways of condensing the process, to produce the same end effect in a shorter time than had previously been expected.

The above exposition highlights the psychoanalytic backcloth in both the assumptions and the process. However, it has also shown that in the focal and short-term approach a variety of therapeutic skills and assumptions are also borrowed from other traditions to help shorten the process. These include cognitive and behavioural ideas, gestalt and art therapy, to name but a few. These other therapeutic tools are called upon as appropriate by the therapist. There is therefore a need for flexibility and expertise in a range of skills on the part of the therapist.

The next section 5.1.3 concentrates on flexibility and techniques from other therapeutic philosophies that have been integrated into psychodynamic brief therapy in order to effect change more rapidly.

5.1.3. Flexibility

The last sections show that short-term focal therapy, whilst owing its heritage to psychoanalysis, differs from psychoanalysis in many ways. It differs for example, in relation to a time limit which was discussed in 5.1.1 and in the embracing of active and flexible techniques more closely associated with other traditions. This section explores how flexibility is seen as a way of shortening the process and of enhancing the effectiveness of brief therapy.

Flexibility as a key principle

Alexander, as we saw in the last section, led the way in the use of behavioural and cognitive approaches and there are many other techniques which appear in the examples of brief work cited. These are flexibly interwoven into the brief therapy process in order to accelerate the process.

Alexander and French are acclaimed as the first to promote this principle of flexibility which they describe as *intrinsic* to the development of the short-term dynamic approach. They presented this as a modification of psychoanalysis rather than as a new model of therapy.

This concept of flexibility was, at that stage of the development of therapy in the 1940s, seen to be quite revolutionary. Alexander tried out a variety of approaches in relation to "frequency of interviews" and the use of "interrupted sessions" and "corrective emotional experience" referred to in the earlier discussion.

Drawing on the work of Alexander and French (1946), Bauer and Kobos in the 1980s see flexibility as a *key principle* of brief therapy:

> Alexander insisted that in psychotherapy the therapist should adapt technique to patient needs. Only individual needs can determine the technique best suited to bring about curative processes (1984, p. 156).

They observe that "though such flexibility may seem obvious today it was revolutionary" at the time that Alexander was writing (1995, p. 35).

Rogawski also draws on the work of Alexander and French and emphasizes that flexibility is a *requirement* for the brief therapist. He reiterates Alexander's stress that it is only "the nature of the individual case" that "should determine the choice of technique" (1982, p. 336). Also, that this flexibility relates even "to frequency and length of sessions" (p. 339). I would suggest that Alexander here is emphasizing the *sensitivity* of the therapist to client need and the importance of being *in tune* with the client.

As Alexander in the 1940s is an early advocate with regard to flexibility of technique, later in the 1960s Wolberg takes up the same theme. Wolberg recommends that: "a degree of flexibility in the therapist is required which enables him to step outside the bounds of his training basis and to experiment with methods from fields other than his own" (1965, p. 136).

He states that this flexibility of technique is vital if real change is to take place as a result of therapy: "Only a therapist schooled in the widest varieties of technique and seasoned through the broadest spectrum of emotional problems can move the patient beyond the comforts of support into areas that hold promise of personality change" (1965, p. 128).

Kovacs too takes the radical view and expects real change to occur from the therapeutic encounter which he recommends should have novel interventions and calls on systems theory saying: "If the therapist provides responses that are novel ... the therapist not only begins to change the organization of the patient but the organization of the patient's entire interpersonal field as well" (1982, p. 149).

Flexibility and integration

Wolberg advances a theory of eclecticism in method but goes beyond this concept in further describing this as a *fusion* of methods. In this he is a forerunner of the integrative approach advocated by many within the wider field of psychotherapy in the 1990s.

Wolberg sees the short-term therapy as combining "procedures from psychiatric, psychoanalytic, psychological and sociological fields. Often utilized in the same patient are psychoanalytic technics, casework, drugs, hypnosis, group therapy, psychodrama, desensitization and reconditioning procedures" (1965, p. 136).

A fusion of methods

Wolberg encourages short-term therapists to understand both the positives and negatives of various procedures. He suggests that experience is required in "blending a variety of approaches for their special combined effect" (1965, p. 195). Wolberg's term "fusion" describes how these come together and he talks of a "fusion of methods, in which there are extracted from the different approaches tactics of proven merit" (p. 136). He adds: "Eclecticism does not sanction wild therapy. It presupposes a scrupulous empirical attitude, assigning the values of the different methods for the great variety of conditions that challenge the therapist in his daily practice" (p. 137).

These ideas are still to the fore in the 1980s where many follow in Wolberg's footsteps. Bauer and Kobos for example understand the brief therapy techniques to be a "distillation based upon the understanding of personality dynamics and patterns of disturbed functioning which traditional techniques have delineated" (1984, p. 153).

Held states that flexibility is "the most important principle" in brief therapy. She proposes a Prescriptive Eclecticism which combines the "individualising" of treatment with the "benefits" of theory and research (1984, pp. 239–240).

Kovacs, also an advocate of flexibility in the brief approach, describes a variety of ways of working with clients. He points the way forward by combining principles from psychoanalytic theory and from systems theory in an attempt to find new strategies that may be effective in short-term therapy. He also refers to the use of gestalt and psychodrama in addition to the well known approaches of the psychoanalytic and humanistic traditions. However, Kovacs takes the concept still further and suggests that newer tactics still may be employed, such as reframing, the use of paradoxical intention and encountering. Encountering is the "forceful and direct expression of effectively tinged observations of the patient by the therapist" (1982, p. 150). Another aspect of encountering as described by Kovacs is the use of the therapist's own humanity. The example he gives is where the patient's non reaction in relation to a particularly sad experience triggers the therapist's own similar experience. The therapist cries with regard to their own sad event and explains why to the client. The client then also begins to relate to the sad feelings that had previously been blocked. This proves a therapeutic process for the client (p. 151).

This involvement of the therapist and sharing of their own pain raises questions for me. It is far removed from the psychoanalytic roots brief therapy has hitherto related to. I see it as moving beyond the realms of brief therapy into a different form of treatment and is not one that I would countenance within the model I advocate and am writing about. Countering the predicted comparison with psychoanalysis, Kovacs reminds us that the method Freud introduced was designed to reduce the intensity of the personal encounter between therapist and client. Freud himself admitted, Kovacs tells us, that this approach came in part from his own personal wish to avoid intense face to face interactions with his analysands and hence the custom of the analyst sitting behind the couch. I remain unconvinced by this argument and see it as over involvement of the therapist. This does not however negate an important contribution Kovacs has made in relation to his ideas on "rites of passage" which will be addressed further on.

Budman and Stone (1983) also recommend an eclectic and pragmatic approach where creative intervention strategies are used. These are taken from psychoanalysis, behaviourism and humanistic approaches. They also include examples of integrative Brief Therapy using family systems approach. They refer to Wolberg (1980), whose leading ideas have been referred to above and who is still a key advocate of the brief approach in the 1980s, and who, despite being a psychoanalyst, uses behavioural and cognitive approaches. These include hypnosis, homework and ego building activities. Budman and Gurman (1983) also work with an integrative brief therapy model using varied techniques.

Thus the short-term therapist will need to be conversant with a range of therapeutic interventions and be comfortable with their use. Budman and Stone speaking in the 1980s predict that the Brief Therapy of the future will be "flexible, creative and eclectic" (1983, p. 945). They suggest that the therapist who uses this approach will need to be open to creative intervention strategies.

Brief therapy in context

The trend towards eclecticism and to integration has been a gradual development and belongs not just to the brief models of therapy but is a more generic phenomenon. Budman and Stone noted that in Garfield and Kurtz' (1977) study of clinical psychologists most described their theoretical orientations as eclectic. The usual reason given was that "it allowed greater therapeutic flexibility and the opportunity to do what works" (1983, p. 944).

Flexibility of the therapist

Wolberg stresses personal qualities of flexibility within the therapist suggesting: "Not only is knowledge of and experience with different procedures important, but their applications ... will require inventiveness and willingness to utilize the contributions of all schools of psychiatry, psychology and the social sciences toward the enhancement of therapeutic progress" (1965, p. 195).

As Marmor (1980) refers to the wide experience required of short-term therapists so Rogawski (1982) sees this approach as placing greater demands on the therapist than the longer-term approaches. He points out that more people will be worked with within the same number of hours. A treatment plan must be devised quickly and the core focal area must be both found and agreed with the client.

Certainly the brief therapist needs to be able to withstand a great deal of loss because of the rapid turnover of clients. The intensity of the working relationship is still present, in the brief contract, but endings are more frequent than for the longer-term therapist who sees fewer clients over a longer period.

Kovacs (1982) also looks at the implications for the therapist of this brief approach. He alludes to the economic uncertainty that rapid turnover of clients puts upon the clinician. He observed that there is a resistance on the part of clinicians to the development of successful brief intervention strategies.

Flexibility required of the client

Sifneos does not refer so much to the flexibility of the therapist but rather to that of the client. He emphasizes the need for the client to be able to address issues "flexibly" and to have the "ability to interpret, to problem-solve and to be inquisitive ..." (1987, p. 108). Sifneos expects from the client a "certain ability to explore new ideas and to experiment with different behavioural attitudes" which "demonstrates not only a constructive and active curiosity but also intelligence, openness and flexibility, personality traits that will help in the task of problem solving, one of the most important technical aspects of STAPP" (1987, p. 45).

Malan also stresses patient flexibility as a criterion for brief work and exploring whether or not such flexibility could be measured at the selection stage. He states that: "It is obvious that the ability to respond to brief psychotherapy must be a measure of some quality of flexibility in the patient" (1963, p. 26).

He observes that Alexander had suggested that a way of "assessing a factor connected with flexibility" exists, that of making "trial interpretations" (1963, p. 27).

Flexibility with regard to timing of sessions

Budman and Stone highlight an aspect of flexibility in relation to the format of sessions. They refer to Alexander's recommendation of: "Consciously manipulating the frequency of the visits. He felt this was an effective way of controlling the transference relationship, limiting regression, preferring the development of over-dependency on the therapist, and fostering autonomy" (1983, p. 940). Alexander points out that "reminding the patient that treatment must be as short as possible discourages procrastination and facing up to important issues ... and advocates the technique of "temporary interruptions" which is "based on trusting the natural recuperative powers of the human personality ..." (1965, p. 90). Alexander further observes with disapproval that "there is a normal general trend towards over-treatment" (1965, p. 91).

Following on from this idea Kovacs suggests that the idea of sporadic therapy or therapy with interruptions may be appropriate. He combines this concept with that of time limits. He suggests that it may be quite usual for a client to complete an aspect of work and then after some time, even years, he may return for further sessions. Kovacs compares this with the concept of rites of passage. Later he suggests that brief psychotherapy may effectively create a kind of "secular priesthood" of therapists. He suggests that clients will keep returning to "see a priest of the rituals of transition" (1982, p. 159).

Budman and Stone fit brief therapy into the developmental process. They refer to unblocking blocks. They see the interrupted sessions as helpful in this regard and liken the concept to that of a medical practice. Here patients come to the practitioner at irregular intervals according to need. Follow up sessions also fit this pattern. Budman and Stone refer to this as "time sensitive" and "cost–effective" therapy. They describe this in both financial and psychological terms. They also refer to time in relation to treatment being rationed. The idea of developmental snags is also highlighted. They suggest that treating the developmental snags enables the therapist to be "brief, timely and judicious". They also suggest that this intervention will have "continuing ramifications for the patient's ability to deal with future developmental problems" (1983, p. 942).

Flexibility of technique

In the last section some examples from the case work were used to demonstrate brief therapy's psychodynamic heritage. Hoch emphasizes that "every technique which is known in the long form of treatment can be used in the short form" (1965, p. 55). Later Marteau concurs with this and includes "interpretation of dreams and fantasies, analysis of resistance, interpretation of the transference, and the link between transference and childhood" (1986, p. 84). In the next part of this section I have chosen case examples to demonstrate the use of a variety of techniques taken from a range of traditions. The techniques are woven together and applied as appropriate for each individual client. They include examples related to the timing of sessions, to dreamwork, fantasy, artwork, use of homework, renegotiating of focus, working through and interpretation.

The word "fusion" used by Wolberg resonates for me as does his emphasis on using tools appropriately and according to the need of the individual. I have separated out the techniques in order to demonstrate the variety that may be used to good effect. I have taken only extracts of the cases in order to illustrate the technique, but am also protecting the client anonymity by using just the extracts. I am giving sufficient contextual information to demonstrate how the technique evolves from the client context and needs to be woven into the fabric of the session. A technique is not something that can be "lopped on" to the work of the session rather it must flow in an integrated manner.

I have selected the following cases Case GD1, J and E to give a range of techniques.

Dreamwork

GD1

Hoch states: "The handling of dreams is the same in short-term as in long-term therapy" and this is evident in the case of GD1 (1965, p. 59).

In the last section, we saw the example, GD1, where in the first session a dream is presented and interpreted within the process of establishing the therapeutic alliance contract and in making "a dent" in the therapy work itself. In the second session a further dream is offered, interpreted and worked with to a successful conclusion. I do not intend to repeat the GD1 case here but it is relevant to refer to, as we examine flexibility in the use of techniques as an example of dreamwork being used to good effect within a brief contract.

Unscheduled short session

CASE J

A different example of flexibility, on this occasion with regard to time, appears in J's case.

> After the first session J appeared requesting a short unscheduled session since lectures had been cancelled and she preferred half an hour now to an hour later on! In this half-hour she talked about how her Dad hurt her by his lack of trust in her, in implying she'd try drugs if her boyfriend did. She also told me about her boyfriend and that her friends had known all about the boyfriend's bad background and drug-taking, but had not told her until after she'd broken with him. This left her with a feeling of hurt and betrayal.
>
> I felt she was testing me out with a number of issues to see how I reacted. The issues did not seem to carry the same emotional weight as had the termination which had been one of the many presenting issues in the first and previous session. When she had referred to the termination the pain had been quite tangible.
>
> She did return to the abortion and how even though it was 4 years ago she cannot forget it and feels upset at remembering it.
>
> I held firmly to the half hour she requested and when the abortion topic came up I emphasized that there was insufficient time at this point to go into such an important matter as that and that we should look at this at the beginning of the next session. This we did, to a very rapid and positive conclusion in two further sessions.
>
> She was I think testing me out with the request to see me briefly to see how I reacted to her "hurt" about friends/boyfriend/Dad, which are not as significant as the pain felt in relation to the termination.

I had agreed to see her, interpreting this request as a testing out situation and instinctively seeing the right response as simply being "there" for her. In the light of the subsequent session when she described how she felt let down by everyone close to her at the time of the termination by their not being "there for her," my instinctive response seemed to be verified. I believe that by agreeing to this unscheduled session the whole therapy process was accelerated and J felt able to go into the most painful issue the termination in the next session.

Working through.   In the next session she told me in detail about the abortion and her feelings in relation to it. That is about the guilt, the feelings of being pushed into it and then having to accept it as it was her responsibility. She related the whole incident, remembering it vividly and becoming keenly in touch with the pain of the actual abortion and of the subsequent loss. Her boyfriend drove her to the hospital, but she felt really abandoned and let down by him. She had forgotten her money for the operation and he had to go and find some. He took all day to do this so was not there when she came round from the anaesthetic. She felt *"deserted"* and found it *"horrible"* being in a separate ward and *"horrible overhearing the groups of women in a neighbouring ward being so glad and relieved as if it meant nothing"*. To J it was a really big thing. She would love to have children and really feels very guilty. This was 4 years ago and still upsets her. She told her sister who was no help at all, but told J how *"terrible"* she was to have a termination. She felt her sister could have at least relieved her of the housework for a while, all she did was swap the hoovering for the ironing but that meant standing.

J had slipped out of the house early telling her mother she was *"going to the market"*. It was a *"horrible experience and having to just carry on as if nothing had happened and feeling really unwell"*.

Her feelings of guilt are strong. We talked about the guilt and about mitigating circumstances, about sorrow and about forgiveness. The one she felt in need of forgiveness from was the child, Oliver Martin as she'd named him.

Together we explored ways of dealing with the guilt and of a symbolic way of making recompense. She agreed that although she'll never forget, she needs to forgive herself. She very much liked the idea of finding a symbolic way of making recompense.

Her poem that she produced for the next session shows a wonderful way of doing this *"every smile and every laugh"*, she tells Thomas Oliver is to be a *"gift to you from me"*.

We talked of her beliefs about where he is now. The "talk" was within the framework of sadness and feelings of grief and mourning and yet we were able to move in and out of the depth of feeling to also explore essential concepts and beliefs at a cognitive level.

We also discussed the importance of ritual and ceremony in dealing with death and the importance of naming the child. She had already done this and was well aware of the day the child's birthday would have been.

Use of homework.   We attempted to move into a Gestalt exercise and to dialogue with the child. This was not successful since she felt he would not understand because *"I denied him his life"*. However, later I suggested that she might do some homework, that is some therapeutic written work she could do during the week. I suggested that she might like to put into words what she'd like her boy to have heard from her if she could speak to him. She found this idea very appealing and resolved to do so. The session ended with her being quietly sad.

The use of homework will be returned to in the activity section.

J followed through on this homework task and in the next session came in telling me she'd written a poem to Oliver Martin which really expresses what she wants to say. She'd like to read it aloud to him somewhere in a church maybe or an open field. The idea of a memorial service or ceremony had made sense to her as an ending of the unfinished business and she saw this as a way of ritualizing the loss.

She plans to do this soon and will tell me about what she does next week.

In fact she did read her poem out aloud in a park surrounded by flowers. *"It really helped"*.

The poem is as follows:

*TO OLIVER MARTIN: **A Gift To You From Me***

I know I stopped you growing
its hard to die before you live
but I know you understand
that I had nothing here to give.
I know that I sound selfish
but all I had was love
and even I couldn't give as much
as you have in your world above.
I'll never stop wanting you
or wishing that you're here
but at least I know that you have
found a purer world that's clear.
Don't think I never wanted you
it's just the time was wrong
but I'll love and pray for ever more
at least my whole life long.
So darling as I write this
rest your treasured head
and wish me please some happiness
to replace this awful dread. You know
you'll never be forgotten put down or
mislaid, ignored or just pushed aside
coz here's a pact we made.
I'm going to place you in my heart
a place that's warm and true
and there you'll stay with me on earth
until my soul joins up with you.
I've never really seen the light and
beauty that you hold
but chose to see a darker side
deathly black and cold.
But Thomas baby now I see
the pain I have inside
isn't something sinister
but your love I tried to hide.
So will you now believe me
when I say with all my heart
that I love you now and always
and that we'll never part.
One day we'll be together
until then just look and see
that every time I laugh and smile
it's a gift to you from me.

I was moved to see that within her poem J had given herself permission to be happy again. She had, entirely alone, come up with the idea that every *"smile and laugh"* would be a *"gift"* to her aborted child. She named him also which was an important step in the process and was glad to know that I would be using her sessions as part of my research. She wanted the name Thomas Oliver Martin retained whilst obscuring the remainder of her identity.

Flexibility and focus.   The other problems she'd referred to move in and out of the central theme. The boyfriend for example had chosen to maliciously, as J felt it to be, send a Valentine's card to her, the day the child would have been born, signed Thomas Oliver, the name she'd given to her aborted child. This led to a brief look at her feeling about the boyfriend.

We talked about whether the other issues are still matters of concern. It was clear, however, that the real issue had been her own guilt, feelings of responsibility and pain of loss about her child.

The "homework" activity undertaken by the client in her own time moved her on to the extent that both she and I felt the therapy to be complete. None of the other issues listed in the first session was any longer significant.

Her relationship with Dad seems to have improved and he is being very nice to her at present. She really feels the abortion was colouring everything else and that she has completed what she needed to and so this was our final session.

In talking about the whole experience and the lack of support she received from her boyfriend and family, and in accepting the reality of the abortion and her feeling of guilt, she was able to address this and move on. The poem served as a bridge to move on with her life—she felt free. J described it as follows:

"*I woke up yesterday as if I were waking up after a long illness*".

I saw her briefly some months later and requested her permission to write up her case and to include her poem. She was happy for me to do so, is still feeling good and is handling her other problems well. She wanted the name Thomas Oliver Martin to be used, using it as a kind of memorial to him.

In only four sessions J was able to put her life back in order. For 4 years she had had difficulties in all areas of her life, but these stemmed from the time of the termination. Once she had dealt with the focal issue she was well able to handle the other issues. These four sessions produced an ongoing change for her.

In addition to highlighting the value of flexibility about time, this example demonstrates a number of techniques being used flexibly, to use Wolberg's terminology, "fused" together to facilitate and speed the brief therapy process. The use of techniques, such as giving homework, exploring conceptual frameworks, with regard to beliefs about death and guilt, involve activity on the part of the therapist and this activity is the subject of a later section.

Use of fantasy work

An extract from E's case demonstrates the use of fantasy work within the brief therapy as one of the many different techniques that might be employed to good effect. It is important that as and when a particular technique could help, it is introduced in a spontaneous and natural manner. The more techniques that a therapist has in their repertoire the more useful this is, provided that the "fusion" that Wolberg referred to earlier is present. The fantasy exercise demonstrated below does not stand alone, but is interwoven with other aspects of the therapy process, such as dealing with transference, the client context, negotiation of contract and issues of dependence.

In order to put this extract in context I am briefly giving a little background to the case.

CLIENT E (MID THIRTIES)

The presenting problem related to exam stress and the first session focused on coping strategies but also touched on past events and past exam times. It was evident that the other issues were contributing to the stress both past and present, and she was offered a therapy contract of five sessions if she wished to explore these issues further.

E returned and requested a counselling contract. She had an immediate concern relating to her family and difficulties with her daughter, which became the focus of this session. This led into our looking at earlier relationships and we decided that relationships would be the broad area for our counselling contract. We agreed four further sessions on a weekly basis.

The focus arrived at by the end of session one was a rather general one, "relationships". Session two explored this generally, looking at some of her relationships in the present and how they related to earlier relationships, her comment at the end was a realization that, *"I don't need to work so hard to succeed"*. We also explored her fear of changing and ended with E finally firmly resolving that she wanted to change how she relates to people.

E said: *"I don't want to be changed, and yet I'm not happy with how things are now"*.

"To be changed" implies that someone will force her to change, it was important for her to realize that she can choose to change or not to change. She rightly assumes that entering into the process of counselling will probably change her, but again she has a choice here. In the statement *"I'm not happy with how things are now"*, she faces the present and rejects it. This leaves the way open for her to change, it is a step leading to a deeper involvement in the process of therapy. This was an important step in creating the working alliance. She needed to face the fear of change and resolve to go ahead with the counselling in order to move out of the "now" situation.

The subsequent session (No. 3) constitutes the real substance of this particular contract and would probably not have taken place without the specific resolve to change that emerged in session 2.

The conclusion of the second session was a firm resolution on E's part that she didn't want to stay where she was at that time emotionally and therefore she was prepared to work to change.

Session three began at that point.

We again attempted to focus down from the broader area of relationships:

Penny. *"What is it you want to change in relationships?"*

As a therapist with this client I was working hard to keep a focus on the material being presented and to relate it to the agreed focus: relationships. E referred to her difficulty in gauging levels in relationships, she explained that she often misjudges the level.

E said: "*I feel unconnected with some people*" and a tear trickled down her face, but only from the left eye—it was flowing quite fast. I wasn't sure if this was crying or an eye complaint because the emotion didn't seem to fit. I checked it out.

At this point there was a change in the emotional temperature in the therapy room. I believe I can best use imagery to explain the concept here. Until these words were spoken there had been a sense almost of two judo experts circling each other, dodging, parrying, approaching, feigning attack and ducking out at the last moment. As therapist I was working hard to maintain the focus almost in the position of agreed combat, but when the client uttered the words above—"*I feel unconnected*"—there was a shift and a new level of being "connected". To continue the above image, it was as if the judo experts now together began to combat the problem.

The fantasy exercise that occurred next evolved from my checking out her "crying from one eye" and is described below.

The client allowed me to be there *with her* as she in fantasy reintegrated those aspects of herself she had split off. In the imagery of the fantasy she led the way, only when she seemed stuck did I facilitate with a suggestion. For the most part I simply accompanied her on this fantasy journey.

P: "*Are you crying?*"
E: "*Yes*" (smiling).
P: "*You're only crying from the left eye—what is that about?*"
E: "*Am I?—I didn't know.*"

We talked a little about the left and right hemispheres and then tried an exercise in fantasy.

P: "*Can your left side talk to the right?*"
E: "*I don't have anything to say.*"
E: (*The left is just cringing in a corner—it's light and round—the other side is hard and oblong.*) "*I want to help but I don't know how.*"
   (*The light side is crying copiously now, not rejecting but not able to ask for what he/she needs.*)
P: "*Does the oblong side want to help?*" ...
E: "*Yes, but doesn't know what to do.*"
P: "*Can the crying one tell the oblong what to do?*"
E: "*I suppose touch would help.*"

P: *"Can you invite the oblong over?"*

E: *"No."*

P: *"Okay, so what's happening now?"*

E: *(The cringing one is just getting smaller and smaller in the corner and crying.)*

P: *"Can we move the two shapes together?"*

E: *"Yes, they are touching now."*

P: *"Can they get closer?"*

E: *"No, it's like there was a glass wall between them."*

P: *"So they can see each other but not get close?"*

E: *"Yes. The white shape is humming. The other is not doing anything."*

P: *"Can you slide the glass aside a little like a sliding door?"*

E: *"Yes, they've moved into each other and they're a squishy shape on the floor—they were greys/whites and blacks, now its's a greenish/grey colour. It hurts a bit."*

P: *"Do they take on a new shape together?"*

E: *"No—it's just there. (pause) It's very dark. (pause) It's taking shape. Oh! It's like a tree silvery/green—between a Doric column and a tree."*

P: *"Can we get more light in there? Sunlight?"*

E: *"I've taken off the roof and it's lighter and warmer. It's not reached the roof yet—it's an old tree quite big and gnarled—with little branches at the top—they are moving around—oh! and it's grown more. It's humming. It's still in this round building—in a wood—not constricted but secure—trees all around."*

P: *"Can you get into the picture?"*

E: *"Yes, I'm leaning against the tree trunk—it's comfortable and safe."*

P: *"Can you take it with you?"*

E: *"No, I don't want to go far from it. I want to move."*

P: *"Can you climb it?"*

E: *"Yes, I'm in its branches and it's nice. It's singing now loudly."*

P: *"So how can you move? Can you be part of it?"*

E: *"No."*

P: *"Can it shrink to size?"*

E: *"No—wait—it's changing shape—it's becoming a horse—now we can go—I'm in a plain now—it's green and there's lots of space."*

P: *"Can you get to the College, to the classroom. Will the horse bring you?"*

E: *"Yes, he's here—I've opened a window and his head's poking in."*

P: *"That's not very practical—can he change again to be closer?"*

E: *"Yes he's changing shape, he's a dragon draped around my shoulders."*

P: *"Can he get smaller; he'll frighten the others."*

E: *"Yes, he's quite small now—under my collar—like a necklace around my neck—comforting."*

P: *"Has he a name?"*

E: *"Yes—Horace. That came up this morning."*

(and she told me of an incident that morning.)

P: *"So how do you feel about what we've been doing today?"*

E: *"Good—it feels like integration. I don't think I'll lose this—it's easier to hold on to images."*

P: *"Have you done this sort of exercise before?"*

E: *"No, but it was easy to do—I could have stopped any time, but if it seems worthwhile, I'll go with things and try it. It seemed to be making sense."*

E: *"Where do I go from here?"*

I suggested E might like to *"write it up to hold it, to stay with it and to dwell on it a little"* as a homework task, another therapeutic tool. We decided to leave the search for a "focus" since what emerged from the fantasy exercise is more important to stay with. Perhaps this is the focal issue. This is also an example of flexibility in terms of renegotiating the contract. We reflected that we have two more sessions contracted for, and I reminded her that the last one would be to review our work together.

This session with its fantasy exercise proved to be the turning point for the client in integrating the split off aspects of herself, she was able to begin to connect also in her other relationships. This was the beginning of the ongoing process.

We opened this next session with a clarification of the number of sessions left, i.e. two sessions including this one and that the last session would be a review session.

I asked E how she felt after the last session.

E: *"I felt languid—lovely for 2 to 3 days."*

P: *"What happened then?"*

E had suffered a setback and felt *"depressed"*. She had felt that she had slipped back so had begun to wonder if after all the improvement she'd noted in herself after session 2 had been real. It turned out that she had heard then of a friend having cancer diagnosed. She herself has to go for a check-up soon and had had a lump last year. This had shaken her considerably. We focused on this for a little while and then by agreement, returned to our work of the previous week.

Focusing down.   We came to the cancer issues by focusing minutely on when she felt good, when she stopped feeling good and what explicitly had happened in between. For example: What had happened? Where had she been? Who had she seen? What had she been doing? This close examination of events brought to light the contact with her friend who had cancer. At this point, she became very clear that this was when she began to feel depressed and then shared the information about her own tests past and pending. Once she had made these links with her mood change, she was eager to return to the therapy work we were engaged in. By separating out the cancer issue from the relationships issue, she was able to re-own the progress previously felt after the last session. On reflection, the "connection" and "empathy" she felt with her friend in this example could have been used as a positive demonstration of her ability to "connect" with friends.

Negotiating and renegotiating the contract.   It is to be noted that the whole exploration of the cancer issue and return to the therapy contract took about 15 minutes only and was sufficient to obtain clear agreement as to the use of the remainder of the session. This continuous negotiation within the contract is an exercise in sensitivity and flexibility for the therapist. It gives the client the choice of what they wish to work on. Once the choice is made, the therapist holds the client to the agreed focus. It is also taking account of the client's external reality. More will be said about this in the discussion on focus.

Taking account of the client's external reality.   It is important for the therapist to keep the client's external life in mind. Clients do not live in a vacuum between sessions and they continue to be bombarded by life events regardless of the intense themes explored within the therapy. The life events need to be acknowledged and, if manageable without the therapist, to be put on one side as the therapy contract continues.

I wondered about the first session we'd had and where it had fitted in with this. She explained that there was a link, always before in relationships she had "split off", now she feels she doesn't need to.

Art work.   She drew me a diagram to demonstrate her experience of the old self and new self. This resembled a divided circle and represented a *"hurt self, a wounded self, an unknown element and the child"*. The *"child section"* was the biggest and is shown as *"split off"*.

She had experienced these separate parts as merging together during our fantasy work, like the fantasy picture *"squishing together"*. Now she sees a different image as better representing her feelings. *"This one is like a circle within circles with no solid edge, it's rather like water. It's flexible"*. E said *"this is representing my creative side and the need to reassert this. It's dark blue outside, this is E, light blue on the middle section which represents the material and the centre is yellow/gold and represents God"*.

We returned to the images we had worked with last time, the horse and the dragon. E finds that both images are needed. The horse is *"fey"* and disappears if she tries to grasp it. It has shrunk in her image to shoulder high and comes and goes, galloping off. E finds it helpful *"to allude to them both from time to time and to experience the feeling of integration"*.

The session subsequent to this was spent in relating the knowledge gained from the fantasy exercise to her daily life and the meaning of the fantasy for her. A great deal of change seemed to have occurred. She felt it had been an *"integrating"* experience.

Since we are nearing the end of the contract of sessions and this has a loss element in it, we looked at loss. She began to cry a little, with tears flowing from both eyes. Was a tear duct unblocked, or was this affirming the integration? Both of us had been alert to observe which eye/eyes were crying and she had moved out of the emotion in her curiosity to observe herself. We laughed about this together and agreed that it could indicate integration. We decided that there is no need to delve further into the past since her present sense of integration seems to have enabled her to handle the present satisfactorily.

Last session of contract.   Dealing with loss is an important part of the work of short-term therapy. Despite the few sessions the depth of the relationship and the therapeutic work is intense, and therefore the sense of loss exists as keenly as if the therapeutic work had been undertaken over a more prolonged period.

We looked further at goals, endings and loss since this session is the last. We had touched on a number of these in terms of her friend and the friend's cancer and her own tests for cancer.

She was unable to be specific but feels the way forward is freer without past shackles inhibiting her. She feels happy about what we've done and well-equipped to go on on her own.

E: *"I feel as if I have gained 'stature', as if the bits that were scattered have come together—and that I have the resources to call upon—I know how to get help."*

P: *"What help?"*

E: *"The dragon and horse—those parts of myself that can cope, they provide a reassuring strength."*

E realizes that these symbols can be dropped eventually when she's assimilated the ideas. She realizes this may take several months.

She had come with difficulties in exams and with relationships and from this we'd looked back to where the difficulties began. We looked briefly at study and exams and she seems clear as to where she's going with this and recalled ways of dealing with the habit of stress in exams. Although we've not focused much on exams in our work prompted by this presenting problem, she feels more confident about tackling them. Her feeling more "together", gives a more solid ground to tackle other problems and issues. Although we seemed to be dealing with past relationship issues only as a way of focusing where the difficulty lay, something of the past has been dropped and left behind. At home things have been both easier and calmer. We looked at where she sometimes gets lost in fantasy, not the work she did with me but on her own, and explored methods of grounding herself.

Conclusion of client E's case.   The fantasy exercise seemed to have allowed the past to rest. E felt it unnecessary at this point to go back and was keen to move on.

She gave her permission for me to write up the sessions and to publish. Horace can stay as a real name, but prefers other names or a code for the rest.

Her comments on a questionnaire completed a few months later were that the most helpful thing about therapy, which she felt was in the top category, i.e. 80–100% successful, was the clarifying of her own thoughts.

The presenting problem

As has already been noted, the presenting problem may not be a real problem at all. In E's case, it was exam stress, but it was quickly apparent that there were other underlying issues meriting attention.

The therapist is required to take seriously the presenting problem and needs to explore this fully with the client. It may indeed be the issue the client wishes to, and needs to, look at. There are not always deep-seated or underlying hidden issues that the client wants to explore. The following story from an ASC newsletter is a salutary reminder about this: In this after about 45 minutes wherein the therapist had helped the client talk about their home and family and relationships and key events the: *"counsellor sums up and says the session is now over and would he [the student] like another appointment"*.

Student then asks: *"Oh, if it's over, then can I have my bus pass?"* (Anon, 1991, p. 11).

However there is often an underlying cause to a problem presented to the therapist. The psychodynamic therapist is very familiar with the ideas of childhood events/traumas influencing adult behaviour and patterns. However, here too I recommend a certain caution before helping the client to explore these issues. It is advisable that much more mundane enquiries are made to ensure obvious life patterns are not being neglected. For example, a student who presents with a difficulty in concentrating and studying may have studied without breaks for 8 hours at a stretch consistently for weeks. This poor study pattern is as likely to be the cause of their problem as is any psychodynamic issue. Lack of sleep, food and exercise also leads to difficulties in concentration, forgetfulness, and depression. It is strongly suggested that prior to any psychodynamic explorations these issues are fully investigated.

Once these immediate and practical aspects to the problems are dealt with, the therapist may begin to explore at a deeper level. Often a client is completely unaware that a bereavement, for example, has an effect on memory, concentration, muscular co-ordination, and decision-making. The client may need straightforward education about loss and how it may affect them. This may be sufficient for the client then to continue on their way without further need of a counsellor. Often clients believe they are going crazy when they are in fact suffering normal symptoms of grief. Some clients, perhaps coping with redundancy or loss of status, go through a process similar to the death of a loved one and need education about this grieving process. They do not necessarily require any more therapy after they have acquired the knowledge.

The reader may at this point be wondering when the psychodynamic therapist is to use the extensive training she/he has acquired. It is my contention that it is the more experienced and qualified therapist who carefully ensures that these issues have been covered before delving further.

Health is another area to be explored in-so-far as someone with flu or glandular fever is likely to feel depressed and unable to cope. People are not always quick to check this out. The therapist needs to be aware of the possible psychological impact of health issues on the client. Where any doubt as to a possible physical cause exists, this should be checked by a doctor before a therapy contract is agreed.

Then to the psychodynamic, the therapist will be looking for unconscious material underlying the presenting problems. Sometimes there are very obvious connections that emerge in answer to a question such as, *"have you felt this way before?"* Often at this point a client refers back to when they were a child and perhaps parents divorced, or a grandparent died, or they were bullied at school. It is very often these events that connect in some way to the present difficulty or dilemma.

With Client E, although some work on early relationships occurred in the intake session and in the first session of the contract, the past was not the prime focus. The work with Client E demonstrates a fantasy method that proved an integrating experience for this particular client. Other clients require very different approaches in dealing with psychodynamic issues.

Dependency and trust for the fantasy exercise

This type of work relies heavily on the therapist and denotes a high level of trust. The therapist holds the reality, the ego, and is with the client in their opening up semi-conscious material within a fantasy exercise. With the therapist present, the client is free to "go with" their imagination and allow images and feelings to surface as a way of exploring previously hidden emotions. As Client E said, *"I could have stopped any time but if it seems worthwhile I'll go with things and try it"*. Client E seems here to be making a statement about trust, dependency and risk taking. It is possible that the step of commitment to the therapy process precipitated a fantasy of playfulness and of imagery common to the world of the child, that is in terms of the "horse" and the "dragon" and the *"cringing one ... in the corner and crying."*

Dealing with dependence

In focal and short-term therapy dependency is an issue that must be addressed as it would also be in other longer forms of psychotherapy.

The client usually is somewhat apprehensive about psychotherapy. It is something new for them, they will have fantasies about it and what happens in sessions. These need to be explored in the initial or intake session. The process of explaining about psychotherapy, allaying fears and replacing fantasies with facts is already part of the therapeutic process. The nature of the fears voiced or fantasies shared gives the therapist a lot of information about the client. Exploring these issues provides the client with a picture of the process they are committing themselves to. It is a time when trust is established. The commitment to the counselling contract by the client is a step in faith and trust. The client "depends" on the therapist to be with them in the exploration. They entrust the therapist with their inner thoughts. Often no one else has ever before been privy to the thoughts and feelings revealed to the therapist. The client entrusts and depends on the professionalism of the therapist to deal with these issues confidentially and competently.

The client relies on the therapist being equally bound by the counselling contract, they expect the counsellor to be on time for their appointment and not to "abandon" them half way. "Abandoning" clients may be unavoidable: counsellors and therapists die, become ill, have to move house or country or have to cease counselling because of other commitments. For the client, any break in counselling is difficult to handle and the counsellor must be aware of this and prepare the client carefully where possible.

In the focal and short-term contract method the ending is built in from the first session. It is therefore possible to build contracts around foreseen ends, such as a move abroad or change of career. Illnesses are not so easy to predict or prepare for. The devastating effect the death of a therapist for example has on a client, points to the intensity of the counselling relationship and the level of dependence existing. As alluded to earlier, the intimate and private nature of much of the content of counselling sessions promotes an *intensity* within the counselling relationship. The client is the one making the revelations and it is the client who comes to rely on the therapist. This as a support, as a guide and at times as a life line, as the client struggles with the particular issue of concern.

Over and above what one might term the natural dependence of the one revealing on the one revealed to, there is the dependence brought about by transference. Here the client puts onto the therapist more or less intense feelings that belong to a parent or earlier parent figure. The nature of psychodynamic counselling or therapy is to look at past events that contribute to present problems. Patterns of behaviour formed in childhood remain in the present. At times these patterns are maladaptive and therefore form problems.

The blank sheet of the therapist enables these transferential feelings to be projected onto the therapist. Within the short-term therapy, transference occurs as in any therapy and at times more quickly and intensely because the focusing and brief contract on the predominant problem concentrates the mind and the emotions. The client therefore may feel like a young child in relation to the therapist and the feelings of helplessness and dependence may be there in relation to the therapist both in the sessions and between sessions. This is not to say that the adult client is incapacitated either during or after sessions, but is to acknowledge that an emotional part of the client is "held" by the counsellor. This bond is contributing to the dependency felt by the client in the course of therapy. It is a necessary part of the therapy. If the client does not allow himself/herself to depend on the therapist, the progress and change is likely to be limited. The client, in depending on the therapist, is also depending on the process and is in part letting go of the "old self" in the search for the new. The therapist becomes a link for the old and the new.

Fear of change

To change is a scary prospect and moving into therapy which is about change is therefore quite frightening. In E's case this has already been referred to above in the preliminary work of sessions one and two. The fear of dependency is one aspect of this and shows itself in various forms of resistance.

The short-term and focal approach is experienced by some as an advantage when facing issues of dependence. Since it is only for a limited number of sessions, the process feels safer. The fear of getting "hooked" diminishes also because from session one the final session is known. The focal issue is circumscribed and so it too has a beginning and end, within that it can seem safe to let go and freely explore the issues. For others the fact that the number of sessions is limited is in itself scary because they feel so helpless that they cannot imagine that a few sessions could enable them to cope. They in fact wish to depend on the therapist for as long as possible. They revel in the idea of an ongoing contract with no clear focus or limit in terms of sessions. For the latter there is a choice of whether they can feel convinced of the merits of working briefly and intensely or not. If after the first session they are not convinced, it is unlikely that a useful short-term focal contract can be made. However, if the therapist believes in the method, here one remembers that short-term includes the possibility of subsequent contracts if necessary, then I suspect that most clients will wish to proceed.

The contract method of fixing a focus for a fixed number of sessions ensures that the client is committed to the task. The aspect of focus will be returned to in a following section. This gets over a natural resistance to change. If the idea of change is too much at the time of the initial interview, there is always the option to return at a later date, when the client is ready. I opt to work with a client who really wants to change and use the sessions rather than spend time persuading the client that the process is helpful. Rather than spending many sessions "working with the resistance", I will challenge the client by suggesting that the client thinks it over and returns if and when they are ready to work on their issues. Some would say that this way of dealing with the resistance is rather harsh. I believe that this depends upon how the therapist says it and the emotional tone that has been established between the therapist and client will govern how the client feels about it and how they respond to it.

The mystery element

This aspect of what happens between client and therapist is the elusive element that is difficult to research and difficult to capture through the written word. Yalom refers to this mysterious element using the following illustration: In attending a cooking class despite following the recipe minutely neither he nor any of the students could achieve the superb results of the tutor: "What was it," he wondered "that gave her cooking that special touch". One day he observed something that seemed to provide an answer. "I saw our teacher, with great dignity and deliberation prepare a dish. She handed it to her servant who wordlessly carried it into the kitchen to the oven and, without breaking stride, threw in handful after handful of assorted spices and condiments. I am convinced that those surreptitious 'throw-ins' made all the difference" (1980, p. 3).

I believe, with Yalom, that it is the same with therapy. What really makes it work cannot be caught and written down or researched, it is a mystery just as all relationships have an element of mystery. With Yalom I suggest "that when no one is looking, the therapist throws in the 'real thing'." (1980, p. 3).

Summary

The above cases show a variety of techniques applied flexibly according to the individual client need. The therapist being *attuned* to the client and using techniques to facilitate the process. For example the extract given in Case E emphasizes that the therapist needs to be free of preconceived formulas about how to help a client in terms of psychodynamic patterns and to be flexible using whatever skills are appropriate with each client in that client's particular journey to freedom. In this case a method that has echoes of gestalt chair work, Moreno's psychodrama and Assagioli's Psychosynthesis. In practice however all that I was doing as therapist was staying sensitively attuned to where the client led and then facilitating when she seemed stuck. This example also demonstrates the *intensity* of the therapy work. In J and E there were examples of *teaching* the client about aspects of the theory of the process of therapy.

Increasingly the trend towards the latter half of the 1990s in the counselling/therapy world and within focal therapy was towards integration. That is a way of working which is influenced by many differing theories of counselling and therapy each of which offers a partial solution. As Nelson-Jones suggest, by selecting the best bits from each, one arrives at an integrated approach which is "more comprehensive than any one approach and yet is derived from the individual counselling theories" (1994, p. 207).

Woolfe describes the move towards integration in the 1990s as "the most significant trend in counselling today and it is reflected particularly in the development of a variety of brief therapies" (1995, p. 34). This integration is described as the assimilation of the "best bits of different systems" which are "accommodated into new principles and practices" (ibid).

There has been much debate as to the move from eclecticism to integration. The former is more to do with the technical and integration more with the theoretical. As Norcross and Grencavage sum it up: "The primary distinction is that between empirical pragmatism and theoretical flexibility" (1989, p. 105). Norcross refers to this with an expressive metaphor: "The eclectic selects among several dishes to constitute a meal, the integrationist creates new dishes by combining different ingredients!" (p. 105).

As seen earlier, I endorse the idea of fusion referred to by Wolberg in the 1960s, which is also the direction of many in the 1990s and the early 21st century.

In this there is a clear move from the commonly held concept of a core theoretical model. Interestingly Feltham, a former keen advocate of a core model, has changed his position and now has "come to believe that there are serious philosophical and clinical objections which lead to the conclusion that training in and support for a core theoretical model are ultimately untenable and even oppressive!" (1997b, p. 121).

I agree wholeheartedly with his emphasis on "empirical listening to client needs and views; on research findings and rational clinical innovation" (1997b, p. 122). I believe the empirical examples of brief therapy seen above adhere to this concept of flexibility.

In these developments with regard to flexibility by therapists in the 1990s there seems to be a return to the aspect of rediscovery mentioned in the history of brief therapy, especially the concept of "fusion" put forward as an ideal by Wolberg in 1965. This flexibility is seen as a key principle or ingredient, in brief therapy, and a key factor in the shortening process.

Many of the techniques applied by the flexible therapist involve a more active approach than would be considered usual in the psychoanalytic field. Therefore in the next section the place of activity in brief therapy is examined.

5.1.4. Activity

In the last section about flexibility it became apparent that many different techniques are used to shorten therapy. These are drawn from a number of traditions and are used flexibly by the therapist according to need. They demonstrate a level of activity in both therapist and client that is far removed from the passivity required in the pure analytical approach. This activity appears consistently in the literature and in the cases as an important ingredient in brief therapy. In the examples of different techniques, referred to in the last section, the therapist challenges, teaches, reflects back, waits, holds the focus and selectively ignores material presented, facilitates fantasy work and interprets dreams to name but a few active techniques. It is this principle of activity that is to be examined more deeply here, as expounded by the key proponents of brief therapy and in the selected cases.

Activity of the therapist

In order to shorten therapy Ferenczi (1919, 1920), one of the early proponents of the brief approach, recommended a modification of psychoanalytic technique. He believed that it was the analytic passivity that led to the lengthening of therapy and he suggested that the therapist should be more active. This activity included, for example, exposing phobic patients to the object of their fear or using led fantasy exercises. It also included the playing of a definite role, in relation to the patient, in order to recreate a particular reaction which could then be modified. Time limits were also seen as part of the therapist's activity. This active approach deviates strongly from the analytic tradition although Ferenczi saw the deviation as elaborating and adapting principles Freud had used. Freud, for example, in his Wolfman case had set a time limit for the treatment.

Ferenczi's method developed around 1918 and was known as "active therapy". Hoch in the 1960s asserted that: "A short form of treatment must be more active than a prolonged form. For instance, it is impossible to utilize some techniques employed in orthodox psychoanalysis where the therapist remains passive and allows the patient to work out his own problems leisurely" (1965, p. 52).

Migone observes that this emphasis on activity is a little confusing because in his view all interventions within psychoanalysis could be termed active, for example, asking the patient to "free associate", or making dream interpretations. So how, he wonders, can activity within the brief approach be distinguished? He maintains that the difference lies in the interactive nature of the therapist's interventions and in their frequency. The short-term therapist will question, provoke a response, limit the focal area, and confront resistance immediately. He concludes that: "The increased activity of the therapist is one of the characteristics by which the technique of STDP is most often defined" (1985, p. 622).

Anxiety provoking aspect

This approach is sometimes seen as overly confronting and certainly Davanloo has been referred to as the "relentless healer" in his persistent confronting of the resistance. Marteau in 1991, at a conference of the Association of Short-Term and Strategic Psychotherapist's referred to "pinning the client down". He used the analogy of "nailing one foot to the floor so that there is free movement only around that point" the point being the agreed focus. These descriptions sound aggressive and Davanloo's approach has been described as brutal. It is certainly incisive and direct, but clients describe the reassurance and relief at being on the receiving end of the therapist's activity. I describe this process terms of "pushing the client up against a wall" so there is no way of avoiding the issue. I too have been challenged on the use of this language which also sounds aggressive and raises questions about power for some. In my view and experience the client does not perceive it as aggressive because it is within the context of the agreed contract and because of the relationship that exists between the client and therapist. Such moments within the therapy are often moments of "magic" such as referred to by BN in reviewing Case J. These are moments when the "connectedness" of client and therapist facilitates the process and achieves change. I suspect that without such intense moments in the therapy contract little will happen, but to verify this would require a separate research project and can remain only a question in this book.

Sifneos whose approach is known as "anxiety provoking therapy" also owns to having been accused by those attending his workshop of being "aggressive" or of "badgering the patient" (1987, p. 112). He describes himself as very active in therapy and he explains the rationale behind his apparent aggression as follows: "an active undermining of maladaptive defence mechanisms used by the patient must be systematically pursued in order to help the patient learn to utilize more adaptive patterns of behaviour and free himself from his neurotic prison" (p. 112).

I referred above to the importance of the contract and the relationship in this active approach and Sifneos endorses this. He sets his activity in the context of the therapeutic relationship and stresses the therapist's *sensitivity* and the provision of reassurance and support. He emphasizes the fact that the therapist may choose to "ignore the 'patient's' resistance and proceed to deal with the anxiety laden content of the material that is avoided by the patient" (1987, p. 113). This will of course be within the "safe environment" of the 'therapeutic alliance and positive transference' (p. 113). To exemplify this Sifneos cites a case of a boy who was talking about his brother's appendectomy and who was resistant to answering questions about this. Sifneos insists on focusing on the appendectomy and the client's resistance to the questions. Through this the client comes to an uncomfortable but important awareness of his fear of castration. Sifneos points out that it "was the therapist's activity, his persistent questioning, and his unwillingness to change the subject that finally gave the patient the clear message of the importance which the therapist placed on the subject" (p. 116).

Migone says: "It seems that by giving the patient a new trauma, namely, therapy itself, we have the opportunity to discern his pathologic and maladaptive reactions better and earlier than under traditional conditions" (1985, p. 623). It is the immediacy of active intervention that is "anxiety provoking".

Sifneos points out that the level of activity on the part of the short-term therapist differs according to the individual therapist. Some notable short-term therapists are less active, such as Malan, Gillieron and Brusset, others more so. "Davanloo, possibly more than anyone else, uses active direct confrontative techniques" (1984, p. 476). Sifneos says: "The technique I use is also very active. Anxiety provoking confrontations and clarifications are made repeatedly and early, but not with as much vigour as by Davanloo. In addition, my emphasis is on active systematic problem solving and insight and on teaching the patient how to utilize it in order to solve new emotional problems after the termination of the therapy" (ibid).

Wolberg emphasizes the need to tackle resistance as soon as it appears since there is simply not time to allow the "patient to wallow in resistance". He advises that it must be "dealt with rapidly through an active frontal attack before it paralyses progress" (1965, p. 135).

Wolberg suggests that the activity required of the therapist is a novel one in the aspiring short-term therapist. For Wolberg it assumes "an involvement of oneself as a real person, and open expression of interest, sympathy and encouragement, are permissible" (1965, p. 135). This is in stark contrast to the stoical and expressionless passivity that somehow has become "synonymous with doing good psychotherapy" (ibid).

Malan highlights the face to face aspect of the therapy context. There is no couch which encourages free associations and self reflections. The fact that the client and therapist are face to face encourages interaction and activity.

Active but non-directive

The activity referred to is not directive and therapists should not be misled into thinking it is. Rogawski makes a clear distinction here: "Being active in therapy must not be confused with giving directions. Dynamic therapists seek to tell their patients what they are doing but not what they ought to do" (1982, p. 343).

The direction of the therapy is agreed with the client at the start of therapy and the agreed general *focus* occurs within the context of the *first session* and in the establishment of the *therapeutic alliance*. All three of these important facets of the brief therapy process merit a section of their own and follow on after this section.

Actively holding the focus

It is important here to stress the role of the therapist's activity. It is to facilitate the therapeutic work around the agreed focal area. This may involve leading a client in an exercise and at all times actively holding the boundaries of the focus and of the work.

Keeping to the agreed focus gives the client respect and shows that the subject they have said they wish to explore, is taken seriously. The therapist in holding the focus and actively using every skill available perhaps by questioning, reflecting back, silence or selective inattention, to name but a few approaches, is creating a safe environment to explore the core issue, where the pain and the cure is likely to reside. In doing this the therapist is enabling the process. By repeating or challenging in a focused way the therapist is actively influencing the direction of the session, the direction being that agreed by the client at the start of therapy. Passivity here would allow the client to lead in any unassociated direction which would inevitably lengthen the process. Malan reminds us of the term for this coined by Pumpian Mindlin called "skilful neglect" (1963, p. 211). BN, one of my external observers, sees it as "ignoring the non essentials".

Experience and skill required of the therapist

If the therapist is to be active, there is less time to consider and one cannot afford to make mistakes and with this in mind the key authors stress the importance of training and experience. One example of activity is the early confrontation of transference. Mills and Bauer observe that: "Such confrontations must therefore be made with skill, care and a therapist attitude of openness to working through the nature of the mutual relationship" (1989, p. 341).

To be able to act quickly, the experience and skill of the therapist are important and the reviewers all allude to this. Bauer and Kobos underline Alexander's view that: "the therapist must know a great deal in order to work rapidly" (1984, p. 156). Hoch states: "A good deal of sophistication is required for short-term therapy. The therapist must be keenly aware of what he is doing since he does not have quantities of time available for experiment. For this reason untrained people are not able to employ the method" (1965, p. 52).

Mills and Bauer pinpoint Malan's view which supports the need for experience: "effective transference work in STDP (short-term dynamic psychotherapy) requires that the therapist has adequate training experiences and personal qualities that enable the patient to feel capable of moving into painful affects" (1989, p. 341).

Contrary views with regard to the experience factor

Van Londen states that: "It is usually assumed that the therapist should be a highly experienced professional who keeps the thera-peutic goals clearly in mind and does not pursue irrelevant subjects. Since, at the start of the treatment, the problems of the patient must be quickly determined, it is obvious that experience is required. It is assumed that a therapist of limited theoretical orientation cannot become a good short-term psychotherapist" (1981, p. 222).

It is not, however, a unanimous view that only the experienced can be most effective as short-term therapists, although Davanloo, Sifneos, Wolberg, Marteau and I myself believe that it is the case. There are some who believe that the training for longer-term work enhances the clinician's defences against the possibility of successful action in the brief approach. Sifneos (1978), for example, observes that inexperienced therapists in their greater enthusiasm may produce good results. Winokur and Dasberg in their paper on teaching short-term dynamic psychotherapy come to the following conclusion: "Having taught both beginning level and experienced therapists, we believe that both groups can learn to become short-term therapists ... beginners are less resistant than experienced therapists to innovative ideas and ... are more enthusiastic about the possibility of rapidly achieving concrete results. Experienced therapists do have the advantage of greater clinical acumen, but their learning is hampered by their ingrained long-term therapy assumptions and by anxiety associated with an experienced loss of competency previously held" (1983, p. 50).

Activity of the client

So far, activity, which is a widely agreed common feature of the brief approach, has been considered only from the therapist's point of view.

I maintain that in this approach activity is equally demanded of the clients. I often remind clients that: *"It is your trip; I am able to be alongside you but you have to do the work."* This can be a timely response when encountering resistance or when teaching the client about the process of therapy in order to avoid the resistance.

Wolberg gives us many examples of activity expected of the client. These activities are what I would refer to as "homework". They are part of the process of teaching the client to become their own therapist—to learn how to observe themselves and begin both to interpret their own behaviour and to choose, if necessary, a new way of behaving. The examples Wolberg gives are as follows:

> Relating outbursts of tension, anxiety and symptom exaggeration to provocative incidents in the environment and to insecurities within the self ... Whenever you get upset, tense or anxious, ... ask yourself: "What is going on? What has upset me?" Keep working at it, thinking about matters until you make a connection with your symptoms and what has provoked them ... Observing circumstances that boost or lower feelings about oneself ... Observing one's relationship with people ...—Observing daydreams or dreams during sleep ... Observing resistances to putting one's insights into action (1965, pp. 171–172).

In this approach the client is an active participant who needs to take responsibility also for the progress made. This begins with the commitment to work on a defined focal area for an agreed time which I will return to later.

Activity in the research cases

Within the brief approach many techniques are employed that involve great activity on the part of the client both within and between the sessions. Some of these techniques as demonstrated in the selected cases have been referred to above and in the previous section on flexibility. In this section the extracts from the cases have been chosen to illustrate the active involvement of both client and therapist. One example of the client working between sessions was already seen in Case J's poem to Oliver Martin and her reading of it in a quiet place, which was referred to in the section on flexibility and techniques.

Case E's fantasy exercise described in the last section under flexibility of technique also shows the activity of both client and therapist, the latter very much as facilitator and holder of boundaries and safety. The client is an active participant both intellectually and emotionally.

Another example of a between session activity or "homework" is demonstrated in research case F. F has been referred to in earlier sections with reference to resistance and the use of teaching to enlist the client's cooperation and melt the resistance. In this section I am giving a further extract of F's case in order to put in context the homework example and to demonstrate other client–therapist interaction. The interweaving of psychodynamic insights and teaching are also demonstrated actively and in an integrated way and follow on from the exposition on flexibility in the last section.

CLIENT F

To recap for the reader, Client F had presented with the statement: *"I'm depressed, I've always been depressed—well since I was 9 years old"*.

She had been quite resistant to the counselling process but, as shown in the earlier section, after some work with me as therapist in that first encounter had requested a counselling/therapy contract.

In session one the resistance was worked with and circumvented by means of a *teaching process* as outlined in an earlier section. A specific contract was formed from within the general focus of "depression" to look at the "9 year old" as she relates to the present day fears and depression. An alliance was made in agreeing the contract both in terms of focus and in the number of sessions to work on these issues.

Focus, therapeutic alliance and the importance of the first session will be covered in greater detail in following sections.

We had agreed to fix four sessions to explore her "depression". F having opted now for a counselling contract, then felt four sessions to be insufficient. The issue of dependency, in her desire for more than four sessions was addressed and challenged. I did not deviate from the offered four sessions.

A brief contract such as this does not preclude further sessions, but is intended to concentrate the mind and encourage clients to do their own work on themselves. In offering the brief contract one is also inspiring hope in the client in that I as therapist at least am confident improvement can occur very quickly.

Use of homework.   As mentioned in the earlier section I set F some "homework" following this session based on the material she had given the therapist.

The homework is to move the sessions on, to enable the client to take responsibility for the work and *to become their own therapist.*

In F's case, it was aimed to help overcome her resistance to the process of therapy and to confirm for herself the validity of some of the information I had given her. The task she was asked to do was to find out dates relating to key events in her life especially around the age of nine, the date of her Nan's illness and death and to list the crises in her life as far back as she could remember, with dates. I anticipated that the important dates would coincide with her known periods of depression and that this knowledge would reinforce what I had said in teaching her about body memory and anniversaries and unfinished business and that this would increase her trust in me and in the therapy process.

The next session began with an apparently quite unconnected concern—a broken relationship. However, the focal and brief therapist will assume that anything raised in the sessions relates to the agreed focus.

The exploration about the relationship was therefore looked at in the context of the 9-year old and Dad. However before going into this seemingly new aspect in any detail I asked her how she had felt after the last session. This maintains the agreed focus.

P: *"F before we go into this* (the boyfriend) *I'd like to know how you felt after last week and what you learned from the'homework?'"*

She had done this, faithfully writing a full 20 pages. She had gone back to being 5 years old. The homework had confirmed all that I as therapist had been saying.

The dates of key events also fitted with the times she was depressed, e.g. May and November were key hard times. As she looked at the events she was able to come to her own realizations about her present fear in her words of the *"world falling apart and never being the same again"* and her desolation and fear as a child when Nan died and Dad walked out and her own "world falling apart".

In seeing this link she is already beginning to cope better with her fears.

F is very quick to "catch on" to the process. She caught herself out using the word depression.

F: *"Well, I'm used to calling it that so I'll do so—when I was depressed in May ..."*

I had in the first session challenged her on labelling herself depressed, suggesting that there was a reason for a feeling. It was this that we needed to discover and work with and which the label obfuscates.

Having looked with her at the homework and her new insights with regard to her "depression" F was keen to return to the issue she had raised earlier in this second session—her boyfriends.

F tends to have a pattern of challenging her friends to declare that they love her. She wanted her boyfriend to reassure her that he did *not* so that they could remain friends.

F: *"I want it to stay as it is—I'm afraid of getting too attached to things".*

She expects and anticipates that they will let her down. I wondered if this was what she felt about Dad. She used to long to tell Dad everything she had been doing all day and he would not be interested. She would then run to Mum. There was a pattern emerging here, the time last May when she had been pushing the boyfriend to declare himself—she had subsequently had the support of a girlfriend. We explored the secondary gain, the friendship of the girl, in her difficulty with the boy and the repeat of the Dad/Mother situation she experienced as a child.

In helping F to look in detail at the one situation, it is possible to help her to see patterns of reaction and to learn to *be her own therapist!*

We observed that the situations with the boyfriends tend to occur periodically. They produce feelings of guilt, anger. We again looked at dates in relation to these occasions. Nan, she had by now discovered, died in late September. She is always depressed in October/November. Grief would produce feelings of guilt and anger.

F is now beginning to understand the psychodynamic implications of past events on the present problems she is dealing with.

F saw that the dates of her hard times in relationships also coincide with those dates she'd discovered through her homework.

The material she had opened the second session with regarding relationships was closely linked with the episodes in her childhood. The same grief and loss she experienced in relation to Nan was repeated when Dad left home. The two events were not unrelated. These events coloured her attitudes to men in the present.

It is significant that once the scene is set in the making of the initial contract, the material the client brings is of immediate significance and relevance, but can easily be missed and seen either as a sidetrack, or as a completely separate issue.

The brief therapist needs to be alert to see how these pieces of the jigsaw fit together to form the whole picture. At some level the client is aware of this and brings the material to the therapist. It is the therapist's astuteness that is required to facilitate the process, weaving each new aspect of the person's life back into the agreed focus.

F was unable to attend the next session but sent me her biography. Nan and Grandad's deaths stand out as highly significant. Mother and Father had a particularly memorable "row" in October and Dad's departure was in May. Her times of "depression" coincide with these dates.

I believe the major part of the work had already taken place for F in the writing of it and it was clear that there was quite a shift even by session two.

The next session (3) was in November, around Remembrance Day and she felt low. She was now also dealing with the emotional upset relating to the fact that a friend of her mother's had died a few weeks ago. It was also the anniversary time of the death of her brother's friend. F began to realize that these real life events have their effect, but also that the past events are somehow resonating. We looked at her biography together and the importance of the deaths and the break up of the family.

There was a great deal of loss in her life at this time and the connection between this and the past losses was explored. The importance of the session was the accessing of emotions about the loss of Nan and Dad—Nan who had died after a period of senility and Dad who had left home. Both these losses naturally instigated many others in terms of social relationships, patterns of behaviour within the family in addition to the loss of the two important people. F began to realize that she had never grieved for these people and that the pain had not therefore been dealt with.

She began to acknowledge and mourn for the losses we talked about, and began to be able to separate the past events and associated feelings from the present.

Since mourning is a natural process the therapist was not required to be alongside her for weeks in dealing with this. She was able to fully acknowledge and accept the loss and sadness and begin to move on from it. My part was in helping her see and realize the block, F was then able to handle the grief, and her relationships.

In the last of four sessions, she had made "enormous strides". She feels more confident and assertive now and is more ready to rely on her own judgement. She realizes how her relationship with her Dad has coloured her relationships with men. She is now able to put her "depression" into perspective and to realize it is really about grief. She has allowed herself to feel the sadness and sense of loss belonging to these past events. She still needs to tackle the habit of responding to men in a pattern formed from the past relationship with Dad and feels more confident about doing this.

F is an extremely insightful client and is very quick to make connections and is catching herself in the act when she falls into a pattern of behaviour she now understands and wants to change.

This was the last session of our contract, we decided that a review session next term, in a few weeks, would be helpful.

The next session occurred after the Gulf War had started. This situation of war had been her worst fear for years. She is coping with it fine. She is amazed at how well she is handling life at present including boy friends. and she feels more free and creative. We made this an end session and I have her permission to publish the material.

CLIENT B

Case B was referred to earlier in the section on psychodynamic roots.

The following extracts of Case B have been chosen to demonstrate activity in relation to timing and techniques. They also show the active involvement of both therapist and client. The chair work undertaken towards the end of the contract demonstrates this especially. Both the client and I are active participants, both are physically moving around the room. I, as a therapist, facilitate her process, encouraging and helping the situation with simple questions: What does this feel like? What do you want to say to her? Go and be her. What does she want to say to you? The client is the active participant moving in and out of characters until a certain integration and peace reigns.

To give the reader some context for the salient extracts I shall recap a little.

> B was a female student in her twenties. Her studies were severely disrupted part way through her course due to emotional difficulties. She had not fully dealt with the underlying problems as became apparent when she called in to see me on an unrelated matter. I asked how she was and received a bright "fine thank you" reaction. It was very apparent to me that she was not feeling fine and it seemed appropriate to pursue the matter further. The tears began to well up and I offered her a counselling contract if she would like it, pointing out that if things were bothering her that it would be good to look at them so they could be understood and perhaps put behind her. We agreed a contract of eight sessions to look at family issues and her relationship with her Mother.

In the session that might be termed a pre-session or intake session, the counsellor is seen to build a rapport with the client. The key issue causing pain is pinpointed and a commitment to counselling obtained. A short contract of eight sessions is agreed. Thus we see the focal area and the time limit fixed from the start.

> B is very vocal in the sessions and talks freely with a clear agenda of her own. I listen carefully, staying closely with both what she is saying or feeling as appropriate. I ask for clarification, challenge gently, reflect back, or emote e.g. *"that must have felt ..."*, or

encourage her to stay with the feelings to allow herself to feel pain and rejection, to cry about it all, or at times to be silent in the remembering.

We talked a little this session about exploring those events which really matter since B was feeling *"disloyal"* about talking to someone outside her family.

B declares that she *"doesn't blame Mum"* for her, at times, rejecting treatment. This does not ring true and we need to look at this again. Where is the anger?

B expressed fears of getting hooked on the counselling and wanted a gap until after Easter. We explored this a little, reviewed our contract—looked at the natural breaks and end, e.g. Easter and her leaving college and finally decided to meet the next week.

The following extract demonstrates the active involvement of both client and therapist as they concentrate on the agreed focus. This case also exemplifies the use of focus which will be covered in a later section.

Session 5.   In session five B begins with two present situations, her boyfriend telling her father of their plan to marry and her fear of parental rejection. She recalled an incident which she cites as an example of her parents' rejection, a birthday card she received on her 21st birthday. She laughed as she said:

   "it, said: '21st birthday, a 9lb boy, Bobbie' ".

I was very aware of and sensing her feelings of sadness, grief, anger, and rejection and checked her laughter—

P: *"that doesn't sound funny to me"*.

The therapist's challenge of inappropriate outward laughter belying the keenly felt sadness, grief and anger at this felt rejection led B to tune into her sadness and anger. She was thus enabled to go more deeply into that episode and experience and stay with her real feelings about it. My response was: *"that is sick"*.

This spontaneous response was rather a strong one and was made in the knowledge of all she had already told me, about rejection and being called different names. We stayed silent for some time in touch with the emotions stirred for B by this 21st card.

The silence within a therapy session is often the time of the most powerful movement. It is not possible to tabulate this or quantify it. It is about the relationship. It does not replicate on a tape recorder. It is here that attempts to document and "research" therapeutic encounters fall short. There is a mystical quality to such moments, and it is perhaps the element in the "I–thou" relationship that is the most healing. Subsequent to the silence B began to talk about her parents and the names she had been called as a child: Bobbie was one of many. Names and being called by different names was an important issue for B. I have, after much thought and with great reluctance, changed the names referred to by B even though I had permission to use the ones she mentioned. I have done so to ensure confidentiality but I am mindful of giving B even more names to contend with. I trust B will understand. These names became a very important theme of a later session.

> Then B began to talk about Mum and Dad always wanting a boy— before her own birth Mum had four miscarriages, all boys, one had gone to a 4-month term. She had often been called by boys names. Her parents' attitude was *"it doesn't matter what you're called"*. I wondered if I had been too blunt in my comment *"that's sick"*. I checked out with her if I'd hurt her by saying this? She said:
>
> > *"No, it—the situation hurt, but it was sick and it somehow helped to hear that said by an objective outsider. It was a relief, it wasn't she who was 'sick', it was Mum and Dad. That hurt too but put the situation in perspective."*

As the therapist here, I was being genuine and by being so both in expressing my feelings and in checking out about the comment later, moved the therapy into new depths.

It should be noted that rejection is still a main theme, but the examples and events of the past become deeper and of greater significance as the sessions progress.

Session 6.   B talks a little about Mother and her fear that the cancer may recur. This is the last session before the break. There is a heavy atmosphere in the room. I'm keenly aware of this. Is it the forthcoming break? Is it the cancer? Is it the matter of last week's session? It seems important to check it out, since the level of conversation does not seem to tie in with the weight in the room.

The "feeling" or atmosphere can often prove the most important element in the therapy. Here this was the case.

I checked out with her if there was something she wanted to talk about or were we dealing with what she wanted. She owned up to a concern about confidentiality and a chance remark she'd made in connection with another girl whom I happen to know. She felt that she shouldn't have referred to the third party.

Issues of trust and mistrust have alternated throughout the sessions. Each new doubt having been explored has then been followed by a greater trust than before. It is important for the intellectual aspects to be dealt with at that level and for the client to be free to challenge, voice doubts, and seek clarification as they need to. The therapist needs to be aware of these issues and not to be in any way threatened by any such questions. The client has a right to know where they stand on all those issues and they need exploration.

I reassured her and the weight in the room vanished. B said she felt very much better this week and that since the last session regarding the birthday card "name", seem to have moved on. There is a sense that we are near to the end of our work together. In fact we have two more sessions within our agreed contract.

Session 7.   The meeting with her parents and boyfriend at Easter was not good, but she felt very free to be herself and to say and do *"her thing"*. This was a new experience and she was surprised that they accepted her firm decisions.

We returned in this session, to the names she was called as a child. She was Rupert and Barry before Bob and almost changed her name by deed poll to Karen, but when her parents agreed to this decided not to. She realizes this was not "normal" behaviour for parents. B said:

> *"that's the last blockage"*

and tears flow freely at this point. We made a contract within a contract to look at names in the next session, and decide that the one after that would be a review session and possibly the end one. I asked her if additionally she would help me with some research work I am doing and if she would be willing for an extra session to look at this and she readily agrees. I asked her if she would like to draw or make notes as a preparation for our session on names.

Session 8.   We began straight away with the names going through them one by one.

"*What's in a name?*"—B's question.

She brought in a list of names by which she had been known and we talked through them.

She had drawn them out too—the pictures were quite illuminating (see Illustration I).

Art—not in terms of artistic merit—but in terms of expressiveness, can be a very useful tool in therapy. It can sometimes help the client to access feelings and thoughts that words cannot express.

She was able to get into the feelings aroused by each of the inappropriate names as she told me about them, showing me how the symbolic drawings fitted with what she is telling me.

Rupert was the first one; she was called this when she was around 6–8-years old, which was also the time when her Mother had her first miscarriage—a boy.

Bob was a name she herself introduced when she was around 9–11, this name represented the mischief boy, B said:

"*the one who turned on the hose pipes or broke things*"

We recalled again the card saying "*Happy birthday—it's a boy 9lb 8oz called Bob*"—that she'd received from her parents, now she can recall this with a quiet sadness, B says:

"*it's just very, very sad*".

She was always **Edith** when things were bad, or when she was in a bad mood. Edith was the one who was mercenary and nasty.

Dad called her **mouth** when she argued with him, here the anger and hurt surfaced. She drew mouth for me, She saw it as "*nasty*", "*unpleasant*" and looking at her drawing she feels "*revulsion*" (see Illustration II).

As B told me about the name, "mouth", it seemed appropriate to move into some Gestalt work using two chairs. In fantasy she puts her Dad on one chair and she tells him what she thinks of his calling

B's Illustration I

Rupert

Bob

Suzanne

B's Illustration II

Mouth

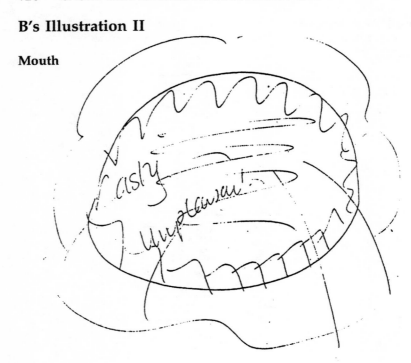

her "mouth". She gets in touch with her anger and is able to get into the exercise readily.

She finally says with a quiet authority and channelled anger:

"don't you ever, ever call me that again, how dare you call me that".

She remembers vividly that on her 18th birthday in an argument he called her "mouth". She is confident he will never do so again since she feels strong enough now to put a stop to it. After the two chair exercise, she feels:

"as if I've got it all out—I feel calm".

In being responsive to the emotions aroused in the detailing of the naming of B as "mouth", the therapy focused for much of this session on this one name. Even though several more names were on the list. It is more important to deal with the heart of what is brought into the session than to complete the "list", perhaps missing the moment when useful work can be done on an issue. The therapist needs to be flexible and to judge the moment to focus in, or the moment to select out, that is for selective inattention. However this list also needs to be finished.

Sue was the next name on the list, this she was called at school which she hated and the name with it. She had no real friends there and when she moved class, it was worse and she finally failed all her "O"'s, her parents "*couldn't be proud of me*". She feels she wants to "*back off from parents*". Although they have both had breakdowns during her lifetime, she had to cope. Neither were in hospital at any stage. She now, as she reflects, finds it hard to recall happy times in her childhood.

Other names, that belong to better times, were **Suzi**, by friends when she left home, and **B**, "unreal" and "explosive", temporarily, at college. Also **X's daughter**. We resolve to look more carefully at the other names next time because the work around "mouth" took up most of this session (see Illustration III, p. 130).

This means that we need to slightly extend the contract to cope with this—she agrees to this. Before we finish we review the dates of Mum's other three miscarriages. She is not sure of these, but we reflect on the boy's names and these dates.

Session 9.   We continue with the names. This time B has brought the sheet of sketches again. She goes this time through the rest of the list explaining how she got the various names. It is non-emotional. She is not sure who she is. This seems to be the key question and it is this that the therapist chooses to focus on.

She is beginning to take very calmly on board that she's "*the sane one*" in the family and really different from the rest—describes the family as akin to "*munsters*". Her father can dramatize and likes to be the centre of attention.

B felt she had to grow up too quickly, that she had to wear ladylike clothes and was not allowed to be scruffy, even though still called by the boy's name. She had had her hair cut in a bob "*like a boy*", she hated it because she never wanted to cut it and liked it really long (like the picture of Bob, she laughed!). She hated the high heels she had to wear.

"Suzi" was her name at the nursing home and she quite liked it. Her boyfriend calls her this.

B's Illustration III

Suzi

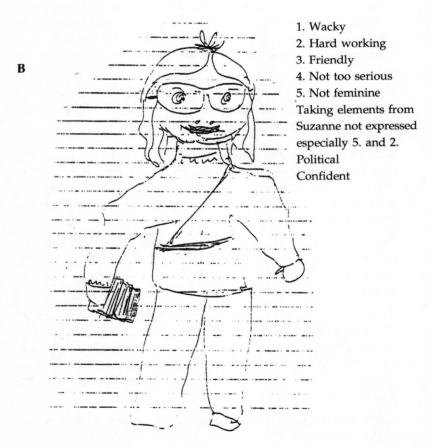

Feminine
capable
sensible
good sense of humour
balanced
happy
self assured

B

1. Wacky
2. Hard working
3. Friendly
4. Not too serious
5. Not feminine
Taking elements from
Suzanne not expressed
especially 5. and 2.
Political
Confident

"B" she sees as only temporary, her friends here call her this—she likes it, but sees it as transient. She's not sure which she is.

I suggested for homework, that she actually draws out on a sheet pictures of herself using imagery, e.g. bird/animal/shape/colour/ imaginative. She immediately saw a *"tree"*, P: *"Okay, which one?"* Over to her. This was the last planned session prior to exams, so we talked about the gap, and holding over "work" until after the exams, so there was a sense of lightening the level of work and focusing on the immediate situation in hand, the exams.

I offered her support sessions through the exam period, but at this stage she preferred not to fix a time in advance. So we fixed a post-exam appointment to continue our work regarding "who am I", probably two more towards our "ending". This to include a review session and one to look back on the sessions for research purposes, this after our work together has concluded formally. (I emphasize the recontracting of sessions and contracts because this process is intrinsic to the focal short-term method. It ensures commitment and effort on the part of the client to the "work" and ensures that I am clear as to how to hold the boundaries of our work and where to direct the "focus," note the focus, not the client.) The focus will be explored further in a later section.

This renegotiating is a more flexible approach than, for example, Mann's more rigid adherence to a fixed number of sessions. I see this as being responsive to client need and appropriately taking account of external reality as shown below.

Session 10.   (Interim appointment, not part of agreed contract.)

B called in for an interim appointment. She had been feeling confused and scared so decided to fix an appointment, not to continue our "who am I" contract, but to deal with *"now"*. Today for her is the anniversary of when she went to the Doctor last year saying she *"needed help"*. The doctor advised her to take a break and to defer the exams, if necessary. She was re-experiencing some of the anxiety of the earlier time and was scared that she was going to fall apart again. She seemed to be experiencing a typical anniversary type reaction. Moving into teaching mode I talked to her a little regarding body memory and anniversary reactions and we began to look at the events of last year, all occurring at this time, the important dates and the similarities of the present time, which contribute to the reactivating of the memories and feelings.

These included, her boyfriend's nanny dying at Easter the previous year—her own Nan dying that April also, as she spoke of this, her negative and angry reaction to an Aunt Edith overtook her and we resolved to return to this subject in due course. Her landlady having terminal cancer was another factor 1 year ago. She was still awaiting being called regarding a road accident that occurred a few years earlier. She had been involved with it in a helping capacity. Other factors included: the exams; her financial difficulties; her landlady's making false accusations, no doubt due to her illness; the time and energy commitment as she looked after the landlady's children and her pending move. At that time, a year ago, when coping with all of these things, she had reached a stage when she simply couldn't cope. She lost interest in herself and in sleeping, eating, washing, and everything. When she over-reacted to another driver at the traffic lights one day she'd realized she must do something and took herself to the GP. She followed the doctor's advice and picked up from there on. We looked at this "package" she'd been struggling with on her own last year and then at the parallels this year. In these weeks she had the landlady's death, looking after the children, a future move, a pending court case, and the anniversary of the deaths in the family. As we talked she began to regain a sense of perspective, to acknowledge the real feelings regarding grief, sadness and loss to be expected following a death and at anniversary times. She also accepted the reality of the stress of exams, moving house again and leaving college. Seeing the realities and normality of her feelings enabled her to accept them without the fear that she was going to *"freak out"*.

In responding to the concrete, real, present time problems and difficulties and in affirming them and B's reaction to them, I enable B to gain perspective on her feelings. Also to realize her strength in coping at a time of exams with such a package of sad life events. This helped B to get in touch with reality and her strength and to be able to cope.

She'd also given thought to who she is, and produced a few sentences she'd written regarding this.

She had prepared a list of *"who am I"* statements, not an imaginative picture and she left that with me at the end of the session. The list is as follows:

B: *"I am a woman, independent, autonomous, K's fiance, unique, child of God—her baptismal name and the nickname most people call her by now—she ends the list—"Who am I?—don't know."*

Session 11.   We brought the following session forward from the next week because B had reason to go home earlier than originally planned. B is thrilled to be going and is looking forward to new life. She has only two more exams one of which is tomorrow and she desperately wanted to see me before she went. It is very important to finish our work and she chose to do so despite the proximity of the exams.

We began with the unfinished business: Edith and names—Who is she? We moved into a Gestalt fantasy exercise again, this time using all the chairs in the room. She physically moved around the room taking on the names she'd been given, throwing out those who are no longer, part of her life, but keeping some in the room positioned appropriately in relation to herself.

We began with "Edith" and how angry she feels regarding the *"nasty"* aunt. She told me what she'd say to her and found it much more difficult to talk to Edith (empty chair) herself and to actually say all the negative feelings as if to Edith in person. However she spoke firmly and quietly about "Edith" and felt as if she'd *"got it out after this and had said everything"*. She experiences "Edith" with revulsion. I asked her to take "Edith's" chair.

P.   *"Can you be 'Edith' and reply to 'B'?"*

B was unable to get into "Edith's" role but supposed she'd say *"why, but I gave you ... or did ..."*

B just wanted to be rid of her. We threw "Edith" out of the room. B moved around the chairs, to "Rupert's" next, sitting on edge of chair, not "owning" any of him either. We threw him out too. B then moved on to become "X's daughter" selecting another chair. Her pose as "X" is a *"superior stance but he got laid back when drunk like this"* she demonstrated as she stretched out in the chair.

B.   *"I can't throw him out he's part of my world."*

I asked *"Where would you be in relation to him?"* B moved to her own chair in the far corner away from "X". Here she is lower, but confident, comfortable and *"far enough away not to be observed too closely"*. She is happy to have him permanently there.

Then we looked at "Bob". B is quite happy to have him around, he is the mischief/fun-loving part of her, she created him as her fantasy brother. She is happy to take his qualities on board, "but not the name"—so we threw the name out!

Then to "Suzanne", she moved to the same chair Edith had been on, there seemed to be no conflict there since "Edith" had gone. She felt okay with "Suzanne", mostly. Some bits she doesn't like, but the serious, hard working part is important and she wants it. That is *"the well-dressed interview candidate, pinstripes etc., I want to keep all of that"*. B no longer wants to throw any of "Suzanne" out and she takes "Suzanne" back to her chair I reflected quietly; *"the super ego and id parallel?"* B agreed saying: *"but people named all these bits for me, I don't need the names. The serious and fun bits are both important."*

P: " 'Mouth' "?
B: *"No, I won't be 'mouth' "* (we had worked on that before).
B: *"no one will call me that again, I'd stop them in a very different way from ever before. At least 'Suzanne' would be with me in the middle and 'Bob' cheering behind!"*

"Suzanne" moved to the fourth chair and felt comfortable and at ease. "Suzanne" is the same as B, *"both are okay, both are equal, they are just two parts of my world—almost in terms of geography."* B returned to her own chair.

This exercise helped her to choose and own those parts of herself that felt right and to discard those bits of herself that others had put on her over the years. However there still seemed to be quite a number of names left in the room. It seemed still a little unfinished. I suggested another exercise in an attempt to remedy this. She agreed. I asked her: *"to go, in fantasy, to meet a wise person in a safe place and he/ she will call you by name."* It is anticipated that the client has the wisdom within them to know the real person and this may be realized in a fantasy exercise such as this.

To prepare her for the exercise I asked her: *"to imagine yourself in a safe, good place, perhaps the country, maybe one of the scenes in the pictures in my room or perhaps the retreat centre you went to. Imagine yourself wondering through calmly and go up a hill to find a wise, old person who calls you by your name."*

She found a good place and the person said:

"Hello, my dear, who are you?"

B said: *"Suzanne"*

and that felt good and right. She told me:

*"I'm Suzanne but when people know me well, **I'll let them** call me 'Suzi' or 'B' I wish my boyfriend would call me 'B' sometimes."*

I teasingly suggested I'd call her by another name to test how solidly she was inside her own place.

P: *"What if I wanted to call you 'Mary'?".*

She laughed because it was one of her other made-up names but said:

*"No—no **I** wouldn't **let** you."*

(This was a really good response!) I reflected back to her the shift here, from *"people can call me anything it doesn't matter"* to *"I'll let them call me."*

She hadn't noticed the shift until I pointed it out but then saw the change clearly. She'd made a huge strides from being prepared to be pushed around by anyone and called anything to being sure who she was and being prepared to defend that. The growth in confidence and certainty about her identity had a knock-on effect on her studies also.

She is no longer worrying if she only gets a 2:2 instead of the longed for 2:1.

We explored the ending of the contract a little, but due to our constant reassessing of the contract and awareness of the brevity of it and of the gaps, needed to spend little time on this.

The ending is, in a sense, built in from the start of the contract and the fact that she was finishing college this year anyway. I expressed a certain sadness that the ending was so rushed, but clearly we'd completed our contract.

I requested her permission to publish the work we had done together. She was thrilled with this idea and that she might have been an interesting case. She wondered why her? I told her that her insight, speed of working on issues and the depth of the issues she was presenting, had made it a very good one to write up for the book and it also demonstrates the considerable movement possible in the short-term focal therapy method.

It seemed that since her own schedule had compressed the time, she had managed to round off the work we were doing together within the one session available. I had previously anticipated that we would need two sessions to complete, one for the Edith issue and one to end.

It is interesting to note that in the multi-chair exercise, B declined to use the chair I usually use despite my vacating it for her use. There was also no mention of Mother in the exercise. It would seem that in the transference, I was Mother for her. Mother who let her be and who approved without intimidating, who supported her and her studies.

Reflecting back to the original contract, that is, the relationships in the family it was apparent that there was a shift. She no longer wants Mother to be a "*best friend*". She wants her to be a "*Mother*". She also realizes that she is well able to stand up for what she wants. She will choose her boyfriend over parents if she has to. She is amazed to find that mother is going along with her. It seems in finding herself she has also begun to find her mother.

Thus in the 11 sessions we have covered a wealth of material and real change has occurred. The natural gaps with vacations means that the 11 sessions cover approximately 6 months. This may be a relevant factor to study.

Summary

In these case extracts giving examples of activity, the therapist employs different techniques drawn from very different traditions. These newer therapies such as gestalt/fantasy work/art are woven into the fabric of the session and fused with aspects of the psychodynamic approach. They blend comfortably in the hands of the therapist as they are used flexibly and *sensitively*, according to client need.

The clients all demonstrate activity both within and outside the sessions and this is seen to progress the therapeutic work. The reader will recall from the section on brevity that my team's cases averaged 6.6 sessions which is much shorter than the other proponents listed. It seems that the level of activity referred to in the case work has an accelerating effect on the process and that my cases indicate full support for Wolberg's statement that "Anathema to short-term therapy is passivity in the therapist" (1965, p. 135).

As the concept of activity has been explored we have seen too, the importance given to the *experience* of the therapist, the *intensity* of the therapeutic process and the teaching element.

Teaching is an activity that figures significantly in these cases, for example in F's case about the impact of the past on the present as a way of dealing with the resistance. In B's case, teaching is again seen as I explain how the process of therapy can work. *Teaching* is referred to by Sifneos as an important element, but I believe that its place is of greater significance, in the shortening of therapy, than has previously been thought.

In this section the importance of actively "holding the focus" has been referred to and the next section examines the importance of focus for the brief approach.

5.1.5. The focus in focal and short-term psychotherapy

The latter two sections focused on flexibility and activity and their impact on the shortening of the therapy process. This is in the context of brief psychodynamic therapy as described fully in sections 5.1.1 and 5.1.2. Each facet of focal and short-term psychotherapy emerging from the analysis of the author's cases and from the key writers is interlinked but in order to gain greater clarity as to each facet each section concentrates on one in particular. This section concentrates on what the activity and flexibility relate to, and that is, the issue or issues that the client brings to the therapy which become the focus of the sessions. In brief therapy a great deal of emphasis is given to focusing the work within the sessions and it is the focus and its place in this shortening of the therapeutic process that is under scrutiny here.

Importance of focus

The importance of a focus is widely agreed by practitioners in the brief therapy approach. It is to Balint in the 1950s that we owe the name "Focal therapy" which emphasizes this facet of the brief method. Eisenstein however, points out that Balint is preceded in the emphasis of a focal issue by Alexander who emphasized strategic planning and the necessity of *limited goals* in brief therapy. "Alexander tended to investigate peripheral issues also, but he always returned the work of the therapy to the centre" (1992, p. 38).

Many others independently have also come to see the need for a focus in this approach. Malan describes the "crystallization of a focus" as the foundation stone on which the rest of the brief therapy intervention rests (1963, p. 210). He refers us to a number of different authors who emphasize the centrality of "focus" in this method of therapy. These authors include: "Barten (1971)" who sees the finding of the focal problem area for the therapeutic contract as "one of the most critical operations of brief therapy" ... Swartz who stresses staying with the focus: "Once the focus is established every effort is made to stay within the chosen area ... The most common focus that is chosen revolves around the precipitating stress" (pp. 108–9) ... Harris, Kalis and Freeman (1963) who state that: "The most important difference between this type of brief treatment and the more traditional forms of psychotherapy is the systematic focusing on the current situation" (1976, pp. 34–4).

In focusing on the current situation however, this is not to the exclusion of the past influences on it. This aspect will be returned to later.

Other key writers such as Mann, Marteau and Sifneos all agree on the importance of a focus in brief therapy and the need for it to be established at the start of therapy. Wolberg puts it quite strongly: "Focused interviewing in the sitting up position is almost manda-tory" (1965, p. 134). He goes on to say: "In short-term therapy, we cannot afford the leisurely pace ... It is essential to focus on areas that will yield the highest dividends. Generally these deal with problems of immediate concern to the patient ... Skill as a therapist is revealed in the ability to establish bridges from the complaint factor to more basic difficulties. Only when a continuity has been affirmed between the immediate stresses and the conflictual reservoirs within the personality, will the patient be able to proceed working on more substantial issues. To focus on what the patient considers to be mere corollaries to his pain, before one has shown him that they are actually the responsible mischief makers, will usually turn out to be an unproductive exercise" (1965, p. 157).

In this passage we note allusions to the *experience* of the therapist and to the *teaching* process in order to engage the client and to enable the process to occur rapidly.

Once the focus is established the key writers are agreed that it must be held to. Malan describes the therapist as pursuing "the focus single mindedly: he guides the patient towards it by partial interpretation, selective attention and selective neglect" (1963, p. 210). He refers also to Mann's insistence on "confining attention to the central issue, and use only those data that relate to it" (1976, p. 34). Marmor maintains that one of the key factors in focal and dynamic psychotherapy is the "persistent focus throughout therapy on the core conflict and the refusal to permit defensive digressions" (1979, p. 153).

Type of focus

There is, however, a divergence of opinion in how the key writers view the depth of the focus. Earlier writers, as referred to above, tend to see this in a more superficial way than those who came later. Brodaty refers to a number of levels of focus and cites a number of early writers associated with these. The most superficial level relates to the current situation only: (Bonime, 1953). The intermediate level refers to a dynamic problem but deals only with its repercussions in the present (Stone, 1951; Gillman, 1965; Castelnuovo-Tedesco, 1965, 1975; Barten, 1971) (in Brodaty, 1983, p. 111). The deepest level refers to childhood (Malan, 1963, 1976a, 1976b, 1979) (op. cit.).

Certainly the work of therapy may be limited to current issues and to more superficial levels, if that is the agreement between client and therapist. However, as emerged in the chapter on psychodynamic roots, the assumption in focal brief therapy, is that the past impacts on the present.

In line with the key proponents Sifneos, Malan, Mann, Wolberg, Marteau and Davanloo, I see the focus as relating to depth issues such as the "nuclear conflict". Malan stresses this psychodynamic aspect and the expectation that the focal issue will relate to childhood, he says "that the most successful therapies reported in SBP were those in which the focal conflict was linked with childhood ... and ... in which not merely derivatives of the nuclear conflict were interpreted, but at least aspects of the nuclear conflict itself" (1976, p. 36).

Marteau reinforces this view that the focal issue is more than the current or precipitating crisis. It is getting to the roots that is the objective. He refers to the "nuclear crisis" as underlying the presenting problem. He observes: "If this presenting crisis is truly nuclear, then getting it out at the roots must be the aim of the therapy while the process will be to reach through the present crisis to grasp the very roots. This means that the presenting crisis needs to be the major focus through which we will attain the roots. The true resolution of the presenting crisis which means reaching the roots, will be the test of successful outcome" (1986, p. 81).

The strategic focus

I make a distinction between what I call the general focus and the strategic focus. By strategic I mean that area in a person's life that is causing the difficulty, the block or pain. I use the term strategic as defined earlier in the section on definitions and if this one area is worked on change can occur in a much wider area. When client and therapist concentrate the work of the limited number of sessions on this focus and on matters directly derived from this, then prognosis of a successful outcome is good. Sometimes it is clear to both client and therapist what the focal area is and sometimes it is less clear. In the latter case the client and therapist will agree a *general focal area* within which to start work together. For example, the client might say they have difficulty in relationships, so this might be termed the general focus of the contract. The therapist will then endeavour to work through this to a strategic focus—perhaps relationships with men may be the problem. This would then become the strategic focus. The expectation of the therapist is that this difficulty will have its roots in the past and this is conveyed to the client. The client needs to understand a little about the process of therapy and how childhood events can affect the present to enable successful work to occur.

Finding the focus

Malan suggests, that in assessing and formulating a therapeutic plan several conditions need to be fulfilled. Three of these relate to the focal issue.

1. *The current conflict.* There is a precipitating factor that gives a clue to the current conflict.
2. *The nuclear conflict.* There are (a) previous precipitating events, (b) early traumatic experiences, (c) family constellations or (d) repetitive patterns, which give a clue to the nuclear conflict.
3. Congruence between current and nuclear conflict. The current conflict and the nuclear conflict are basically the same (1976, p. 264).

Wolberg describes the process of finding the focus as follows.

2. Arriving at a tentative diagnosis.
3. Evolving with the patient a working hypothesis of his psychodynamics.
4. Circumscribing the problem area as a focus for exploration. Elucidating neurotic patterns and encouraging the patient to observe himself for these (1965, p. 142).

Who chooses the focus?

Wolberg emphasizes the element of client choice in the area to be focused on.

> The particular area to be addressed is, therefore, more or less of the patient's own choosing. Often this deals with the *precipitating stress situation*, ... An endeavour is made at a working through, at least partially, of the conflicts liberated by the stress situation. These, derivatives of and related to fixed underlying core conflicts, are handled as autonomous sources of anxiety. Historical material is considered only when it is bracketed to the current problem. Not only may the patient be brought back to emotional homeostasis rapidly, particularly when he is seen immediately after the stress situation has set in, but inroads on his deeper conflicts may be engendered. ... Another focus in therapy is on *distressing symptoms* (1965, p. 159).

Mann and Goldman focus on the underlying pain presented by the client and therefore sees the choice of focus to be more in the hands of the therapist than the client. He recommends that the therapist refer to the focus in terms of "the present and chronically endured pain". This statement of the central issue needs to be "in the nature of a clarification that the patient readily recognizes". He says if this is made appropriately it "reverberates from the deepest levels of the unconscious ... It spans from the patient's experience of time from the remote past to the immediate present to the expectable future ... *With few exceptions, therefore, the central issue as formulated by the therapist in time-limited psychotherapy will be very different from the problems that the patient states as his reasons for seeking help"* (1994, p. 23).

This formulation is to be arrived at by the close and sensitive attunement of the therapist to everything that the client presents and to the underlying messages beneath the words.

Mann and Goldman highlight the fact that this method of working with the focus "expressed in terms of the patient's chronic pain and negative self image, induces a treatment experience that rapidly becomes intensely affective for both patient and therapist" (1994, pp. 27–8).

I agree with Malan that the formulation of the focus requires all the skill of the therapist, and I would add *"and the client"*.

I contend that the establishment of the focus is as much the client's decision as the therapist's. Indeed, more so than the therapist. The client needs to be made aware of the process of therapy, the possibility, for example, of the past impinging on the present, or the significance of anniversaries, or the pattern of grief, to name but a few. Then the client is expected to apply their own skill, knowledge, experience and analysing ability to the task of fixing the strategic focus. They will no doubt have an idea as to why they decided on therapy at this time, what the precipitating crisis is and have at least a vague idea as to where the problem lies. With very little help from the therapist the client will be able to make connections and select their own strategic focus. The therapist's task, in my view, is to facilitate this, helping to clarify, define, circumscribe and, at times, confront resistance or give feedback to help the client's awareness. It is not, in my view, the task of the therapist to "redefine the problem in oedipal terms" (Davanloo and Sifneos) or in "separation terms" (Mann) but rather to stay alongside the client sensitively in tune and alert to underlying feelings and pain and to facilitate the process.

Some therapists laid a particular emphasis on one type of focus. Sifneos for example in his early work in the 1970s laid great emphasis on patients with oedipal foci, he said: "It is generally agreed that the specific psychodynamic focus during the course of the treatment is a *sine qua non* for individual short-term dynamic psychotherapy. Most investigators also agree that the foci which respond best to brief interventions are: unresolved oedipal conflicts, loss and separation issues and morbid grief reactions" (1984, p. 474). However in his later work Sifneos acknowledges that the "vital role played by the Oedipus complex in the psychic life of everyone ... seems to have decreased during the past forty years" (1992, p. 41). He has broadened out the foci that he now, in the early 1990s, sees as responsive to brief therapy!

I have no specific preconceptions when working with clients as to the root cause of their focal issue. It is my contention that such preconceptions limit the process and inhibit the client, leading to a less effective outcome.

Rogawski points out that: "For a good prognoses in short-term dynamic psychotherapy: Therapists should be able to abstract a circumscribed core problem from the patient's initial presentations. In the evaluation process, therapists should recognize a central issue and agree with their patients on what is to be accomplished in the limited treatment period" (1982, pp. 339–340).

The focus is the client's choice

It must be remembered that the focus should be the client's choice— not the therapist's. The therapist may well think the issue raised is less important than another and it is certainly appropriate to share such an observation for the client to consider. Having done so, however, the therapist's task is to help the client to work on the issue the client wishes to.

As Wolberg, Sifneos and I stress, reaching the focus is a "joint" enterprise, and the client is the one who makes the final choice of circumscribed area to explore. I see it as a negotiated process:

Focal therapy is a psychotherapy approach where client and therapist work together on an agreed focal area of the client's life. They do this within an agreed and limited time-span.

The "focal area" is negotiated. Often clients present an initial problem which is bothering them. This may then become the initial general focus of the sessions. However, as exploration goes ahead, it may become apparent that there is an underlying problem relating to the initial focus. This will then become the specific focus of the remaining sessions of the contract.

The term "contract" is used because in this approach, the mutual agreement as to the focus of the sessions is important. Once client and therapist have agreed on the general area to be explored, it is then the therapist's task to ensure that this happens. If it becomes apparent that the agreed focal area is no longer relevant, a revised contract is negotiated" (Rawson, 1995, p. 8).

Sifneos gives an example of how the evaluation elicits the focus from the client—some are quite straightforward.

A 25-year-old graduate student had presented her problem at the beginning of the evaluation interview as follows: *"I am anxious in my relations with my boyfriends because I tend to put on an act and pretend that I am someone I am not. It is like wearing a mask. I want to free myself from this pattern of behaviour."*

Sifneos goes on to show how after talking for a while with the evaluator the client was able to see the patterns from her past she now sees

"that this behaviour pattern of mine, . . . has its origin at the time when I was young and when I was trying to impress my father" (Sifneos, 1987, p. 21).

I would reframe this process in terms of a general focus with regard to the pattern of behaviour and her relationship with her father the strategic focus.

My cases C and *"I"* are equally straightforward as the extract below show.

Client C had a clear issue she wished to work on. *"How can I be more confident and why don't I like myself?"* This became the general focus through which we reached the nuclear conflict—relationships with mother and siblings.

Client *I* knew that she wanted to look at the childhood abuse that she had suffered in an appropriate situation. For her the focal issue was not in doubt. It was the context that was. Did she need to see a psychiatrist, a social worker or a counsellor/therapist? Once clarification as to the process of therapy had been achieved she was ready to work on her issue, i.e. child abuse and its ongoing effect on her life.

Others however are less simple and need more assistance from the therapist—or evaluator—as Sifneos describes the therapist at this stage. Here is an excerpt of a report from Sifneos, 1987.

"A 30 year old female housewife was unsure as to which of the several problems that had brought her to the clinic bothered her most. These included her anger at her mother, her difficulties with other female employees at work, and her problems with her husband (1987, p. 20)."

Sifneos records the discussion as follows:–

"Patient: *All three problems seem to be equally important to me.*
Evaluator: *I understand, but let's look at it this way. Now, what was it that prompted you to call the clinic to set up this appointment?*
Patient: *The fight that I had with my mother on the telephone.*
Evaluator: *So maybe this is the most important problem.*
Patient: *No, because as I mentioned before, I had a fight with one of the girls at work which preceded my fight with my mother. She yelled at me for no apparent reason, and I kept thinking about it all day. When I talked to Bill, my husband, he was sympathetic, but I knew that he was busy. He has a lot of work to do for his bar exam. I was tense and I wanted to talk to someone. In any case, Bill isn't a good listener. He doesn't like people who complain, and that's another problem.*
Evaluator: *Is this then the problem?*
Patient: *Oh, no. I did think I needed some help, so I thought of calling my mother and asking her advice.*
Evaluator: *So?*
Patient: *Well, I did, and guess what my mother said? She said it was all my fault.*
Evaluator: *So the question is whether you were more angry at the girl at the office or at your mother after that telephone call.*
Patient: *It's interesting the way you put it. I hadn't thought of connecting the two episodes. I had looked at them separately. Actually, the girl at the office was criticizing me for being a victim in the same way my mother did. So the anger at both of them was the same.*

Evaluator: *So what is it that you want to accomplish out of all these things?*

Patient: *I want to get rid of everything.*

Evaluator: *You must choose only one. Which one will it be?*

Patient: *You aren't very helpful.*

Evaluator: *I really am. You see, helping you decide to place priority on your most important problem is giving you the right perspective on your difficulties, and you keep the decision in your own hands.*

Patient: *I see what you mean ... well, the anger at my mother, I think, is the key to all the other problems. It's been simmering for a long time. I suppose that it's my main difficulty, and I want to understand it* (pp. 22–23)."

Here we see the therapist helping the client to focus down on the pressing issue, that I would term the general focus. Through homing in on this in the questioning and pinning down the client, the client comes to see the underlying issue—her anger at her mother.

This issue with Mother is what I describe as the strategic focus. Other authors as we have already seen might refer to this as the nuclear crisis or the focal issue.

In my Case J, referred to in some detail in the section on flexibility, we see a similar situation to the client referred to above. J presents a range of important issues. It is important to ascertain from these which one is to be the strategic focus.

She is in her early twenties but presents as a younger person.

Client J: "*I am never good enough for Dad. I thought I'd get away from all that, but I have to phone two times per week and go home at weekends. They chose the course for me. I wanted to work with children! Dad is very negative about nannies and teachers.*" She regretted that her boyfriend was in prison for drug-taking and that her Dad demanded that she give him up.

Client J: "*It's all my fault.*"

This seems to be the message she receives from everyone. At the mention of the abortion her eyes filled with tears and there was a sadness in the room. She moved on to tell me that it was 4 years earlier. She is not sure if this is the course for her—and that the careers officer had suggested she took science.

These various issues came tumbling out in rapid succession. Towards the end of the session I helped her to list the issues referred to, drawing her attention to her own emotional response to the mention of the abortion. I talked about the reasons for therapy and about the idea of formulating a focal area for the sessions and contracting a number for these.

The issues referred to were as follows.

1. The abortion—August
2. The boyfriend 2 years later—July
3. Dislike of the course—
4. Not knowing what you want to do—
5. Suicide attempt, causing liver damage—December
6. Coping with Dad

I read the list back to her for her to choose the key area. At first she wondered about No 6 (coping with Dad) but as I observed and reflected back her reactions, that is, tears when she first mentioned the abortion and tears again at the mere mention of the abortion, she decided that this was the issue that was affecting her the most deeply. We agreed that we would start with making this the focus, for four sessions. The last of the sessions would be a review and if she still wanted to look at the other issues we would investigate them.

Factors and criteria in choosing a focus

In the above extract from Case J, I help her to select the focal area to work on in the sessions. The one finally chosen is the one where most emotion seemed to reside. At first the client wanted to avoid this one and look at another area but I confront this resistance by gently observing that the emotion seems to lie with the "abortion" and explaining the process of therapy. However, the choice of focal area is left to the client to decide and on reflection she chose this issue.

In the final review session the other topics listed in session 1 are again looked at to see if J wishes to explore these further.

She describes how she now feels as follows: *"I woke up yesterday morning feeling as if I were waking after a long illness"*. Her eyes were glowing. J and I both felt that the work was complete and somehow the other issues listed in session 1 had faded away.

The striking element in this particular case study is the fact that focusing on the "one" most central focal issue enabled the client to go on her way well able to manage the other issues she mentioned initially. I call it the "ripple effect".

The client presented several key issues in the first session. Any one of them could have become the focus of the sessions but only one was charged with emotion. This was expressed in her body language and tears and in her voice tone. That was the abortion. This aspect will be returned to in the section on the importance of the first session.

However, it is by working on THE focal issue that the process of therapy is completed in a relatively short time. If this key focal issue is dealt with the client is usually empowered to cope with the other problem areas on their own without requiring a therapist's intervention. This is the strategic focus.

By the end of the first session sufficient trust had been established to agree a contract of four sessions to look at the abortion issues as our main focus. The other problem areas that had been enumerated at times would have a bearing on the main focus and in the second session she was able to talk about her boyfriend and her father. Her feelings about being trusted by parents and being able to trust friends and herself were being explored. This session, shortened at her request because of other commitments, was also a session where she was raising some of the lesser problems as a testing ground for dealing with her real issue, the abortion which was reached in the third session.

This may be what I would term the general focus that encompasses the other issues referred to. In exploring related issues the client is at times preparing the way, trying out the therapeutic situation and gaining trust for dealing with the strategic focus.

In the third session she began to tackle her feeling about the abortion.

Choosing the focus—depth of pain

It may be noted here that this is an example that does not appear to be a nuclear conflict. It does relate to a past event, however, of some

4 years earlier. It was chosen because it was where the emotion—the pain—resided. It is this depth of pain that is, in my view, the key criterion as to where the work of the therapy lies and where the strategic focus will reside. It is not always tears that are the indicator of the most painful issue. It could be expressed as, with another client, in a shift of body position.

To elaborate on the aspect of body language I am referring to another case, client Y.

Client Y curled up into an almost foetal position at one stage in the session. This was the most important thing to then focus on, in my view. Until that point the conversation in this first session with the client had been in relation to leaving an exam early.

P: *"Has this ever happened before?"*
Y: *"No."*
P: *"Sometimes there is some past event that links with a situation like this. Are there any echoes for you?"*
Y: [Silence—client curls into foetal position, hair completely hiding her face.]
P: [Silence for a while]—*"Stay with that feeling."* [Silence]—*"What's happening?"* [Silence] *"What are you remembering?"*
Y: *"My sister"* [beginning to weep] ...
P: *"Something very sad happened?"*—[Gently]
Y: *"She killed herself when I was doing my 'A' levels."*

That was where the pain lay—the unfinished work of grieving. We therefore focused on this.

This client only had the time for this one session since she was going away immediately. Prior to any work, I had established that she did realize that therapy could be upsetting. We established that she did wish to try one session. It was also established that, if need be, a second session could be fitted in later that day.

We looked at the sibling's suicide, the family's non-coping and blocking of emotion, and the pattern in relation to the exams. Tears flowed. We then looked at strategies to cope with going home, with the family, with her needs in relation to her family's refusal even to mention the sibling's name. She left the office knowing she could make a further appointment if she wished. She left in control, sad but calm, determined to change things at home and to re-sit her exams.

I saw her briefly by chance in a corridor several months later. She told me she had gone home, talked to the family about the sister. They had all shared their loss/sadness and given each other new support and a demonstration of love. She had re-sat her exam, passed this and was feeling very different and free. She thanked me for the one session that she believed to have enabled all that change.

One session can, indeed, be enough in this approach. The client can do their own work, once they have released the block. I call this the log boom effect, and I will return to this in a later section on the importance of the first session.

Finding the strategic focus

When the presenting problem appears vague, as in F, it is the therapist's task to help the client to focus down to a more defined area in this focal and short-term approach.

In the search for the strategic focus, the therapist will be alert to any sign or indication of emotion, for example, tears, silence, body language. Rather than allow the conversation to drift on, at the slightest sign of the client being in touch with their pain, the therapist will challenge or encourage, using whichever skill seems appropriate in order to bring the feeling to the client's consciousness and into the session. This immediacy of approach is one of the features of this method and is one of the factors that accelerates the process. This was important in Case J referred to earlier where the tears welled at the mention of abortion, and here in case F this immediacy is observed where very close attention was paid to the opening sentences that F spoke which held the key to her problem.

There will be clients who have no idea what is causing their problem, as in F's case. They simply feel depressed or anxious and want help to sort this out and to feel better. Here the therapist needs to flexibly apply whatever skill or technique seems helpful to find the focus. The general focus in this case might be to work out what is causing the depression. Sometimes in a case like this, as the client talks, the therapist becomes aware of an emotion in their own person. For example the therapist perhaps suddenly experiences a deep sense of loss or fear. He/she knows this feeling belongs to the client and by reflecting this back to the client, the therapist may be able to bring into the client's consciousness the issue they are grappling with and thus a strategic focus may be found. This aspect of transference known as "projective identification" is a most useful way to speed up the process. Another indicator may be when the client, whilst describing their situation, shifts their posture towards the therapist. This movement needs to be noted by the therapist since it often occurs as the client is touching on the issue of concern. Then the client needs to be helped to further explore the topic. As I—Rawson suggest: *"Every word, expression, hesitation, body language and the emotional atmosphere need to be monitored carefully by the therapist. In so doing, important clues are gained to move the therapy on so that positive results are achieved"* (1995, p. 8).

In examining the cases selected there are a number of examples of how the focal issue is arrived at.

Too narrow a focus—assumption of necessity for an oedipal crisis

An interesting case Sifneos refers to in his exposition bears some similarity to one that I have chosen to analyse. Sifneos's example states:

A 25-year-old male engineer was very close to his mother, but he was also happily married and seemed to have good relations with people at work. It was after his mother's sudden death in an automobile accident that he became depressed and sought psychiatric help. During the evaluation, his relations with his mother, his wife, and women in general were scrutinized, but no significant problems were encountered. He was also thought to fulfil the STAPP (Short-Term Anxiety Provoking Psychotherapy) criteria for selection ... He made rapid progress in terms of understanding the importance of his attachments for his mother. ... As soon as the therapist mentioned the possibility of ending psychotherapy the patient became angry, claiming that he did not want to stop (1987, p. 53). This client eventually discontinued his therapy stating that he had found a private psychotherapist who was willing to see him "as long as he needed to be seen".

Sifneos sees this situation arising as a result of a "defective evaluation". The therapist who had taken on this client confirmed that the client "did not have an oedipal focus" and it is this that Sifneos sees as making the evaluation defective.

The real work or focus required with the client was, according to the other therapist who was seeing him long-term:

"pre-genital and characterological in nature, having to do more with the early loss and separation of the patient from his grandmother, who brought him up and who had died when he was 4 years old. His subsequent attachment to his mother, which appeared at face value to be oedipal and which had misled us during the clinical evaluation, was really a dependent substitution of his mother for the dead grandmother. It appeared that the patient's mother had an important job when the patient was born and did not want to give it up. Having divorced his father, she asked her widowed mother, the patient's grandmother, to live with them and take care of her son. The grandmother readily agreed and took care of the patient, pampering him and acquiescing to his demands. When she died, his mother grudgingly took over the care of the patient. He, in turn, repressed the painful and ambivalent feelings over the death of his grandmother. This important information was unavailable to us, possibly having been missed because of the repression during our evaluation of the patient. The sudden death of his mother which brought the patient to the clinic, and at the time was thought to be a good therapeutic focus to concentrate on, was obviously a repetition of a much greater pre-genital trauma which he had experienced at the time of his grandmother's death. Because we subsequently had similar difficulties with patients who were selected for STAPP whose therapeutic focus was a "loss of a loved one", we decided to exclude such individuals from our *research* study because it was thought that they required a longer time to deal with their reactions to separation, and for that reason they were not thought to be ideal STAPP candidates" (Sifneos, 1987, p. 54).

SUCCESS OF FOCAL THERAPY WITH ISSUES OF LOSS—A WIDER FOCUS

It is my contention that Sifneos' approach is overly restrictive and that many more can benefit from the brief approach. The examination of case F in relation to the focus, will be shown to support my view. Case F bears some resemblance to the case cited above and yet *was* dealt with within the brief framework. Indeed, in four sessions the client showed a marked improvement and ability to cope. This was despite a great deal of resistance initially in reaching either a general or strategic focus.

Case F has been seen earlier in the sections on psychodynamic roots and activity and is returned to here for further analysis. Initially "depression" was the problem presented but this soon revealed a deeper issue of "loss".

At times the client is less clear than the therapist as to where the focal issue lies. F was an example of this. F had been referred by the doctor to me on account of her "depression".

> F stated that: "*I am depressed and I've always been depressed—well, since I was 9 years old.*"

> I explored with F the events that took place when she was nine. These events related to the loss of her Nan, firstly in a partial way as Nan became senile and then when she died. Nan had lived with them at home and this affected the whole family and consequently F's childhood. These events had been compounded by a further traumatic loss when her father left home, a few years later. It became clear that this earlier time was affecting her in the present and seemed the likely root of her depression. After a process of teaching, and of homework, aspects of the focal approach which were covered in the section on activity, the client eagerly contracted to look at the events occurring at 9 years old, and subsequently this became the focal area of exploration.

Often the journey towards the key strategic issue is a progressive process.

In case B in the intake session the client was clear that the area she wished to look at related to "*family issues*" and her relationship with her mother especially.

In the session, therefore, the therapist enabled the client to explore these areas. In the last chapter the psychodynamic roots of the approach were examined in detail, and here an example of this is to be seen. Here in case B, as the client is facilitated in looking at the "family issues", she freely and easily relates incidents from her childhood that are impinging on the present and her current distress.

TOUCHING THE PAIN

> Case B desperately longs for her parents' love and approval and feels lonely and rejected without it. Approval or support makes her dissolve into tears. At one point in the session she said "*I expect you disagree . . .*" I said: "*No, feelings are okay, there's no right or wrong.*" And the tears welled.

MOMENT OF HEALING

This silence is a powerful healer. It is almost tangible between client and therapist and is perhaps the moment of "mystery" when healing occurs. I am unclear how such moments can be quantified or tabulated. It is a factor within the therapeutic alliance and I assert that it is a powerful moment within the course of therapy, maybe even *the* moment at which change/healing occurs. In some sense it is recognizable to the outsider. Certainly, one of my external non-therapist reviewers B.N.1994 observed this. He described the idea of talking to the child, in Case J's homework exercise with the poem as *"a touch of magic ... with the very beautiful and poignant poem being a fitting end to a quick and successful therapy"*.

As a validating measure, I asked several independent people to read one particular case and make their observations about the process. They largely endorsed the points that I had brought to light. This *"magical"* or *"mysterious"* almost *"mystical"* moment as they described it was apparent to each of them.

As observed earlier, it is not always so clear what the focus of the sessions should be to either the client or therapist. At such times *it is the skill of the therapist that enables the most strategic focus to be found*. At times finding the focus may become the "focus", and within that contract the "work" of the sessions will hopefully bring to light the strategic issue that needs to be faced. In Case E this, indeed, was the case.

RESISTANCE

With Client E the focus arrived at by the end of session one was a rather general one,—"relationships". In the first of these we attempted to get a clearer focus area to work on together. We explored further some of her relationships in the present and how they related to earlier relationships. Her comment at the end was a realization that *"I don't need to work so hard to succeed."* We also explored her fear of changing which I referred to earlier as resistance.

> *"I don't want to be changed—and yet I'm not happy with how things are now."*

This was an important step in creating the working alliance. She needed to face the fear of change and resolve to go ahead with the counselling in order to move out of the "now" situation. We were now closer to a clear focus—what is it in the now that she wants to change?

Session two explored this generally, but the more important element of the session was related to dealing with the resistance. That is, resistance to change, and since she assumed that therapy would lead to change, resistance to the work of therapy. The conclusion of the second session however was a firm resolution that she didn't want to stay where she was and therefore was prepared to work to change. Teaching about the process of therapy, about fear of change, the unknown and issues of trust, was given by the therapist to assist E in overcoming her resistance. Subsequently there was a clear commitment to the process of therapy. In the next session therefore we began at this point and again attempted to focus down from the broader area of relationships. What is it she wants to change in relationships? As a therapist with this client I was working hard to keep a focus on the material being presented and to relate it to the agreed focus: relationships. When the client said: *"I feel unconnected with some people"* and a tear began to trickle down, there was a change in the emotional temperature in the counselling room. This is another example of that mysterious moment when the pain is touched and shared within the warmth of the therapeutic relationship and contract.

It was here that the real work of the session began and the point was reached by holding to the agreed focus and then in focusing down within the agreed general focus "relationships" to what she wanted to "change" about her relationships. This was what she wanted to change and it was this that I would call the strategic focus.

Multiple focus

At times more than one issue becomes the general focus agreed as the contracted area of exploration. Generally, they will interlink and lead to a more specific strategic focus. This is the situation with Client M.

M presented as very withdrawn with very little eye contact and defensive body language. She had been referred by a tutor. She is in her early twenties. She feels really miserable and under pressure to do well at college. She feels pressured by friends, tutors, course mates and family and does not want to be here. She finds herself unable to concentrate. This has been the case since last year. She was abroad then and in June her parents divorced. She heard this by accident from a friend of the family. Her mother had kept this news from her because of exams.

M felt it must be her fault because she had often had the role of being between her parents. Dad would attack her about study and Mum would defend her. This was especially the case when she was 10/11-years-old and again when she was 18-years-old. *"So it must be my fault."*

I challenged this by moving into a fantasy exercise with her. She has a niece aged about 10-years-old—I asked what she would say to her if her niece was telling her that it was all her fault. M reluctantly smiled and agreed she'd try to convince her that it was *"not her fault"*. She slowly began to see the parallel for herself.

I challenged her also by reflecting back to her what she had told me that she takes responsibility for things that are not her fault, i.e. the parents' divorce, and not those that are. That is, she could leave and relax, get a pass degree, go and live the life she pleases, she does not have to accept the pressures and expectations of others. This approach took M somewhat by surprise. She began to express concern about talking about her family to anyone, even to a "counsellor". *"You won't tell Mum, will you?"* I reassured her regarding confidentiality and also about the appropriateness of talking about things that bother us and impede our work/concentration and happiness. We then summarized the issues that had emerged so far, i.e.:

(i)   the divorce and the fact she is still grieving about the loss of the family unit;
(ii)   the feeling of guilt regarding the divorce;
(iii) her unhappiness regarding the pressures on her to do well and difficulties in concentrating; and
(iv)   responsibility issues.

I then suggested that if she would like to look at these areas we would make a contract for a number of sessions to do so. It has to be her choice, both to engage in the therapy contract and to decide what areas she wishes to explore. She chose to have a therapy contract, therefore I suggested that she might think about what areas she wants to focus on and to let me know in the next session. It is important for this to be her choice and her responsibility.

Although there are four clear areas they seem to interrelate sufficiently to leave all four as the focal area for further exploration.

Additionally I was very aware of the non-verbal evidence of great distress and the need to be supporting client M's ego strongly. At this stage, to attempt to focus down further might have proved counterproductive in heightening M's defences. M's commentary on her experience of the process of therapy appears in full in Chapter 6.

Summary

In this section I have drawn on my own and other writers material to examine the place of focus within the Focal and Short-Term Psychotherapy. Whilst all are agreed as to its intrinsic place within the approach there are differing assumptions as to the underlying pathology and as to the depth that can be reached in a brief contract.

My approach is at the radical end of the spectrum. That is, that the roots of the problem will be in the past and, as Marteau says, it is by reaching through the focus to the "very roots" that a successful outcome will occur (1986, p. 81).

I also have no basic assumptions as to whether the focal conflict must be oedipal, pre-oedipal or involve loss or separation. I stay with the client focusing down more and more until the strategic focus is reached. Inevitably this will link to the past, not necessarily back into early childhood, although this is often the case. This section has drawn on some quite detailed examples from one of the key proponents: Sifneos. This is not just to underscore the importance of a "circumscribed" focus, to use his term, but to reinforce the fact that my own empirical work reflects a development beyond the earlier restrictive thinking about suitable foci. The empirical work shows that this can be much wider than the early proponents thought. The importance of the focus in brief therapy is reinforced, as is the aspect of therapy being a joint enterprise. The finding of the focus requires skill and *experience* and a great deal of *sensitivity* on the part of the therapist to *tune* into the client's need. Also, as pointed out by Mann, this focused work brings about a most *intense* therapeutic experience. These aspects of working with the focus may contribute to the increased brevity shown by the empirical work, over and above the earlier proponents, and therefore may be considered important in the shortening effect of therapy. The next section explores further the joint aspect of the work as the "therapeutic alliance" and its place in brief therapy is examined.

5.1.6. The therapeutic alliance and motivation

This section returns to the key proponents on short-term therapy and to the selected cases to examine more deeply what they understood by the therapeutic alliance in this context, and how motivation figures within this understanding.

In the preceding section 5.1.5, the focus within focal and short-term psychotherapy has been examined in detail. The focus, however, cannot be arrived at in isolation, it involves a joint process between the client and therapist leading to an agreed focus for the therapy. The process towards agreement involves exploration and the establishment, not just of the central issue but also of the suitability of the client. Assessing suitability for therapy refers to both the client's psychological state and also to their motivation for change and intention to apply themselves to the therapeutic process.

When client and therapist jointly agree that they can work together on the particular circumscribed focus, this is called the therapeutic contract, and the relationship established between client and therapist, the therapeutic alliance.

Psychotherapy as a joint venture

Sifneos stresses this joint nature of psychotherapy and suggests that it is important to obtain from the client: "an agreement to work cooperatively with the therapist in order to resolve the emotional conflicts underlying the specific focus which is considered to be responsible for the psychological difficulties" (1992, p. 2).

Motivation in the therapeutic relationship

Sifneos also stresses the importance of motivation and the fact that this should be "motivation for *change*" not merely "motivation for symptom relief" (1987, p. 42). He summarizes the criteria relevant to motivation as follows.

1. Willingness to participate actively in the evaluation process.
2. Honesty in reporting about oneself.
3. Ability to recognize that the difficulties are of a psychological origin.
4. Introspection and curiosity about oneself.
5. Openness to new ideas and willingness to change, explore and experiment.
6. Realistic expectation of the outcome.
7. Willingness to make a tangible sacrifice (1992, p. 42).

The importance of motivation had not really been fully understood until Sifneos discovered from the results of follow up interviews that: "many patients emphasized ... that their original intent to understand themselves was very possibly the single most important factor in the ultimate success of their treatments" (1984, p. 94).

Client commitment—motivation

The term "contract" that is used, when agreement between client and therapist has been reached as to the focal area to be worked on, implies active involvement and commitment on the part of the client. I—Rawson—suggest it is a term chosen: *"because in this approach, the mutual agreement as to the focus of the sessions is important"* (1995, p. 8). It is this agreement and commitment that lies at the heart of the therapeutic alliance and it is this that acts as a powerful motivator for the client. It is important because at times the work of therapy is painful and it takes courage to persevere. As Sifneos observes, motivated patients are willing to fully enter into the process of therapy and "are willing to experience some pain in the process of extricating themselves from the neurotic chains that tie them down and that keep them from expanding and using their talents" (1992, p. 42).

The concept of motivation, as the reader will recall from the earlier chapters on psychoanalytic roots and the literature search, is not a new one. Rank in the late 1940s developed the concept of "will therapy". He endeavoured to mobilize the patient's will and thereby was able to shorten the length required for the therapy.

Transference in the therapeutic relationship

Malan too highlights motivation and stresses the importance of transference as well. He suggests that successful therapy is most likely when: "the patient has a high motivation; the therapist has a high enthusiasm; transference arises early and becomes a major feature of therapy; and grief and anger at termination are important issues" (1963, p. 274).

Davanloo, another key proponent, also sees both these factors as important in the brief approach: "In terms of technique, I have emphasized the importance of the therapeutic alliance, which is generated by a dynamic interaction between the patient and the therapist, the active utilization of the transference relationship, with active interpretation of transference resistance and the active avoidance of a transference neurosis. One works actively on the triangle of defence/anxiety/impulse feeling and on the triangle of transference/current/past" (1980, p. 70).

Wolberg further describes how the transference can influence the therapeutic relationship: "The aspect of the relationship embodying expectant trust operates automatically at first, but soon this is reinforced or neutralized by activities of the therapist and by transference, which in short-term therapy is less of a hazard than in prolonged treatment due to the time limitations" (1965, p. 132).

Therapeutic alliance—a "relationship situation"

Wolberg refers to the therapeutic alliance as a "relationship situation" which is "a significant healing force" (1965, p. 31). Within this relationship the patient finds: "asylum, a refuge from the devils that stir him up from within. This tension resolves as he puts himself into the protective sweep of the therapeutic alliance ... The mere process of talking to an interested person tends to bring relief" (p. 132). He goes on to say that: "Human warmth and feeling, experienced by a patient in one session with an empathic therapist, may achieve more profound alterations than years with a probing, detached therapist intent on wearing out resistance. This does not mean that one should be neglectful of the unconscious. For within a short span of therapy, repressed psychic aspects may still be elicited and handled" (p. 138). Winokur and Dasberg refer to this intense empathic support required in brief therapy as a "collaborative alliance" (1983, p. 45).

When working within the brief therapy context Wolberg stresses the need for a working relationship to be established very quickly. He suggests that this is enabled as detailed below.

a. Sympathetic listening to the patient's story.
b. Communicating understanding.
c. Communicating confidence in one's approach.
d. Reassuring the patient that he is not hopeless.
e. Structuring the therapeutic situation (1965, p. 142).

Involvement

Malan takes the aspect of relationship further. He postulates that from all the research and examination of the evidence there is: "a single unifying factor of extra-ordinary simplicity: That the prognosis is best when there is a willingness on the part of both patient and therapist to become *deeply involved*, and in Balint's words 'to bear the tension that inevitably ensues'" (1963, p. 274).

Malan goes on with some words of caution about the nature of such involvement and the need for awareness on the part of the therapist of countertransference reactions: "Each must become involved in a special way: the patient must bring to the therapy his intense wish for help through insight, and to the relation with the therapist both his neurotic difficulties and some of his dependence—but dependence that is neither too intense nor too primitive; while the therapist must bring his human sympathy, his therapeutic enthusiasm, and his willingness to interact "objectively", and he obviously must not become so involved that—for instance—he is resentful if therapy fails, and still less must *his* involvement be seriously complicated by unconscious reverberations from the past" (1963, pp. 274/5).

Specific factor in brief therapy

Malan suggests that, within brief therapy, this is a "specific factor ... a special variety of this involvement on the part of the patient, together with insight into its meaning; i.e. the transference experience accompanied by transference interpretation, and particularly the experience and interpretation of the negative transference and of the therapist–parent link" (1963, p. 275).

Caring support

This "*involvement*" incorporates care. Malan refers to one of his patient's comments on the therapy: "For her, one of the deepest experiences in therapy ... (was) the realization that the therapist *cared*, that it really mattered to him how therapy turned out for her." (1963, p. 275).

This patient's comments reflect my own experience. Repeatedly on evaluation sheets completed after brief therapy contracts, the client's comments were: "*you cared*" or "*you really understood*" as being the most important facet of the work together.

Reich and Neenan also endorse this view, stressing the element of patient/therapist interaction as an important patient selection variable. "If patients do not feel the therapist truly understands their problem or are uncertain of the therapist's interest in them, then the chances for a successful therapy are much reduced" (1986, p. 64).

This is supported by Strupp who shows failure linked to: "therapists" negative responses to difficult patients" (1980, p. 954). The client who terminated therapy early said of his counsellor: "I'm not sure whether or not he likes me" ... he "seems rather cool and distant" ... and "does not make it easier for me to talk about things I find difficult to talk about" (1980, p. 948). Strupp and Hadley had earlier observed that success, on the other hand, is seen to relate to "the healing effects of a benign human relationship" (1979, p. 1135).

Intensity in brief psychotherapy

There is wide agreement amongst the key proponents that there is a particular intensity about the brief therapy process. This is highlighted by Sperry: "In brief therapy, similar processes of engagement and exploration are involved, but the time, intensity, and content tend to differ ..." (1987, p. 240).

Winokur and Dasberg believe that this intensity is enhanced by the time limit which: "adds to the intensity of the experience and increases the work accomplished in both the therapy and learning situations" (1983, p. 39).

I also see intensity as an important ingredient in the brief approach and one that places a particular demand on the therapist: "*This is a particularly intense form of therapy and requires alert attention to every aspect of the therapeutic relationship*" (1995, p. 8).

Therapist as facilitator

Marmor reminds us of the need for "respect" for the client's "capacity to be autonomous" (1979, p. 153). The client must choose to collaborate and to participate actively in the process. "It is their trip" as I have heard Marteau say many times.

This aspect was commented upon by C.S. (1994), one of the external observers on case J. She says: "The therapist at every stage enables and leaves her free. The therapist facilitates the client, it is J who chooses the focus, the contract and the way of working". Like Marmor above, C.S. sees this facilitator role as showing "respect" for the client in "helping the client to listen to herself". CS observes, that this respect for the client requires a certain humility on the part of the therapist: "The way the therapist has dealt with J allows her to be fully herself and to do as she wishes to. This is very significant and is an indication of the level of relationship. J receives the strength to do what she resolves to do. I note that the interesting thing is the "humbleness" of the therapist. The client J is on her own, the therapist stands back and facilitates the relieving of the person. Enabling the person (J) to stand on her own feet, being vulnerable but with strength".

Bennet also underlines the client's involvement and the patient's own power to heal. He refers to the therapist as facilitator. He reminds us that the role of therapist is to apply "the least extensive and intrusive intervention capable of removing the obstacle to normal growth" (1984, p. 176). Bennet prefers not to over-emphasize "the therapist as a healing force" but rather as "an adjunct to the patient's own recuperative or health-seeking initiatives" (p. 176).

The selected case extracts below, are intended to demonstrate aspects of the therapeutic alliance and its development and relate also to client motivation.

CASE M

The case demonstrates the difficulty of this exploration. How does one begin to fathom the development of the relationship which precedes the development of the therapeutic alliance? Since I am the therapist I can reflect back on the non-verbal communications and my own experience of the situation. This is of course subjective and therefore limited.

M presented as very withdrawn with very little eye contact and defensive body language and given the demeanour of this client and her reluctance to talk, the case notes show a surprisingly quick move into therapeutic work.

I deliberately tried to maintain eye contact, gently encouraging the client to meet my gaze. I am aware of a softening of tone in my responses to the client despite, as the notes state, my gently "challenging" her. As therapist I was aware of the need to coax and encourage and be *sensitive* and yet to help M to deal with the issues she was bringing and hence to challenge as required. She needed to see the possibility of change from the first and needed to see how therapy could help this, and we "made a dent" in the problem by moving into the fantasy exercise referred to under the section "Focus". This idea of "making a dent" will be returned in the section on the importance of the first session.

This constituted the initial step in the process towards the therapeutic alliance. As we looked together at the issues we had touched on in the course of the first session, it was agreed that there were tasks that she could undertake between sessions to help move the therapy on. In her agreeing to do this and on the area to look at, the therapeutic alliance is confirmed. I suggested that she could, for homework *"look at dates that might be significant in relation to any of your relatives to see if they can help you to understand this present 'misery' and secondly that you might try writing to yourself as the 10-year-old child."*

Towards the end of the session I also directly addressed the lack of eye contact and endeavour to meet her eyes. She tried to respond. This too is a step towards strengthening the therapeutic relationship and alliance.

In the next session she tells me of even more painful episodes—e.g. *"a suicide attempt at 18 years old and a stay in the psychiatric hospital."* This shows a deepening of trust almost despite herself. *"M says that she feels both guilty and relieved to be talking to me and is amazed she is telling me so much."* She told me that *"her previous psychiatric encounters decided they were unable to help because she wouldn't talk!"*

She told me that, after the last session when she'd told me of very deep secrets, she felt *"initially drained for a few days and then much better."* This encouraged her to go deeper in the next session.

My contention is that the less definable aspect of the client/ therapist relationship that I referred to earlier is paramount. The aspect that governed the way that I, as therapist, related to her is the key to her opening up with me and to enable the therapeutic alliance to be formed. I simply cared and this message was clear to M and was enabling. It is difficult to quantify or record.

M has written up her experience of the therapy. She does not refer initially to this caring aspect of the relationship rather to an *"apparent harshness"* that she experienced. It was this in the second session that she describes as the *"turning point in the counselling!"* *"Penny seemed to be particularly harsh in asking me why I did not just give up and sit at home all day. She told me that I did not have to do what I was doing if I did not want to, but that I was a free person. I left the session feeling very upset, maybe even angry. Perhaps it was my pride that was hurt and the idea of her suggesting I stay at home doing nothing all day. This really made me think and I realized that I knew I was capable of doing more than that and did indeed want to. (From that point on, I was determined to pull myself together.) I think Penny's use of the phrase 'top yourself' also made me want to overcome my problems. Once again, I felt as though she were using this phrase to annoy me and make me see how awful it is when people commit suicide.*

In short, I do not know whether I am correct, even now, but I feel that this apparent harshness really 'brought me back to my senses'."

M also observed that *"the idea of a fixed number of sessions was very good."* M: *"It made me realize that if I did want to be helped, I had to start talking and not waste the counsellor's time."*

M's commentary appears in full in Chapter 6.2.

The fixed number of sessions therefore also facilitated the therapeutic alliance and the process of therapy. M will be returned to in the section on the importance of the first session.

CASE J

Client J presented a number of issues which were concerning her. I encouraged her to look at the one causing her the most pain. This was expressed in her body language and tears and in her voice tone, and was *"the abortion of 4 years ago"*! This became the topic that we agreed to focus on. This was possible because a relationship of trust had very quickly been established. In the setting where I worked with the client, the counselling service was well advertised and known to the clients—a university setting. I believe that some of the testing-out that takes place in private practice is not needed in this setting since the institutional setting acts as guarantee for the client. It gives the therapy service an official stamp and standing, and contributes to the quick establishment of the therapeutic alliance. In J's case however, there had been a kind of testing out as seen earlier in the request for a half hour session where issues other than the abortion were referred to.

C.S., one of the external observers, comments: *"The therapist saw this for what it was—a sort of testing out ... The fact that J shares as she does in session three shows the importance again of the second (short) session. The trust she shows in session 3 is amazing and shows that the therapist has made her feel safe"*.

B.N., the other external observer, said that *"it struck him as strange, going along with a lack of discipline in letting her have her own way with the half hour session. However it proved to be a good decision as in the next session she reached the heart of the matter. He noted that the therapist maintained a measure of control over the boundaries of the session by not allowing the important issue of the abortion to be discussed in the half hour and wondered why not if it is so important"*. I did not in fact allow it in the half hour because it was too important to be rushed.

CASE F

In F's case it was necessary to overcome quite a lot of resistance to the therapy process and in order to facilitate this I explained the process. This explanation was intermingled with encouraging the client to tell me about her situation and, indeed, starting the process of therapy. It is important to begin to deal with the client's issues at this early stage to enable the client to begin to hope that there are solutions and that change can occur.

> I had set F some homework after the first session. This was to move the therapy work along and to let her take responsibility for the work. The homework had been to find out when her Nan died and to list the crises in her life as far back as she could remember—with dates.

She had done this faithfully, writing a full 20 pages. She had gone back to being 5 years old. She had begun to see that the losses that her family had suffered could link with her fear of the "world falling apart" and "never being the same again". In seeing this link she is already beginning to cope better with her fears.

The fact that F did the homework showed that she had really engaged in the therapy process, was motivated and that the therapeutic alliance was quite strongly in place by the end of session 1.

CASE E

Case E had come to see me as therapist about exam stress for a one-off session. In dealing with this, other issues emerged and a contract to look at these was offered. Some time elapsed before she returned requesting a counselling contract. This interim period, I believe, is connected with her ability to engage in the therapy process wholeheartedly later and to move rapidly within the ensuing four sessions. Although clarifying the focal area took up a large part of the first of the two sessions of the contract, a level of trust existed from the first.

In the first of these we attempted to get a clearer focus area to work on together. We explored further some of her relationships in the present and how they related to earlier relationships—her comment at the end was a realization that: "*I don't need to work so hard to succeed.*" We also explored her fear of changing. "*I don't want to be changed, and yet I'm not happy with how things are now.*" This was an important step in creating the working alliance. She needed to face the fear of change and resolve to go ahead with the counselling in order to move out of the "now" situation. We were now closer to a clear focus—what is it in the now that she wants to change?

The next session moved into a fantasy exercise in which the "work" of the contract took place and contributed to the required change. This has been presented in full in the section on techniques within flexibility.

CASE I

This client needed to check out what counselling/therapy was and how it differed from psychiatry or clinical psychology and social work. Once this had been clarified, she blurted out that she needed *"to explore issues around child abuse"* and would like counselling for this. As a preliminary step before reaching my door she had talked to the Student Union who had checked with me whether therapy would be appropriate. It was after this that Client *I* had made her appointment.

These two steps towards fixing on a contract with me were, in fact, an intrinsic part in the establishment of the therapeutic alliance. Often one might be unaware of external factors or people contributing towards the client's approach to therapy, but this is another example where it is possible to pinpoint.

Case B

Client B originally made her approach on an unrelated issue, but as she spoke I noticed tears were beginning to well up in her eyes. I gently asked what was happening and suggested that if there were things bothering her it might be a good idea to fix some counselling sessions. Then in the therapeutic context the issues of concern could be looked at, understood and put behind her so that she could get on with her life unhampered.

In recognizing that there is pain and a reason for the pain and by explaining how therapy might help and in giving hope that things can be better, my intention is to help the client to make a decision to choose counselling. In this process of "teaching" the therapeutic alliance is being established, resistance is being overcome and the client, by being in touch with the pain, is made more aware of the pertinent issues that need to be explored. The client's tears already indicate a measure of trust in the therapist and in the therapeutic situation.

Client B and I talked a little about the issues, about therapy and its length and finally agreed a contract of eight sessions. These were to look at family issues and her relationship with her mother especially.

We see both a general and specific focus here. There is also a clear statement with regard to duration. That is the expectation of working in a concentrated way on the agreed focus. The expectation that a positive outcome is possible in that time scale is also implied. The realities of the pending end of term were taken into account and the eight sessions timed to be completed in time for the client's departure from town.

It is always important to have some awareness of the client's social context in setting up such contracts. This aspect of timing has been covered elsewhere. The therapeutic alliance is now established and in the clarity of the strategic focus and the commitment to the eight weeks the motivation of the client is demonstrated. The client's determination to complete before leaving London also gave evidence of motivation. All these factors are significant in the expectation of a successful outcome. At the next meeting B talked freely about the family, recalling painfully a number of events from her younger years. In this first of the eight agreed sessions, the "work" began intensely and immediately. The depth of the session was only possible because of the strength of the therapeutic alliance already established.

I suggested earlier in relation to Client J that the institutional context is a factor in speeding up the establishment of the therapeutic alliance. Clients F, C and E had all had an earlier contract with the service, a gap and then the formal request for a counselling/therapy contract—second time around, all being very clear what they wanted and all three prepared to put energy and intensive activity into the process.

This may also reflect the importance of interruptions in therapy referred to earlier. Such interruptions may provide the client with a period of latency in which the therapeutic alliance may be strengthened.

Summary

To conclude this section on the therapeutic alliance, there are a number of facets to this as both the literature and the case references have shown. The therapeutic alliance is fundamentally about relationship and as Butler et al. state:

> This therapeutic bond far outweighs specific interventions, length, or type of therapy. In practice, this quality of the relationship is often based on the patients feeling of being listened to and understood. This, above all else, impresses us as the essence of therapy, and the effectiveness of any dynamic therapist, brief or otherwise, is ultimately limited by his or her ability to establish this connection with the patient (1992, p. 91).

The aspect I wish to emphasize here, as it emerges from the cases and the literature, is its rapid establishment in brief work. It is the speed with which the alliance can be formed and therefore the focused work to begin that enables good results to be achieved in a short time.

A *teaching* process was often seen to be present as a way of building up the therapeutic relationship and enhancing the client's motivation to achieve change. This was often accompanied by a *sensitive* awareness of the *pain* or other emotion that the client was experiencing. The communication of this awareness combined with teaching about the process of therapy motivating clients to commit themselves to the therapeutic contract. The therapeutic alliance works in parallel with establishing a clear focus which forms the contract. That is, the decision of client and therapist to work on a particular issue for a certain period of time. It also encompasses aspects of trust, dependence and hope.

This need for speed in the early stages of the therapeutic work leads on to the next section which examines the importance of the first session in brief therapy.

5.1.7. Importance of the first session

In the last section the need for a rapid establishment of the therapeutic alliance was found to be an important element in brief therapy. This leads us to examine the first moments of the therapeutic encounter and what goes on in the first session.

This section therefore returns to the literature and to the cases to examine the first session and its significance for brief therapy.

It is interesting to note that, in the *majority of the early writers* and commentators about the focal and short-term approach, the importance of the first session is *not* highlighted. Only Kovacs and Bauer and Kobos refer to it as a significant factor (See Table IV). However the analysis of the selected cases showed it to be a *very significant factor in every case* (See Table I). When the works of the key proponents were examined against this key theme it was found that only four of them, Sifneos, Mann, Davanloo and Kovacs, acknowledge its importance, but they each see the value of this initial session in differing ways. Indeed, in the case of Kovacs and

Sifneos, they are diametrically opposed. That is, whilst agreeing that the first session is important, they recommend completely different approaches within the session itself in relation to the taking of a history, or in beginning the true work of therapy.

First session as start of therapy

Kovacs exhorts us never to "squander" the initial visit. He likens it to any first moment of meeting in ordinary relationships from which lasting impressions are formed. He stresses that the first session "should *never* be given over to our exploration of the patient's history or to some systematic survey of current strategy and functioning" (1982, p. 148).

Sifneos on the other hand takes exactly the opposite view. He stresses "history taking" as "probably the single most important aspect of the psychological evaluation" and states that it "can become the basis of understanding the nature of the patient's difficulties as well as solving them" (1987, p. 16). He tells us that "it should take place sometime during the middle of the first interview, after the patient has had an opportunity to describe his presenting complaints" (1987, p. 16). In this Sifneos sees the history taking and the first session as diagnostic and disagrees with Kovacs by placing this as central to the first session.

Kovacs holds an opposing view and is emphatic that the first session's:

> "over-arching purpose is to begin the true purpose of psychotherapy (as opposed to diagnosis). And in order to achieve this purpose, four tasks have to be mastered effectively by the psychotherapist.
>
> 1. The therapist must develop the capacity to make some preliminary formulation about the nature of the developmental crisis which has brought the patient into the consulting room.
> 2. Having done so, the therapist must next do *something* to demonstrate to the patient that s/he has been understood. The beginning development of an empathic bond during the first session is a *sine qua non* for the continuation of further brief psychotherapeutic work.
> 3. The therapist must then undertake some intervention during the first session which begins to make at least a small dent in the stasis into which the patient has been locked for some time now.

4. And finally, the therapist must give the patient some assign-
ment to carry out in the patient's real world before the time of
the next visit (if any)" (1982, p. 148).

In these four tasks it is clear that Kovacs places diagnosis within
the first session but in the context of making therapeutic interventions sufficient to make a "dent" in the blocked situation.

I contend that, if the therapist does not engage the client and
begin work on the real issue in this first session, the work will not be
as brief as it could otherwise be. It is by doing this that the therapist
demonstrates to the client that they are understood. Kovacs' second
point is that it is in this work that the *intensity* of the therapeutic
alliance is established. This intensity, alluded to in the last chapter,
contributes to the rapid results achieved within the focal approach.

It is important to obtain a history in order to set the patient's
problems in a context, but I believe that this is secondary to the
points Kovacs makes. The history can be obtained through the
opening work of therapy. To leave aside the client's initial
expressions of the key issues that have brought them to therapy,
in order to take a history, would be to dismiss the importance of the
issue. The step of trust that entering therapy and telling their story
involves for the client is better nurtured by immediately responding
to the issues presented. The task Kovacs recommends for the client
to work on by the next session takes the presenting issue seriously
and gives power back to the client to work on their issue before the
next session. The client's activity is engaged and the therapeutic
alliance enhanced. Sifneos's more formal history taking allows a
more passive role for the client and may delay the intensity of the
relationship required for rapid action.

Comparison of Davanloo's and Mann's emphasis on the first session

Davanloo and Mann both lay stress on the importance of the first
session in terms of it being an active start of the therapeutic process.
Rasmussen and Messer, note that Davanloo "avoids colluding with
his patient's intellectualizing defences by forcing her to examine her
immediate feelings about talking with him (the therapist). Only
minutes into the session Davanloo confronts her resistance and
begins to work with her transference" (1986, p. 173).

One of Davanloo's techniques is described as "chasing the evasiveness with forced dichotomies and pinning her down on very noncommittal, vague response" (p. 173). For example, at the same time as he relentlessly challenges each vague generalization asking for specific examples or definitions, Davanloo acknowledges the client's pain, giving support and care. There is, Rasmussen and Messer state, an "emotional *intensity*" in this approach "possibly unparalleled in other forms of therapy" (p. 174).

Rasmussen and Messer compare Davanloo's challenging approach to Mann's who they see also as an "active interrogator", but as more gentle. Mann's method is described as more "incorporative, soothing and affirming in contrast to their description of Davanloo's as "penetrating and relentless" (p. 181).

Davanloo's first session as trial therapy

Davanloo is one of the more recent of the short-term therapists who has discovered the importance of the first session. He refers to this as a trial therapy. Within the first session he employs the same techniques that he would use in later sessions. He uses the first session also as a process of selection. Davanloo says: "One persistently confronts the patient in the face of vagueness, avoidance, and passivity, and further leads him with relation to significant people in his current life, such as his boss, wife, etc. This might mobilize anger in the transference as well as defence against anger; and this is brought into focus the moment it arises. One persistently confronts the patient, asking what he really feels rather than interpreting it to him" (1980, p. 46).

Davanloo sees this process as a gentle one despite his critics seeing it as aggressive. Davanloo says: "The patient is gently but relentlessly confronted with his feelings in his current situation, in the transference relationship and in the past, and whenever possible links are made among these three areas" (1980, p. 51).

Davanloo describes himself as the "relentless healer" (1980, p. 53). This seems an apt description as he relentlessly pins down the client to examine minutely the feelings described. This heightens the *intensity* of the process. The client tends to feel increased relief when he manages to focus on key issues and feelings because of the questioning and holding to the focus.

One session is sometimes enough—catalyst—Sifneos

Returning once again to Sifneos, we examine this time another aspect of the first session, that of the catalyst effect. Sifneos highlights the therapeutic value of just the initial interview. He points out that the therapeutic impact within this one session is sometimes sufficient and precludes the need for further sessions.

It may be that the client, either in the session or subsequently, gains sufficient insight to change the unwanted situation. He cites the example of a girl whose prior relationships with men linked to her desire for her stepfather. Once the link had been made, she could unravel and change her patterns of behaviour—and one session was sufficient. Sifneos sees her as one of the "individuals who are ripe for a simple psychodynamic confrontation that acts as a catalyst in setting in motion the resolution of their psychological problems" (1987, p. 88).

Sifneos challenges the medical profession with this stance and reminds us of their difficulty in accepting these cases. He observes that: "Psychiatrists who have been trained to believe that psychological reactions take a long time to be modified become suspicious and tend to undermine the patient's confidence by implying that they represent a 'flight into health' or a 'counterphobic reaction' or doubt that positive results will be maintained" (1987, p. 88). Sifneos's follow-up interviews however, show that improvement is maintained. For example, the patient referred to above had ceased to fight with her stepfather, had left home appropriately and was engaged to an American and so had found an enduring relationship with her fellow countrymen where previously she could not (p. 84).

Log boom effect—one or more sessions as catalyst—

I fully support Sifneos's concept of the one session being the catalyst. I refer to this process as the "log boom effect". I wondered, however, how effective the first session would be in this regard if time out was to be taken from the key issue to devote to history taking, which Sifneos advocates, and I am pleased to note that Sifneos nonetheless observes the effect.

What have log booms to do with focal and short-term psychotherapy? This is an analogy I often use with clients to help

them to understand the process of therapy. I explain this as follows:
Rawson:

> In Canada it is a common sight to see log booms floating by at a steady pace down the river. Log booms are like rafts; they are made up of some 20 tree trunks tied together. Needless to say, these booms will pick up river debris as they travel and this may slow the pace, but they generally keep going. Now and again, however, the debris is such as to bring the boom to a complete standstill. ... It then blocks not just the one log boom but several others also.

> At this point, to restore movement, it requires the location and removal of the strategic obstruction. When this is done, the log boom or booms move on at the pace dictated by the river.

> As I watched such booms on a recent visit to Canada, it seemed to me that here was an analogy of the work of brief and strategic/focal psychodynamic therapy.

> Mostly people will be travelling along through life flowing with the "stream of consciousness", William James. They can go on their way alongside others adequately. Then some event occurs in their life or relationships and they become stuck and hampered in their everyday life. This is just like the raft accumulating debris on its passage through the river. Often the stream of time, the ebb and flow of life itself, will shift the block and they move on adequately. This is like what happens on the river when the strength of the current is sufficient to clear the debris. Sometimes, however, the blockage caused by some past event impedes movement in the present. This analogy is one that clients seem able to relate to and one which enables them to feel empowered and it inspires, I have found, hope and I explain that the therapist can facilitate the process to free the block. It is this that sometimes eases the client to commit themselves to the therapy ... often one session is sufficient as has been stated (1990, p. 10).

First session as part of the selection process

The first session is of course part of the selection process and establishing that the client is a suitable subject for therapy and for the brief therapy approach. There is wide agreement amongst the key writers that one is looking for the ability to focus on a circumscribed issue, the signs of motivation to change and the willingness to consider past events in relation to the present using the ability to enter into the therapeutic alliance and the ability to form relationships.

Davanloo includes a selection process in the first session where he begins the therapy work immediately. I also believe that both the process of evaluating the issue and that of selection occur during the therapy which begins from the first moments of the therapeutic encounter. They are a simultaneous process that is encompassed within the work. If the client presents a variety of issues or an unclear statement, these are clarified, challenged, played back as the therapist tries to make sense of the client's view of his/her inner world. If, for instance, no focal issue can be pinned down despite the "relentless" confrontation described above by Davanloo, this would be an indication that the client is not suitable for the approach; also, if evidence of psychotic breakdown were apparent in the initial presentation. If either of these excluding factors were evident, then the process would be concluded and appropriate referral made.

Sifneos states that, in the focal way of working, psychotherapy must be a "joint" venture which explores an agreed "circumscribed" problem area (1987, p. 16). He observes that quite independently he and Malan had come to the same conclusions about selection criteria. The following summarizes the selection criteria in Sifneos' words:

"1. The patient must be able to circumscribe the presenting complaints.

2. The patient must have had at least one meaningful (give and take, altruistic) relationship during childhood.

3. The patient must relate flexibly to the evaluator, demonstrating that he or she can experience and express both positive and negative feelings appropriately.

4. The patient, must be fairly intelligent and psychologically minded enough to comprehend psychotherapeutic interactions.

5. The patient must be motivated to change and must not expect only symptom relief through psychotherapy" (1992, p. 20).

He reminds us also that the patient needs to be able to tolerate a certain amount of stress in brief therapy which he describes as "short-term anxiety provoking therapy" (STAPP). This type of "psychotherapy utilizes the patient's anxiety as a motivating force to help him resolve his difficulties" (1987, p. XIV).

Mann stresses additionally that the client needs to have the "capacity for ... rapid affective involvement and equally rapid disengagement—a measure of the capacity to tolerate loss" (1991, p. 91).

Patient selection

When looking at patient selection for brief therapy, one needs to bear in mind basic criteria for *any* type of psychotherapy. There are, according to Marmor, "five qualities" "that are essential factors in the selection of patients for any form of dynamic psychotherapy, long-term as well as short-term" (1979, p. 152). These factors show a remarkable similarity to those referred to above, by the proponents of the brief approach and include:

"1. Evidence of ego strength (e.g. intelligence, level of educational achievement, sexual adjustment, type of work, ability to assume responsibility).
2. At least one meaningful interpersonal relationship in the past, indicating a capacity for basic trust, which is essential in the psychotherapeutic process.
3. The ability to interact with the therapist in the first session (i.e. the capacity to form a positive transference).
4. The ability to think in psychological terms (i.e. the ability to accept interpretation or, as it is sometimes called, the capacity for insight, which is usually tested in the initial interview by making a tentative interpretation and evaluating the patient's response to it).
5. The ability to experience feelings (i.e. the degree to which the individual seems to be in touch with his own emotions)" (1979, p. 152).

It would seem that the real areas of difference highlighted relate to the ability to circumscribe a focal area for the joint work and the ability to enter into the therapeutic relationship deeply and quickly and also to "disengage" from it quickly. These factors involve the ability to tolerate anxiety as Sifneos observed and to tolerate loss as Mann points out. The marked similarity of the other criteria perhaps suggests that more clients may be helped by the brief approach than may have been acknowledged previously.

Ability of the therapist to tolerate loss

In addition to Mann's observation above about the client's capacity to tolerate loss, I suggest that the possession of a high capacity to tolerate loss is of paramount importance for the therapist who chooses to work within the brief focal model. The brief and dynamic approach enhances the intensity of the therapeutic alliance and therefore heightens the loss experienced by client and therapist at the conclusion of the short number of sessions. The rapid turnover of clients means that this demanding process is also repeated very much more often than would be the case if clients were seen for a long time. The therapist needs to be able to let go and needs to be very clear as to any counter-transference issues that might make this difficult. Few of the authors stress this aspect, although this is alluded to by Demos and Prout (1993, p. 20).

I further suggest that the therapist in this method needs to be able to convey all the skills of the therapist rapidly and needs to be able to move into therapeutic intervention with courage and certainty. As Wolberg puts it, "The tolerances in short-term therapy are fine; there is place for only the barest margin of error" (1965, p. 128). In this approach one must keep the focus and the end in mind. If the process is to proceed rapidly, the therapist cannot afford to allow the client to meander and needs to be ready to be the "relentless healer" of Davanloo referred to earlier. The therapist needs therefore solid training and experience to intervene in this way. The client will discern this and I believe that in the first session there is a testing out process undertaken by the client and the therapist also.

This aspect is apparent in the selected cases which now come under scrutiny.

First sessions in my casework

The analysis of the casework revealed many of the aspects which are referred to above and which can therefore be seen to be endorsed by the key proponents. However the reader is reminded that, although in the write up here the discoveries from the literature are reported first, the examination of the cases took place before the detailed analysis of the work of the key proponents. This fact is significant since the findings in relation to my colleagues and my cases also highlight aspects of the first session that the earlier authors have not commented upon. The testing out process is one such aspect.

Client's testing out of therapist and therapy situation

The following case extracts taken from the clinical work give instances of the client testing out the therapist and therapy situation.

CASE C

C had had counselling a year earlier in relation to a specific relationship issue. She had moved on successfully after two sessions. This time she came with a clear focal issue to work on, namely: *"How can I be more confident and why don't I like myself?"* I asked whether she'd got what she needed from her previous encounter with the counselling service. She said she had and she admitted that on the earlier occasion she'd been *"testing out the service"*. Now one year later she wanted to bring the *"real issue"*. Is the time lag a significant factor? Does it perhaps allow the client time to gain courage to broach the painful issue? It became apparent there was another factor influencing her decision to come for counselling at this time also—her return to her own country in a number of weeks. The "deadline effect", referred in an earlier section, was at work.

It is interesting to note that she had adopted the language I tend to use in briefing clients about the focal approach offered by the service. She brought the issue she wanted to *"focus on"*—and had in mind a *"contract"* of six sessions. This number seemed appropriate to me for the issue presented. I only discovered later that, for her there were only 6 weeks before she would be away for a while, so the deadline was built into her mind. As the case evolved, it was clear that the "deadline effect" pushed her to bring out the painful issues she'd been trying to avoid previously. The imminent return home is also connected to her issue about confidence and this served as a "clue" to the focal issue. When she returns home she is confronted with her relationship with mother whom C described as *"a machine"* and as *"someone who never had time for me. I long for mother to really listen and talk to me."* She referred to her younger sister's assault incident that had occurred a year before C left home and how she'd felt she'd had to *"cope"* and be *"good"*.

Within this session were the seeds of the important issues for her. As the session evolved the depth of "loss" experienced, the importance to her of the word "coping" became apparent, underlying her lack of confidence and dislike of herself. The big thing she needed to deal with was fear, ultimately linked with fear of loss and her lack of confidence. The word "coping" was an important indicator. The concept of clue giving in this testing out process is taken up again later in this section.

(Client C's own commentary on the experience of therapy is seen in full in Chapter 6.1.)

CLIENT *I*

As we saw in an earlier section Client *I* also adopted a tentative testing out approach to therapy. She firstly sent along a friend to ask: *"How can someone be referred to a psychiatrist?"* I suggested to the friend that she asked the person concerned to come to see me herself although I also gave an outline about how a referral might work. In addition I pointed out that there were other options open to the person such as counselling. This, I would describe as a teaching process.

Client *I* eventually came herself and told me that she was the aforementioned *"friend"*. Her question was: *"How can I go about seeing a psychiatrist?"*

The client describes this encounter as follows:

I felt apprehensive as I knew no one who had been before. Also being a fairly cynical and cautious person who usually weighs up the pros and cons before doing something, jumping feet first into counselling was quite a risk.

Teaching. In response to the testing out in Client *I*'s case I talked about therapy/counselling and psychiatry—how I understood the differing roles and how I myself worked. I offered her the opportunity of therapy if she wanted it.

There is a teaching element in the therapist explaining therapy and what it is to the client. This process engages the adult part of the individual. It contributes to the process of developing the therapeutic alliance and facilitates this building up of trust. It is also intended to inspire hope.

This explanation of the process seemed to reassure her. She decided there and then that she'd like a focal therapy contract and would like to begin straight away. This we did. Client *I* began at once to tell me about the abuse she and her sister had suffered at the hands of her stepfather and that this was what she wanted to talk about.

Why does the client "test out" in the first encounter? It is my assumption as therapist that clients are somewhat fearful about entering into therapy because it is a largely unknown quantity. The process is unfamiliar as is the therapist and they may have many fantasies as to what happens in therapy. They know that part of it will involve revealing very personal things about themselves to a stranger.

A section of Client *I*'s own commentary on the beginning of therapy endorses my assumptions about some of the fears clients have.

I had previously seen it a weakness to need counselling and regarded it as something for manic depressives and the suicidal to attend.

My first thoughts were that I would be confronted by some "holier than thou" do-gooder who thought they knew all the answers and be someone I could not relate to at all. These feelings not being surprising, considering my previous experiences with so-called "welfare people". So in I went carrying a 5lb bag of King Edwards on my shoulder, which achieved nothing. This made the first few sessions seem like a war of wills and I would try and devise more ways to defend myself against this person who apparently wanted to know all my faults and weak spots. Gradually my mistrusts seemed to lessen as all that I said was not going to be thrown back into my face.

As my trust grew, I worked harder at the task in hand. This led to changes in my everyday environment and I became more relaxed in company, which close friends commented on ... Eventually talking became easier and I found myself **saying the unspeakable** which amazed me."

(Client *I*'s complete case and her own commentary on the therapy experience appears in full in Chapter 6.).

Client sampling therapy

Quite often a client will present with a problem that is the trigger for their making an appointment but is not the real issue. This proved to be the case with Client E.

Client E's presenting problem was about exam stress. It was quickly apparent that there were deeper issues causing concern.

In E's case the teaching took place because of issues about exam strategies. In exploring these, we talked of past events and previous difficulties with exams. I suggested she might wish to explore these and explained the counselling process, offering her five sessions. This was not agreed at the time but left open should she wish to take up therapy. She, in fact, did return and began to look at issues concerning relationships.

The client was left free to return for a counselling contract or not and in fact some weeks elapsed before she returned. It is not uncommon for there to be an initial interview such as this. It is helpful for the client since they can assess the therapist and clarify for themselves what it is they want from therapy. For the therapist it is a time to assess the suitability of the client for this type of therapy. An initial relationship is established. The presenting problem is explored and if relevant, links to past events are made. If the client is thought suitable a therapy contract is made.

As we saw earlier the therapist will have a number of questions in mind as to whether the client is suitable for therapy. For example: Is it possible to establish a rapport with the client? Does the client wish to change? Can the client understand that past events may be contributing to the present problem? Is it possible to come to an agreement as to the focus of the sessions i.e. is it possible to establish a "working alliance"?

"Can the therapist perceive and handle my pain?"

Client B first made contact with me as therapist by requesting *"time with me as senior counsellor of the department to discuss a project she was doing on counselling"*. This proved to be her form of testing out. However her situation brings in a different facet of this. Here she is testing if the therapist can detect the pain that she is experiencing.

In B's case in response to a general unrelated question about how she was getting on, I received a *"Fine, thank you"* reaction.

Since it was clear from the tight way she replied, as if to hold back tears, that she was not fine and it seemed appropriate to comment on and to acknowledge the pain. The fact that she had chosen counselling as her topic and requested a talk with me was a clue to her particular situation. Another clue was her demeanour and an almost tangible sense of pain that emanated from her momentarily and which I believe she permitted me to be aware of at that time. I use the work permitted advisedly since I see this unveiling of pain to be another clue and test that clients allow the therapist. It challenges the therapist to be sensitively aware, in tune and alert to the present moment in order to acknowledge that something important is happening for the client and to open the way for the person to go deeper if they so wish. To be attuned, acknowledge pain and to be in relationship have all been examined earlier. I return to it here to stress the importance of such an encounter in the early stages of therapy if it is to be a brief process. Having acknowledged awareness of her pain I then talked a little about therapy and how it works and that it could be helpful to talk about things that might be bothering her in order to understand them better and put them behind her. She readily agreed. We decided to meet for eight sessions to look at family issues and her relationship with her mother especially.

Clues as to the strategic focus

Another aspect of the importance of the first session, which forms part of the testing out, is the giving of clues as seen in Case B above. The client is checking out: Will the therapist pick these up? Is he or she sufficiently alert, perceptive, sensitive and in tune? This may be a quite deliberate exercise on the part of the client. Clients have told me:

"I gave you a few clues to see how you would react".

At other times the leads are given by the client quite unconsciously and here it is doubly important for the therapist to be alert to them within the first session in order to speed the process.

It is sometimes not so easy to take note of this. I suggest that at times the therapist is too busy taking note of the history or the selection criteria to pay full and total attention to the client and what they are revealing verbally and non-verbally in these first important moments.

It must be borne in mind that the client has come at this point in time for therapy because they are now ready to do so. Therefore, when they approach the first session, to some degree what they tell the therapist has been rehearsed. Winnicott as we saw in an earlier section refers to this as the "sacred moment". They want to be helped and therefore consciously or unconsciously give the therapist the clues.

The client very often gives the pointers even within the first few sentences as seen in the following example.

CLIENT F

In F the key to the whole of the contract was encapsulated in F's opening statement: *"I've always been depressed—well, since I was 9 years old."*

It was the latter part of that sentence that held the key to most of the later work. The events that occurred around the 9 year old were the cause of her depression. She herself was unaware of the connections in a conscious way but in those words she gave me the clue. From a psychodynamic viewpoint the expectation is that some past issue is impacting on the present and that, if this can be accessed and understood, the blocked pain can be expressed, released and left behind enabling the client to move on.

CLIENT J

In Case J, we again see the clues. J's opening words were that she was *"never good enough"* for her Dad. She regretted that her boyfriend was in prison for drug-taking and that her Dad demanded she give him up. Her boyfriend paid for her abortion and then blamed her for it. She said: *"It's all my fault."* That is the message she received from everyone. At the mention of abortion her eyes filled with tears and there was a sadness in the room. Her opening words linked in with this and her sense of guilt.

The abortion became, after some discussion, the focal issue for the therapy contract—and this was examined in more detail in the section on focus.

The first session—beginning of therapy

In each of the above cases there was an initial testing out of the relationship and the process and then the commitment to it. In the process of the testing out, it is my belief that the therapy process has begun. It is especially I believe the acknowledgment of the pain by the therapist, as seen in B, that helps to form the alliance and trust. This "human to human" level of communication provides an empathic bond to which the clients B, C and E responded by initially committing themselves to the process and later by going deeper into their issues.

My explanation as to the process:

In explaining the process which I refer to as a *"teaching* exercise" and in my responses to their immediate presenting statements/ issues/questions and body language I aim to put the client at ease. The client then has the choice to become a partner in exploring the issue knowing a little of what the process involves. There is a level of trust in the therapist and in the process and in the belief that the therapist knows, not only what they are about but that the therapist can withstand the pain. This is enhanced by the acknowledgement of pain and the anxieties and enables the client to commit him/ herself to the brief therapy contract. The fact that the process is expected to be brief is reassuring to clients in that they are given the hope of being out of their pain in a short time. This is enabling in terms of accepting the painful aspect of going into the pain in order to eventually leave it behind. Not all clients find this helpful initially, some fear that there will not be enough time to deal adequately with their issue. This fear needs to be acknowledged and worked with. I believe that the therapist's attitude is of great importance here. If the therapist does not believe in the brief approach the process is unlikely to be brief!

In the extracts that follow I have selected further examples of different aspects of the first session.

Immediate establishment of focal issues, time limit and therapeutic alliance

The immediate establishment of a focal issue, time limit and a clear therapeutic alliance seen above is typical of focal and brief therapy and is a necessity. It is helped as seen above by a process of teaching, being in tune and a certain intensity that the immediate start of therapeutic work brings.

Rapid intervention

Client M

M who has already been referred to in earlier sections to demonstrate other features of the approach shows how rapidly the therapeutic work begins. At the risk of being repetitive I am recapping some of the important elements covered in the first session to show the importance of getting on with the work from the start. This takes place at a number of levels. It involves the establishment of the relationship, the agreeing of the focal areas and making "a dent" by both touching the pain and enabling greater insight to take place. And importantly, in the homework, inviting the client to *become their own therapist*.

M presented as a very pretty, tall woman in her twenties. She was withdrawn, having very little eye contact and with defensive body language.

Initially I listened and encouraged but did not hesitate at the appropriate moment to challenge, to use a fantasy exercise with her and to encourage eye contact as an active part of the session.

M said she was feeling *"Miserable"* ... *"under pressure"* and *"can't concentrate"*.
P: *"When did the feelings begin?"*
M: *"Last year when my parents divorced"*.

M felt that the divorce must be her fault because of a childhood pattern and events that took place especially when she was *"10–11 years old"* and *"18 years old"*—*"so it must be my fault"*.

Early challenge. I actively challenged the *"it must be my fault"* statement by moving into a fantasy exercise.

P: *"What would you say to a child in your position?"*

Gaining of insight. M realized that she would immediately try and convince the child (she had interposed her niece into her fantasy picture) that *"it was not her fault"*. She also recognized the parallel between herself and this scene and was able to begin to see that it had not been *"her"* fault.

Relating past and present. I linked this inappropriate taking of responsibility with a present situation where she is, also inappropriately, refusing to take responsibility and thereby is being pressurized—*"by friends, tutors, course mates and family"* in that she does not want to be at college. I reminded her that she is free to make her own choices about staying or leaving.

Engaging the adult/issues of trust. The approach I took in challenging the issues of responsibility engaged the client's adult and freed her then to explore her fears about confidentiality. She needed to be sure that her parents would not hear of her sessions.

Contract. I summarized the issues and checked these out with M and we both agreed the areas to be covered. A number of sessions were than agreed.

Homework. I suggested homework in relation to the key issue of the session that would probably be the core focal area as the sessions progressed, i.e. what was going on when she was 10 years old—could she write about significant dates and the 10 year old. I suggested that she might talk to one of her family about what was going on. M replied: *"We never talk about anything that matters in my family."*

Early challenge and relationship. I rounded off the session by lightly endeavouring to deliberately engage eye contact, talking to her about this with a touch of humour. In this I was being quite confronting but lightening this with the humour and attempting to "engage" the client and to deepen the connection between us to enhance the therapeutic relationship. M tried to respond somewhat sheepishly.

This first session has encompassed a number of elements of the therapy and had highlighted key areas the client wished to explore. By responding in some measure to each of these and making contact with the "child", in a safe context, the therapeutic relationship has been quickly formed and trust established.

I was aware of the comment at the end of the first session, *"we never talk about anything that matters"* and prompted the client to talk about the key issues—in the second session, asking about the homework and the 18 year old. My hunch was that this sentence was a *"clue"* and that she had something that especially "mattered" that she wanted to talk about. This was indeed the case and transpired that the client had overdosed and her parents had divorced in that year.

Making a dent.   As therapist with this client I judged that, as Kovacs describes it, it was crucial to "make a dent" in the issues of concern in the first session. This particular client was highly intelligent and needed to be challenged intellectually as well as facilitated emotionally. M acknowledged that things shifted a little for her after this one session. M wrote in her commentary:

> *"With regard to my parents splitting up, I feel that the example Penny gave me, involving my younger cousin, was very good. From then on, I really doubted that I could be entirely to blame. After speaking about the awful experiences I had during my childhood, I no longer knew why I wanted Mum and Dad together anyway."*

CLIENT B—EARLY CHALLENGE

In Case B also there is a clear example of early challenge as a further example of rapid intervention.

B talked freely about the family, recalling painfully a number of events from her younger years. These she began by recounting with a bright smile or laughter which masked her distress. When I challenged that contradiction—*"You're telling me of very sad events yet smiling and laughing—I'm feeling sad for the little girl—who was only trying to help"*, she allowed herself then to own the pain and to cry a little about the situation. This related to an incident as a 7-year-old when she'd offered to pay for some toys and Dad became upset by this. This episode was referred to earlier, in the section on psychodynamic roots. She had in this episode experienced *"ultimate rejection"* as her father told her to *"Go to Hell"*. Rejection was and is a common theme for her. At school she didn't fit in, she was *"the one at the big house"*, her friends tended to be the other ones who didn't fit who she could *"help"*.

In both examples M and B the client moved beyond the words into the pain. In both cases they were in touch with the pain experienced by the child. The detail of this was brought into consciousness to be experienced and made sense of, and in the process catharsis occurred. B's first session covered a number of incidents that were still reverberating pain, the bottom line being parental rejection and the ensuing loneliness and loss.

It is perhaps appropriate to look in greater detail at the process taking place in this first session.

Selective inattention.   The therapist needs to know when to select out the information given. It is noted, stored for use but not opened up for exploration unless of relevance for the agreed focus. B also mentioned in this session her father having been in hospital and her mother having had a breakdown. These important facts, too, were noted and passed over for the present.

Her parents once threw her out from home saying they *"grieved for (her)".* All she felt was rejection. She anticipates rejection and is overwhelmed when the therapist is warm and accepting towards her and agreeing with her views. The therapist, in being genuine in supporting her client's views where this is appropriate, can begin to model a "good parent"—an accepting, non-judgmental parent. Even in this first session the flow of tears at this accepting comment is indicative of the strength of the positive transference.

Intensity.   There existed from the first session a powerful bond and intensity. The close focusing and concentration required of client and therapist contributes to this. The brevity of the contract assists in concentrating the mind and in facilitating a circumscribed focus.

Strategic questions and dreamwork in the first session

To look now at colleague's cases, it is clear that here, too, in a variety of ways rapid therapeutic intervention occurs as an intrinsic part of the first session and in the formulation of the therapeutic contract.

CLIENT GD1

This example was explored more fully in the section on psychodynamic roots where the dreamwork was examined. The therapist's questions led quickly to the heart of the matter. They were:

"When did you first notice the lack of feelings?"

and

"Was there anything else going on around that time?" GD1

These questions asked in the first session helped to move the process on and the answers provided clues as to the root cause of the presenting problem. These clues enabled the therapist to interpret the dream the client shared later on in this session in a way that the client found helpful. It is interesting to note that the therapist did not hesitate to use dreamwork even in a first session and used it to good effect. The dreamwork helped to "make a dent" in the problem and enabled the client to link his present feelings—or rather lack of feelings, with a past situation.

The client's comments, at the conclusion of the first session, show how much he has learned already.

"He said he found the session very interesting and was clearly quite thoughtful about the idea that his present emotional state could have something to do with events 4 years before."

AM1

In the case of another colleague's case AM1, we see two simple but key questions which help the clients to open up and the therapy process to begin rapidly. These are:

"When did the problem start?"

and

"What made you come for therapy now?"

This latter question, asked in session 1, focused the couple on their present relationship problem and a miscarriage. This linked up for them with the early years of their marriage and, for the husband, the miscarriage had echoes for him. Many years before a former girlfriend had had an abortion without telling him and the miscarriage brought back all his feelings about that earlier episode. This contributed to his overwhelming sense of loss at the recent miscarriage which had affected him more than his wife.

Influence of context for speed of the therapy

The setting where the counselling occurs I believe makes a difference as to the extent of these early explorations in an intake or initial session. In a GP surgery context, or a college or hospital, I believe much of the "testing out" of the therapist will be taken for granted. In private practice, I believe the client is more likely to need a little more time to establish trust and to discover how the therapist works. In a college setting, students will be familiar with the counselling service and would expect the qualifications of the therapist to have been assessed by the educational establishment, so minimizing the questions on these issues. Therefore it is not surprising that there is little reference in the selected cases to these sorts of questions. This also contributes to the rapid progress.

In whichever setting therapists work, they should be prepared to talk openly about their training background/experience and methods of therapy.

I do not make a clear demarcation between an "intake session" and an "initial interview" or "first session". This is because the client's referred to within this book came from contexts where the two functions occur within the one session, and the counsellor who first sees the client will always continue with that client. Certainly, at times, a client has an initial session that precedes the full counselling contract but this is, as referred to above, seen as a sampling session. I always assume the first meeting to be the start of therapy in this brief approach. The aspects referred to earlier need to be covered, but often this is dealt with very briefly and so the formal "intake" session or the "initial interview" as it may be called, is here always seen as the "first session" of the therapy contract.

Summary

As shown in the introduction to this section the key writers in general did not lay great emphasis on the first session. The few that did had differing views as to how the first session should be used, whether for case histories or for an immediate and intense start to the therapy process. One session was seen to be, on occasion, sufficient to enable the client to go on alone.

The differentiating aspect of selection for brief therapy, as against the criteria for non time sensitive therapy, centred on the following: establishing a circumscribed problem area, working towards its resolution as a joint endeavour, and being able to move in and out of the therapy situation rapidly. The latter aspect requiring both therapist and client to be able to establish relationships quickly and to sustain loss. The initial analysis of my chosen cases showed that in *every case the first session appeared as very significant*. In this deeper analysis of the first session a number of facets have emerged. In line with Kovacs and Davanloo getting on with the therapy from the start is seen to be important. The being in tune or sensitivity, the teaching element and intensity are highlighted.

However my analysis of the case studies revealed a number of other aspects relating to the importance of the first session. The following Table VII summarizes the most significant of these.

Table VII
Important aspects of the first session as seen from the selected case work

a)   The client's assessment of the situation
    i)   Learning what therapy is
    ii)   Testing out the therapist and the therapy situation
    iii) Deciding if it's trustworthy
    iv)   Deciding if it meets their needs
    v)   Giving clues

b)   The therapist's role in the situation is:
    i)   Teaching what therapy is
    ii)   Demonstrating what therapy is by getting started
    iii) Enlisting the adult as co-therapist
    iv)   Helping the client to become their own therapist
    v)   Dealing with the defences
    vi)   Recognising the client's pain and issue and communicating this
    vii) Assessing if client is suitable for therapy, i.e. is the client motivated/insightful/able to relate/has an issue to work through.

c)   The joint task
    i)   Client and therapist seeking and finding the focus
    ii)   Client and therapist agreeing to the contract in relation to the focal issue and the number of sessions.

They include the client's need to test out the situation and the therapist. The therapist in turn needs to establish a relationship, explain the process of therapy and meet the client's challenge. This is achieved by understanding the feelings involved, touching the pain and interpreting the clues appropriately to make sufficient progress with the client to promote hope. It also encompasses teaching the client to ultimately become their own therapist.

Not only is the first session a time for assessment, formulating the contract but also for beginning the actual work of therapy. It is in this session that the therapeutic alliance is established. In the first session also, the client gives the therapist pointers that are necessary to help to uncover and resolve the difficulties. The therapist needs to be *finely tuned* to every communication, verbal and non-verbal, of the client, because herein lie the clues for the successful progress of the contract. To achieve this the therapists will actively employ their expertise and knowledge flexibly, using whatever skills and techniques move the process on.

It is not unusual in brief psychotherapy for sufficient insight to be gained and sufficient emotional catharsis to occur in very few sessions to enable the client to proceed on their own. In fact one session may enable the client to change what needs to change in their lives by themselves and without further need of a therapist. Thus the first session might be the only session. It is a key session and for the brief approach is perhaps *the* session that enables the contract to be brief. The *first session* could therefore be described as the *microcosm* of the whole contract.

This concludes the in-depth analysis of the seven combined key themes that were drawn from the cases and the literature in the earlier phases of analysis.

The next section, Chapter 5 Part 2, summarizes the findings from the in-depth analysis and preliminary conclusions.

Part Two: Summary of the findings from the in-depth analysis of the key themes and provisional conclusions

T his section summarizes the main findings and provisional conclusions about each of the key themes studied above and highlights the significance of the subsidiary themes.

5.2.1. What is understood by short-term?

The examination of the empirical work suggests that between four to six sessions is the median to aim for, in the short-term approach described. The average number of sessions in this small sample was 6.6. This differs from the key proponents who expect to have considerably more sessions and despite the lack of a general consensus in the literature many expect the median to be from 15–25 sessions. The brevity of my examples suggests that within this clinical work there exist clues as to the shortening of therapy.

Since there is no consensus as to the number of sessions in the literature, Budman and Gurman conclude that the terms "time sensitive" or "cost–effective" are useful in describing short-term therapy.

5.2.2. Psychodynamic roots

The form of therapy referred to in this book is, as Malan puts it, a "technique of brief psychotherapy based on that of psychoanalysis" (1976, p. 281). The casework supports this view by revealing examples of transference, resistance and transference repetitions. However whilst highlighting the psychoanalytic backcloth this approach goes beyond its roots and also adopts a flexible and integrated use of other therapeutic skills and assumptions borrowed from other traditions to shorten the process. It also shows different ways of dealing with some of the psychoanalytic concepts such as the use of a teaching approach to circumvent the resistance. This is one example of teaching and in analysing both cases and literature the sensitivity of the therapist was also evidenced. Both of these were subsidiary themes highlighted in the clinical work and in this further examination were seen in both the case work and in the literature.

5.2.3. Flexibility

The indepth analysis demonstrates that the brief therapist uses a number of different techniques as and when they are appropriate. This requires a certain flexibility on the part of the therapist, who needs to be more concerned with being and keeping in tune with the client, than remaining loyal to any one school of therapy. Flexibility is required of the therapist in embracing important concepts and therapeutic tools from traditions other than the psychoanalytic to inform and speed the process. Wolberg aptly uses the word "fusion" to describe how the different techniques might be applied and suggests that this requires an "experienced therapist schooled in the widest varieties of techniques" (1965, p. 128). I, too, believe that flexibility takes for granted the experience and substantial training needed. That is in order for the therapist to work with the range of skills and to creatively adapt these to the needs of each client.

References to some of the subsidiary themes have been noted in the further exploration of flexibility and include the experience of the therapist, the intensity of the process and the educative aspect of therapy. The latter especially helping the client to "become their own therapist".

5.2.4. Activity

The analysis found that activity is seen to be an inherent part of brief work and is a factor in the shortening process. Activity however, is not just for the therapist but is also expected of the client. The client is expected to take an active part in the therapy process, for example undertaking homework tasks that also help the client to gradually learn the techniques of therapy and soon to dispense with the therapist to become their own therapist. For example, they learn about their own emotions and patterns of behaviour and ways of changing these. In this way too therapy can be seen to have a teaching component. I often say to clients "This is your trip; I'm able to be alongside you but you have to do the work". In being alongside the client the therapist needs sensitivity and needs to be in tune with the client in order to be able to utilize the appropriate response to move the client on. The examples demonstrate a number of skills and the intensity of the encounter between therapist and client. Thus once again the subsidiary themes are evident.

5.2.5. Focus

The section on focus found that all the proponents agreed as to its intrinsic place within the brief approach. There were differing views however as to what constitutes a suitable focus. The empirical work shows that the focus can be much wider than was thought by the earlier, rather restrictive view as to what was appropriate for brief work. There were also varying opinions as to how the focus was to be found, whether this initiated more from the client or therapist or both. The idea of therapy and finding the focus as a *joint enterprise* is one that I support and the empirical work shows. The importance of *circumscribing* the focus, to use the term coined by Sifneos, is emphasized by all. Once more the subsidiary themes, that is: experience, sensitivity, attunement and intensity were able to be pinpointed.

5.2.6. Therapeutic alliance

This section observes that as for any form of therapy, it is the relationship between the therapist and client that enables the therapeutic process. Within the brief approach it is the rapidity with which it is established that is of significance. The therapeutic alliance also has a key place in coming to an agreement as to the focal area to be explored. A teaching process is often used to help motivate clients to undertake sometimes painful work and to commit themselves to the therapeutic contract. Therapist sensitivity to the client's pain and generally being in tune with the client, contributes both to finding the focal area and in forming the therapeutic alliance.

5.2.7. Importance of the first session

The first session, emerges from the research to be of far greater all embracing significance than earlier writers have given it credit for. The findings too bring to light many interesting aspects not highlighted in the early literature. Where *some* of the findings in the preceding sections develop the thinking about brief therapy, in its emphasis *the whole of this section's insights* could be said to do so. Every one of the selected cases showed the first session to be significant. Table VII (p. 192) summarizes some of the important aspects which include the testing out process, the giving of clues and the getting started. The analysis also highlighted the rapid formation of the therapeutic alliance and the need to jointly establish a circumscribed focal area for exploration. The factors that helped the therapy to proceed rapidly were: therapist sensitivity and being in tune especially to the client's pain; the intensity of the relationship and the activity within the sessions; teaching and enabling the client to become their own therapist. These latter factors were all included in the subsidiary themes to be looked at in the in-depth analysis of the key themes. Although some or all of these subsidiary themes were apparent in the analysis of each of the key themes, in this section on the first session their significance to the shortening process became more clear. I believe that they deserve a much more prominent place in the thinking about what short-term therapy is and what shortens it.

Summary of the subsidiary themes and their place within brief therapy

These subsidiary themes, as listed above, had been elicited from the clinical work. Since they were deemed to be important features of the work, I was alert to any references to these aspects, in the in-depth analysis. There proved to be considerable evidence of these aspects in the analysis of the key themes. They are features which do not so much stand alone as permeate the fabric of the sessions in the clinical work. In returning to the key proponents with these facets in mind it was found that there were many references to them there also. However I believe the clinical work indicates that these aspects merit more importance than is allotted by the key proponents.

It is not so much that these are new or different features within the brief approach, or indeed one could argue within therapy as a whole, as that their importance brings a new dimension of short-term work into the foreground. I suggest that it is an appropriate combination of these aspects, in addition to the principles emerging from the key themes, that may contribute to the shortening of therapy. A summary of the findings in relation to the subsidiary themes follows below.

The teaching aspect of the therapeutic work

The analysis has shown teaching to be of great significance. The earlier writers did not attach so much importance to it. It has its influence on all the other principles and holds a key place in the all important first session.

Becoming their own therapist

Another major feature emerging from the above analysis is the giving of control to the client. The therapist is enabling the client to become their own therapist. The teaching element supports this as does the use of homework and the enlisting of the client agreement about focus and time limit in the therapy contract.

The therapist's role is to walk alongside the client in their journey to freedom using skills and therapeutic knowledge flexibly in this enabling process. It is the role of a facilitator.

Intensity

Intensity is often referred to. As a participant observer in some of the clinical work I am able to comment from an inside perspective. The case commentaries and case examples can give the reader a more objective, outside view. Intensity is evident as I analysed the content of the cases of colleagues and also appears in the literature. It is not an easy aspect to quantify and relates to some degree to the mystery element discussed within the analysis. This applies both to the therapeutic relationship and to the process of therapy. It is an aspect of the process that is recognized by clients and therapists. It relates especially in the brief approach to the limited number of sessions for the encounter. This makes for a more condensed process. The circumscribed focal area that helps to concentrate the minds of both therapists and clients also has its impact on the intensity.

The rapid establishment of the therapeutic alliance and the immediate start of the therapy, even from the first moments of the first session contribute to this particularly intense form of therapy.

Experience required of the therapist

The conclusion, from the analysis, that experience is required of the therapist for this approach, relates to the other important features of brief work. This includes the limited time available for the therapeutic contract, which means that the therapist needs to be rather precise with the interventions made. This requires skill, which assumes training and practice to acquire and inspire confidence.

The sensitivity of the therapist in order to be in tune with the client

To achieve the effective operation of the key principles, sensitivity is required to enable the therapist to be in tune with the client. This is evident in all of the cases. Sensitivity is not unique to the brief therapy, but, within this approach, it is seen as an accelerating factor enhancing all of the above principles. This needs to be present from the very first moments of the therapy contract and enables the rapid establishment of the therapeutic alliance and also the intensity of the experiences referred to above.

*   *   *

The next chapter (Chapter 6) records some client commentaries on their experience of brief therapy and an example case that is included in full, in addition to that client's own commentary. This provides the reader with the opportunity to verify, or having the advantage and disadvantage of an "outside" perspective, to challenge the above preliminary conclusions with different interpretations.

CHAPTER SIX

Client commentaries: C, M and *I* and a complete case example: Case *I*

What clients C, M and I said about their experience of short-term therapy

H aving analysed the individual elements of short-term therapy and the key components that make for the shortening process, this chapter gives three examples of how the process is experienced by clients: see commentaries 6.1 Client C, 6.2 Client M and 6.4 Client *I*. Extracts of these have already been used to illustrate earlier points. Here the commentaries are included in full, without further comment, and allowed to speak for themselves. Clients C and M's commentaries are followed by a case example where many of the key elements are seen to be integrated in a real situation.

Case *I* has been selected for inclusion here, in its entirety, because it is a case already in the public forum as a result of a court case. This therefore minimizes problems related to confidentiality referred to earlier.

Client *I*'s commentary is also included in full after the case report.

The case demonstrates how the key principles outlined in

Chapter 5 are used in an integrated way to achieve a very positive outcome in a limited number of sessions. It is one of the longer cases examined and therefore enables a wider range of skills to be demonstrated than would be possible in one of the cases with maybe only four sessions, which have been used to demonstrate various points in the earlier sections.

Client *I* chose the letter *I* to represent her case for this book since she felt it demonstrated how she now perceives herself. In view of the fact that the choice of this letter *I* represents a clear statement for the client I have kept to that letter in the case notes. To avoid confusion for the reader, I have differentiated Client *I* from references to me (I) by the use of lettering style, using bold italic for Client *I*.

6.1. Client C's commentary

It used to come just like that. That cold, piercing fear. It could come quickly or slowly, brought on by who knows what.

Usually it would take me by surprise. In a quarter of a second I would be changed from a fairly calm person into someone so scared and horrified that the only thing I wanted was to hide away from everything.

I suppose the fear of the fear itself sometimes was worse than anything else. Not knowing why I suddenly turned cold, and felt that I was going to die, imagining awful things happening and believing I was physically ill of an incurable illness.

I so desperately wanted to enjoy life, enjoy it to the full. But the black cloud, my fear, was so powerful. It was at a stage where I was constantly scared and felt that my feelings totally controlled me, and not vice versa, that I decided to seek help.

Without turning it into a too dramatic thing, I went to get an appointment with a counsellor at my college that I had been to briefly the previous year. What actually encouraged me was the fact that earlier that term everybody had been asked to seek help there if they felt they needed it, "even if you don't really know what's wrong with your life and just feel like talking".

Initially the counsellor and I decided on six appointments, I quickly felt that time was running out.

I never seemed to get to the point, there was instead a lot of talking from my side about my relationships to other people particularly to my mother.

During those weeks of counselling, I started to realize things about myself. I have always been good at school and came from a privileged home, but feelings have never played an important part of my life. Plain feelings. I remember coming home from school at the age of eight or nine crying because some older boy had been nasty to me. My mother reacted by being angry. Maybe not with me, I realize that now, but rather with the whole situation. "Don't let them be nasty to you, be tough and proud" And I felt ashamed. Ashamed of being a victim, ashamed of being weak and terrified of mentioning anything similar in the future. I already then made up my mind, nobody should ever catch me being weak.

The counselling made me realize gradually that being weak and allowing yourself to show your true feelings is actually being strong in many circumstances. Allowing myself to loosen up I found that people would more easily relate to me. I realized the obvious and painful truth, that we are all human beings, including myself. And I was allowed to be a human being, not a machine, which was new to me.

I started trusting people more. I talked to a few friends and they responded with care and warmth. That helped me trust them, and feel more free. Free to feel. Free to cry. Free to speak out.

I suppose that is when I finally managed to tell the counsellor of my fear. The fear that I felt was so destructive and that I was so ashamed and scared of. "It couldn't be natural to feel such a piercing, overpowering fear".

Just mentioning my fear of dying helped, saying it out loud and getting a response and not a shocked expression made it all easier. Then it all came out at once, my fear of cancer, Aids, my fear of being abnormal, turning mad. Things I had never dared say to anybody.

What I didn't expect was the counsellor's reaction. Instead of brushing it away she realized that this was important to me. At the same time she didn't turn it into a big drama, something I would have hated.

Instead she asked me when I felt that mind blowing fear. When? I had never thought about that, the fear itself had been so hard to cope with I hadn't been able to analyse my feelings.

Asking when and why I was so scared was a new experience. What did I think brought this on? In what situations did I typically turn cold? Did I associate the fear with any particular people?

I soon realized that certain things triggered the fear, such as things that had been said and things that had happened that I couldn't immediately cope with. Especially if close friends had been involved.

And the fear of physical illness was a way of moving my fear over to something that was understandable. After all, illnesses that are physical can be diagnosed more easily than things to do with the mind.

The counsellor told me to try analysing my feelings when I was scared. Ask yourself why? And take the time to analyse yourself. Treat yourself nicely, she said, don't be too tough, after all you're only human.

The last session I suddenly realized that the reason why I was so desperate to get rid of this cloud in my life was that I love life so much.

I am very much a person of the extremes, I like to live fully, to feel one hundred percent. The counsellor expressed this so beautifully, by saying that if you want to feel extreme happiness you must expect to feel the total opposite too, fear and unhappiness.

And that was the turning point. I could see everything in a new perspective. Of course everything didn't feel right straight away. But I could see that positive side of things. The positive was stronger than the negative. And being able to understand my fear didn't stop it suddenly coming, but it made it easier to cope with it.

I feel that I have now accepted myself and I feel so much freer in expressing both good and bad feelings. I am free!!

6.2. Client M's commentary

Since my Mum had left my Dad in May 1990, I had felt awful. I felt as though everything was entirely my fault and that I did not want to go on. I even planned to commit suicide one evening in Germany where I was studying at the time, but after drinking too much on that evening, simply found myself still alive and very ill the next morning. I was unable to admit this during counselling with Penny as I still felt ashamed of it. I preferred to convince her and myself that I was well past having such thoughts. However, looking back at what I planned to do in Germany, I do not think that I had felt the way I did when trying to commit suicide at 18.

I feel that, in Germany, if I had ever stopped to think, I would not have done it—mainly as I would never do anything that might hurt my Mum. At 18, on the other hand, I thought that no-one in the world would care anyway.

After that evening and for the entire summer I was very upset. I tried to avoid people and locked myself away to be upset alone. I had no idea what I could do and only after arriving in France in October, I considered counselling. My course tutor organized an appointment for me in France but I did not go.

The time in France caused me to seek help in religion and I spent much time with students of a university of theology. I gave up this and going to church with them due to the relationship I was having with my boyfriend.

The problem seemed to worsen in France whilst I was away and after a trip back to England I split up with my boyfriend (as I hated anything to do with marriage and relationships).

Finally, I was referred to Penny by a teacher. It took courage to go to the first session, but I had no choice as I knew the teacher would be after me if I did not. After the first session I felt awful and wondered why on earth I had sat and told a stranger things that I had never told anyone before. I still do not know why; but I went to the second session. Maybe it was because I thought there would be no other way out. I think, however, at the time I was deeply confused. On the one hand I wished I could just die, but on the other hand I really did want to live.

I think that a turning point in the counselling came in the second or (third?) session. Penny seemed to be particularly harsh in asking me why I did not just give up and sit at home all day. She told me that I did not have to do what I was doing if I did not want to, but that I was a free person. I left the session feeling very upset, maybe even angry. Perhaps it was my pride that was hurt and the idea of her suggesting I stay at home doing nothing all day. This really made me think and I realized that I knew I was capable of doing more than that and did indeed want to. (From that point on, I was determined to pull myself together.) I think Penny's use of the phrase "top yourself" also made me want to overcome my problems. Once again, I felt as though she were using this phrase to annoy me and making me see how awful it is when people commit suicide.

In short, I do not know whether I am correct, even now, but I feel that this apparent harshness really "brought me back to my senses".

After that session, I feel I began to co-operate more and even tried to think more and write things down at home. At times, though, I still found myself very upset, particularly when people were arguing around me.

With regard to my parents splitting up, I feel that the example Penny gave me, involving my younger cousin, was very good. From then on, I really doubted that I could be entirely to blame. I soon realized that I did not want my parents to be together any more anyway. After speaking about the awful experiences I had had during my childhood, I no longer knew why I wanted my Mum and Dad together anyway. I think, as Penny suggested, that I had built up my own image of a perfect family. I was determined to have this and completely overlooked the fact that my family could never be like that.

It was, however, still hard to let go entirely of my dream of a happy family. It did not happen until Christmas when I saw my Dad after he had drunk too much. I had been so happy and excited (although nervous too) when I went to see him on Christmas Eve. I was shocked and upset by the encounter, but then realized that what I was looking for could never be.

However, I did not feel that all my problems could be solved unless my Mum would speak to me about the past. Once again, Penny's counselling here was invaluable. It made me realize how much I needed to talk to my Mum and gave me the courage to do so.

Finally, there were some things, such as violence and abuse, which I never managed to talk about. I did, however, write many things down and this was a great help to me. I realize, however, that these probably were two of the main things affecting me. As Penny had said, "You leave out the important bits."

I could not talk about such things as I felt so ashamed about them. I had been able to talk about some of the things Dad had done to my Mum or my dog. The idea of talking about things done to me personally made me feel ashamed and embarrassed.

I think that I may be "normal" again. I do not know exactly what I want from life, but I no longer feel sad. I have had the confidence to attend interviews and am also able to have a relationship again.

In addition, I have been exploring religion a little more. Thinking and talking of awful things made me really think that there must be "something else somewhere".

I thought that the idea of having a fixed number of session was very good.

It made me realize that if I did want to be helped, I had to start talking and not waste the counsellor's time.

Spacing out the sessions with a gap of 2 weeks was good too. It made me less dependent and gave me more time to think.

Note

When M shared her commentary with me we talked about the "missing bits". She had had enough to cope with during the last months of her college course and perhaps had instinctively felt that this was not the time to address these issues. We agreed that a time might come when she will want to talk about these—perhaps with me—perhaps with another therapist. When the time is right, she thought that she would not now be afraid to seek help.

6.3. Client *I*'s complete case demonstrating key elements of short-term therapy integrated in practise

Client *I* was referred to see me. She had no concept of what counselling was and at her initial interview, began by asking how to go about seeing a psychiatrist.

I explained the distinction between psychiatry and psychotherapy/counselling. I also explained the way in which a focal/short-term therapist works. She decided after this resumé of the therapy field that she would like a short-term therapy contract. We began this straight away.

Session 1

She was quite nervous about the idea of talking to a counsellor/ therapist.

She explained that she and her sister had been abused by her stepfather from the age of about 8 years.

When she was 18 years old, that is, relatively recently, her sister (who was 16 years old at that time), confessed all about this abuse to a social worker and started police action. *I* was consequently contacted *"out of the blue"* by the police. They wanted a full statement from her about the abuse that had occurred in the past. This had been a total shock to her since she had received no warning that the whole of her past was suddenly to become public. It was a traumatic experience relating the events of abuse in the giving of her statement. She was not given any help or advice by the police regarding counselling and felt that they simply abandoned her. Neither did she hear the outcome of their enquiries immediately. She did, however discover later that her stepdad got no jail sentence at all. This angers her.

Her sister, because she was under 18, had a lot of help and was seeing a social worker at the time. These facilities were not available automatically for *I*. She feels somewhat bitter about the way this happened. She was so distraught at the time that she rang her real father who lives some 2 hours journey away. She told him what had happened with the police and as a child with regard to the abuse. He said: *"I'll ring you back in a few minutes"*. He did so, saying *"I am coming for you"* and he was there in a matter of hours. He took her back with him to his new family and she stayed there for some months. Whilst she liked being cared for by Dad, she was away from friends and had nothing to do, so this period is described by her as a *"really bad time"*.

Session 2

I was somewhat wary about counselling. She was aware that she needed something and was resentful that her sister had everything. She told me that her sister had written to mother about the abuse, when they were younger, but mother refused to believe her and had hidden the letter under the mattress. Her sister tried to overdose a couple of years before she told the police. When *I* visited her in hospital, her sister's eyes said, *"don't tell"*. She and her sister never talked about it. *I* at times feels guilty about not having spoken up and she wonders if her sister would not have suffered, if she had. We explored that a little, looking at the powerful reasons for why she held back.

Her stepdad had had a separate room built on downstairs. This became *I*'s room and made it easier for him to come to her room. It tended to happen when he was drunk and was more touching than rape. This was traumatic enough. She, on recalling this, was physically aware of hands on her.

It was the *"humiliation"* that was the enduring pain.

Once mother really knew what had happened she did throw him out, but another man was soon on the scene for her.

I had brought with her some drawings she had done prior to the session. She is something of an artist and these are a combination of art and emotion. She feels entrapped as the pictures depict (see Illustrations IV and V, p. 211 and p. 212).

She moved on then to her habit of playing "mind games". She analyses people and plays games with them—especially with men. She referred briefly to a man she had a relationship with, who repeatedly attempted suicide. She has now finished with him. She does have a boy friend whom she's *"horrible to"* and whom she plays *"mind games with"*. She tests her own strength with him and is scornful of his weakness. She tells me she spends a lot of time sorting out other people's problems. These examples show different

I's Illustration IV

Entrapped

I's Illustration V

Imprisoned

ways of not relating, especially to men, and is something we agreed to focus on in due course.

She agreed it was important to start into the feelings earlier in the session.

Session 3

I arrived a little late and asked for a glass of water. She described a good but scary experience she had had the day before. A black man had been deliberately frightening people by approaching them, coming up close and staring them out. She had outstared him. She had been scared but had not shown it. She told him *"you're pathetic"*. He eventually went away saying, *"you are strong"*. She felt she had proved herself. She'd been strong with not just any man but with a big bully of a man whom she knew to be dangerous (he had been reported earlier to have pulled a gun on a group recently). This chance encounter had been like a stage-managed therapeutic replay of the type of situation she'd had to experience with stepdad as a child. Then she'd been too small and weak to challenge. She realizes that this episode has changed her and her need to put down the young man who she has previously been "horrible to".

She is still unsure if she could see stepdad and be as strong. She used his name for the first time in the session. She said she had not used his name for a long time. She is not now so much afraid *of* him as of what she would *do* to him. She feels murderous towards him. When she was 16 years old she did hit him and floored him. He never touched her after that but turned to her younger sister. She is really afraid of the extent of her anger and of losing control. After the last session, she told me she was full of anger because she did not use the session sufficiently. I suggested she "use" the session earlier. We then went into a longer discussion about anger/depression and the consequences of holding it in—a pressure-cooker effect. We explored ways of expressing anger, perhaps with a Gestalt exercise, or by writing down her feelings and then putting a match to them— or talking to an empty chair here in the therapy session. Here I am the safety container. As I described the latter method, she said she could see him on the chair near me, but was unable to speak to him although some of the anger surged up. She said *"I'd just want to know why?"*

She raised doubts about whether she can get anywhere in such a limited number of sessions. It is not just my limitation she is going home, so there is an external deadline also. I confirmed that I believe we can. Certainly she reluctantly admits that what we've talked about makes sense to her. She feels I *"read her"* and she doesn't like that and yet she knows that she needs what we are doing. She returns again to her wish that she'd been helped years ago and her anger that no one suggested counselling or any sort of help.

Session 4

I had remembered about beginning straight away, but it was 10 minutes past the hour when she arrived and she was yawning. She did begin and told me of her anger after the last session. She felt empty and was handling a crook-lock with anger; she then "borrowed" a friend's magazines and tore them up. Friends don't say anything—they just accept it—but it's aimless non-directed anger.

I asked what she would want to do to "X". She replied, *"Smash his face in and laugh! Take a gun and shoot him and laugh. Let him feel what I did"*. She has done a lot of writing and drawing since last week. *"I did let a little out then, but boiled all week."* She says all she'd do to X, using his name now with no show of emotion at all and I can't feel it either, so I challenged her regarding this. She began to back off.

We had 20 minutes of session left. I said *"we have 10 minutes to get back together and 10 minutes to work, or 10 minutes to discuss why we shouldn't work"*. She was scared of being vulnerable with me and afraid of the power it could give me since she doesn't know anything about me, etc. She agreed to work. She didn't want to say anything but I was pushing her into the anger using phrases like *"let's stay with the anger"*. She got in touch with it and described X hitting her, she felt vulnerable, humiliated, laughed at. She said *"the worst was when Z laughed as well at X's lies"*. She couldn't bring herself to tell me the episode, but she recalled the pain of the situation. She said, *"I've never told anyone about what I'm angry about, I've never shared it,"* so all her habitual defences—*"I'm not going to show anyone"* came back.

P: *"Okay, could you draw out the anger—are you in touch with it?"*
I: *"Yes, it's like a pressure-cooker going to explode."*
P: *"Okay, what colour do you want?"*
I: *"Black"*.

I gave her paper and pen and she drew:

I: *"Now he feels as I did–X shot in pain and crying and myself laughing on top"* (see Illustrations VI and VII, p. 215 and p. 216).

I really scribbled away hard with the pen and I could feel the anger in her. I spoke as she drew, reminding her of the painful episodes:

P: *"X getting at you, the injustice, mother doing nothing, the physical abuse, the laughing, the crying."*

She drew and was almost shocked that she'd shared it with me.

I felt so in touch with anger she said, *"Now what?—how do I stop it again—I feel like a bottle of vodka now—to drown it out"*. P *"the pain"*. I said the word "pain" in a way to convey empathy, to restate the anger she is feeling, as pain and to help her to own it in order to be able to deal with it. I observed that I keep talking about the pain and she keeps talking about the anger. She recognizes that the anger covers pain and this needs to be emphasized.

I's Illustration VI

X Shot

I suggested she drew *"a good place—safe, peaceful, happy."* She drew Illustration VIII (p. 217), entitled "A safe haven" of a boat and sea in blue and she visualizes herself with dad—they sail all day when she visits and she has him all to herself. *"It is like a safe haven."*

She feels vulnerable with me now so I ask how can I help? I share that I'd like to come and hold her hand. She doesn't want me close and tells me that a friend will be around for her after the session and will give her a hug and that's what she needs. She is feeling a slight sense of relief at sharing the Z thing since she has never told anyone at all before.

I's Illustration VII

Real Justice—Ha Ha—Now he feels as I did

I is aware that a little of the anger is out, she also says she's never told anyone why she's angry before.

I tell her how I feel like crying for her yet she doesn't feel like crying. Why do I? I try and explain my awareness of the wounded child in her that we've been in touch with, and the adult now and the instinct is to pick the child up and cuddle it. She looks as if she sees this as sentimental rubbish so I verbalize this for her and say it's real. I collect the crayons and paper and need to reassure her that I won't touch her.

I's Illustration VIII

The Safe Haven

As I collect the two drawings together, she sees the picture Illustration VII and gets in touch with the rage again. I apologize and show her the boat picture again and she became calm again. She's realizing she's got a way of calming herself down again—a tool. She goes out determinedly *"in the boat."*

She expressed great disgust at mother during the session. Mother never believed her, stepdad never hit her in front of mother. *"So mother is powerful"*, I observed. She disputes that.

"Mother always believes his lies, never intervenes if he's shouting etc. Can't live without a man—she's so weak."

Yet *I* still has a place for her mother in her heart—*"well she's my mother"*.

Session 5

The session started late and she was absolutely fazed with alcohol, caffeine tablets and "pro plus". She had been working very, very late to complete assignments to be handed in at 1.00-ish that day.

She talked about her mother whom she sees as pathetic and hates her ineffectualness, her need of a man and despises her, *"yet she's my mother"* and she loves her too.

She sees tears or anger as weakness and so is fighting for control. She feels guilty *re* her sister. She believes that its all her fault that her sister tried to kill herself. I suggested that this sister could have been upset at a number of things and I rattled off a few possibilities, e.g. she could have been bullied at school, pregnant, etc. At the time she said nothing regarding this, but later in the session managed to tell me that these *"slights"* on her sister had made her rage defensively for her. She felt I was saying her sister was a tart. This is what stepdad was always saying, so there are echoes here. Her feelings about this were so overwhelming that she was absorbed in them and this really prevented her hearing what I was saying about her feelings of guilt. We explored this a little and the importance of challenging me. I understood her point, so hopefully my positive response to her anger helps the pattern change just a little. She showed me the pictures she'd been drawing during the week. She kept practising looking at the one of stepdad and could do so each time with a little less anger. She also showed me Illustration IX: when will it end (p. 219) and Illustration X—the key (p. 220).

In illustration X, the key in the hand belongs to the past when she was 18 and also to now. She felt the social workers *"thought they'd given her a key to a future, but I didn't know how to use it to unchain the past"*. She half thinks *"the counselling may be another key"* and is hopeful that it will release her but doesn't know.

I asked to photocopy the work—she refused at first—then agreed *"what the hell, it should be known"*. She also asked me to read what she'd written about the anger and pain. She is still not quite admitting the pain. Last week after the session she had not been angry but had been in touch with the pain and had cried copiously with someone who she'd been helping last week. She felt *"embarrassed, vulnerable, weak"* and knows she's fighting not to cry here. Towards the end of the session she came out with the view that she was seeing this session as wasted because she has not said what she had planned to say.

We looked at the positives of what we'd talked about. She then came out with the topic area, telling me she had been trying to blurt it out

I's Illustration IX

When will it end?

When will it end?
Asked the young girl
Who only ever desired
To be free
To create
Her own destiny
Instead of existing
To help others create theirs.

I's Illustration X

The key

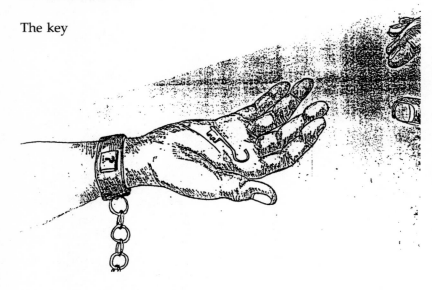

all session—I'd given several opportunities for her to lead the session. She had just not been able to but now it is near the end it is safe to do so, perhaps? I suggested she had had such a heavy week and was so tired that it was best not to have too heavy a session today, so we'd begin next week with what she wanted to talk about. She wanted to tell me why the episode where Z and X laughed at her together was so very humiliating. *"I want to tell you everything about it"*.

We agreed this would be the start next time. (She's here for June only, so time is really very limited.).

Session 6

I had gone home at the weekend to her mother. She had found her sister stoned and unable to communicate. Mother had W and his brother and sister there, so lots of strangers. Mother was totally unresponsive to her even when she showed her her hockey trophy, Mother just said, *"put it up near W's trophy"*.

I feels really let down/out of place/not getting mother's attention as she wants. There are cultural problems at home now also, since she is the first one to go to college and they don't understand. They call her a snob. She is now embarrassed by some of the things mother does but none the less does not consider herself a snob. She preferred to stay with the feelings about the bad weekend rather than talk about the episode she'd avoided last week.

I emoted a lot for her about her rejection; the little girl inside wanting support and someone to listen, really wanting her "mummy". I also endorsed the reality of being the first person to study in the family and also the image of the capable person that she presents to everyone. We talked about the paradox of strength in weakness. She really wanted to say to mother, "*this is silly, can we go and have a chat somewhere*". She wonders aloud, "*Is it worth it?*" She feels very alone in her London flat and doesn't fit at home and dad has his new family. In a way she has three families: through dad on the Isle of Wight; mother who has said "*come for the summer*", and another family she nannied with who are taking her on holiday.

She felt so bad yesterday that she came to see me at 5.30 p.m., without an appointment, but the doors were locked, so she went home and got stoned. She wouldn't have if she'd got in to see me. She would have given me the matchbox of dope to throw away (N.B. I would have made her dispose of it since I would not wish to handle illegal drugs).

I told her she could always try rattling on my window—if I'm there I'd let her in.

I hope I'm modelling a different type of mother figure, for example, I am interested in her hockey trophy, etc. I would listen and give her time even out of hours.

This session she was very near to tears but didn't let go.

She told me she was holding on tight to the boat in the last few minutes before she went off to work and the hockey match.

I observed that there are a lot of phallic symbols in her pictures For example, tower spikes, guns and hockey sticks. She ignored this which seemed odd but we were near the end of session. It was subsequent to this that she mentioned the boat. I wondered if she was angry and noted this to perhaps return to in a later session.

Session 7

She'd made contact by phone with her sister and has patched things up. They had a really good talk and have arranged to keep in touch. Her sister is going to talk to mother for her. Mother rang and tried to be interested in her achievements. They are not really communicating yet but some improvement.

Session 8

The home front is still her major concern at the present and her new boyfriend, with whom she had had such a good time and who had restored her trust in herself and men a little—turned out to have a girlfriend already. So she's chucked him. She tries to brush it off— it's life! We looked at this and the need to acknowledge the pain— even if this sort of thing is indeed a part of life.

Session 9

Mother phoned her *re* exams and almost embarrassed her with wanting to know about the results, etc. Some progress towards communication with mother. This relationship is very important— she frequently says *"well she's my mother"* in the same breath as saying she could walk away from her without looking back.

Session 10

I had great difficulty looking at me today, this is the penultimate session. She appears quiet but not "tired", rather sort of restrained. She wants to tell me about something stepdad used to say to her that makes her feel *"so cheap"*. She has been rehearsing it all week and wants to tell me but can't say it out or write it. Did say it to the police and had to re-read it. She feels if she says it out it will be another milestone.

We touched on other subjects—her *"anger at stepdad—would like to kill him"—feels he deserved a goal sentence and he didn't get one.—Tore up the compensation papers yesterday—really angry."* She feels no compensation could ever be enough for the damage he caused.

She was "stoned" and not very conscious at the time he said the offensive words to her. She was followed to her room; he was sober and he pinned her to the bed and was kissing her all over—she does not remember getting undressed but was naked—she was aware of lapsing in and out of consciousness—she is not sure whether he did more to her than just kiss because of her state. The offensive words that stick in her throat are: *"You've nice boobs"*. They don't sound so bad, but in saying them she was jolted right back to the *"not there"* feeling she'd had at the time.

The words came out so quickly. She knew she'd only be able to say them if she didn't look at me. She was afraid to see compassion and sympathy in my eyes and that this might get her in touch with her tears and sadness. She has not smoked dope for 2½ weeks and declined some recently for first time ever. She has also stopped the shorts—drink-wise.

She feels she still has not got her self-respect back. She hears her stepfather's cruel jibes and comments in her ears pulling her down all the time. This is getting better. *I* finds compliments difficult to handle—even her mother's new attempts to praise her—she rang her to congratulate her on her exam result (she had hoped for a distinction so is disappointed with only merits).

She wants to know *"why people do things that are so bad."* Would like to ask stepdad, why?

Session 11

This was the last session. *I* was a little pensive and quiet. She has done a lot of thinking since last week and was surprised that she did not feel like crashing out after last session. She'd said the most difficult thing for her, having revved up all week to say it. It had lifted a further weight off. She had gone out smiling, feeling really high, later had felt down and then evened out. She was a bit puzzled that this tremendously awful thing she'd had to say seemed so insignificant retrospectively. We looked at the things that matter to a child that may be of less significance to the adult. She is sad and happy to end the therapy. Glad to be done with the things we've talked about—yet sad to lose the contact with me. I shared this feeling. We've done some intense and important work together. We reflected on the sessions—the milestones were the fact that she was coming to counselling at all—then sharing the humiliation of being laughed at and finally what stepdad had said about her as he abused her; *"You've got nice boobs"*—the way he said this and the wrongness of the situation that went with these words—she's aware other people might say this in different circumstances and she would have no reaction at all.

She had been helped because I *"understood—she felt as if I'd been alongside her as she relived the bad experiences, so she was not so alone with it."* It was as if she had had a suppurating wound that needed to be re-opened and cleansed to heal properly, now the scar needs to heal.

She thought she saw stepdad recently and, while her first reaction was to attack, her second was almost to shrug and to let it all go. She is aware that she has moved on and that she need not look back.

She has quit the vodka and the dope and sticks with beer now and goes for a cycle or to play sports if she's fed up or angry. She is able to own hurt feelings and told a recent boyfriend how he had hurt her. She is writing and drawing out her feelings still and finds this therapeutic. (She may send her reflections to me to publish or use in research.)

She is aware there is a lot to do still but feels she can do this. She is changing courses so feels she has a new beginning in September. Now she feels ready to address herself to work and achieve her potential—a new chance.

She has also begun to be less hard on herself about some of her past escape routes such as drink. She realizes it was not really her fault. She knew no other way to drown the pain.

I wondered what was helpful or unhelpful in the counselling? She appreciated especially the way I helped her voice her worst "secrets".

She is a bit scared of the future and what will she be doing when she's 40. Her immediate goal is the degree.

In whatever career she does she wants *"to be good at it"*. We talked a little about these fears; until now she never dared to look beyond coping with today and trying to block out the past. She described her previous insecurity *"like standing on a carpet someone's going to snatch away any minute. Now I've stepped off it into the unknown"*.

She chose the letter *I* for denoting her case study because she feels as if *"from here on I can be myself without shame or pretence."*

Another symbol of the change is that she spent £56 on a haircut and colouring—the first time ever she's spent that much on herself as a woman.

She was able to shake my hand as she left, and we agreed a follow-up session for approximately 2 months from now to see how things are progressing.

Client I unscheduled session

I came in one day soon after the Christmas break in a panic because her sister, who was due to stay with her, had vanished without letting her know where she was or what was happening.

She needed to check out if she was doing all that was necessary and to share her anxiety a little.

Session 12—Review

In this review session she told me of her progress.

She has begun to go to AA, having finally accepted that she does indeed have a drink problem. She has found two good groups, one in Chelsea, with a large number of young people, and one in Acton which is smaller and perhaps more intimate. She has needed the support and encouragement of the AA group and her Christian group.

She is convinced that without her new-found faith in God, she could not continue to be sober. She calls on God's strength to help her when she feels the need for a drink. She has given up her drinking haunts to make it easier and is beginning to realize that she has friends who also appreciate her when she is sober. She now sees the drinking side as shallow. She is helped by the fact that she knows what triggered the drinking, i.e. the child abuse that she feels she has come to terms with successfully. It is now more the habit she needs to break than a need to hide from her emotions.

She has also decided that she will after all go to the claims court for compensation. Previously it would have felt contaminating to have money related to her past experience. Now she just sees that the money would be useful and that it's a demonstration of where the blame lies.

She will be seeing the social worker regarding this over Easter.

She plans to ask her why she was not referred to counselling when the news broke about her stepfather.

6.4. Client I's comment on the therapy experience

Counselling helped me to see that everyone has strengths and weaknesses. Acknowledging your particular combination is to really know yourself. However, this may take a frustratingly long time, but patience is needed as well as a determination to do justice to yourself.

The first few sessions were for me the worst. I felt apprehensive as I knew no one who had been before. Also being a fairly cynical and cautious person who usually weighs up the pros and cons before doing something, jumping feet first into counselling was quite a risk.

I had previously seen it a weakness to need counselling and regarded it as something for manic depressives and the suicidal to attend.

My first thoughts were that I would be confronted by some "holier than thou" do-gooder who thought they knew all the answers and be someone I could not relate to at all. These feelings not being surprising, considering my previous experiences with so-called "welfare people". So in I went carrying a 5lb bag of King Edwards on my shoulder, which achieved nothing. This made the first few sessions seem like a war of wills and I would try and devise more ways to defend myself against this person who apparently wanted to know all my faults and weak spots. Gradually my mistrusts seemed to lessen as all that I said was not going to be thrown back into my face.

As my trust grew, I worked harder at the task in hand. This led to changes in my everyday environment and I became more relaxed in company, which close friends commented on.

The intensity of my anger and resentment gradually began to fade, as at last its foundations were being confronted and dealt with.

Some sessions were very difficult and the will to continue often wavered. I knew however that it was not going to be easy, and that at times it would be painful, but finding the determination to carry on often seemed impossible.

The most difficult concept about counselling is that for the first time I was able to continuously "take" from one person, without any pressure or need to give emotional support back. In everyday relationships, friends lean on each other through stressful times, but counselling seemed to me very one-sided and I found this uncomfortable at first.

After a particularly difficult session, I felt emotionally drained and exhausted and needed quiet hours alone to put my confused mind back into some logical order, to lick my re-opened wounds and sometimes to cry.

Often a day before an arranged session, I would roughly decide what I wanted to say, which helped me to find the courage to keep going. Most of the time I'd end up sitting there with the words stuck in the back of my throat. I would then feel frustrated and angry with myself.

*Eventually talking became easier and **I found myself saying the unspeakable, which amazed me.***

Re-living the blocked-out past in such vivid detail, brought old feelings of helplessness and despair flooding back. This time, however, I was not alone and an older, wiser person from within myself could now be in touch with the pain. But first the covering layer of anger had to be dealt with and removed.

Working between the sessions is important and speeds up the recovery process. I used my love of drawing to visualize my feelings and be in touch with them. This can be helpful if you find it difficult to express your feelings in words.

During stressful demanding sessions, I became obsessed with how my counsellor sat in her chair and any sudden movement made me nervous. Moving to sit on the end of her chair suddenly closed the distance between us and made me panic. Then the impulse to run out of the door and to keep on running was almost impossible to control.

Whilst talking about the most painful memories I found myself unable to sustain eye-contact. I felt I would be judged, be made to feel guilty for what happened even though I know it was not my fault. But the most important fact is that I had eventually said the impossible. It was as if I was experiencing the memory once more, but this time I was free to leave when I wanted and that if I couldn't there was someone there to pull me back to reality.

*If I were to visualize the whole experience I'd say it was as if I was trying to paint my life, but the only colours I had were black and white. Counselling gave me the primary colours to add depth and texture, **but most importantly I held the brush.***

After reading the report my mind began to remember how I felt during those sessions and this seemed so far removed from what I feel today. I realized I was justified in being so angry and that I used this anger to shield the pain. When reading this there was no pain, no anger, only sadness about this "stranger's" childhood and the solace she sought in drink and drugs.

21.05.92 (Commentary written by *I* when she read the write-up in May 1992).

*   *   *

This concludes the detailed case example and client commentaries. In the next chapter the key principles that have been discussed in the preceding chapter and which have, in part, been demonstrated above, are located within the latest thinking in the field.

CHAPTER SEVEN

The analysis within the wider context of the latest thinking in the field

T he last chapter included client commentaries and an example of a complete case to show how my discoveries fit within the real context. The reader has now had the opportunity to partially assess the veracity of my findings by reading Case *I* in full. Since other possibilities and avenues may subsequently have emerged, it is important to turn attention again to the task in hand. That is to find and analyse the key principles of short-term psychodynamic psychotherapy and what it is that especially contributes to the shortening of the process.

Summary of key themes

In order to refocus I am summarizing below the headings under which the themes have been studied and the principles that have emerged from my analysis so far:

What is understood by short-term? Psychodynamic roots; Flexibility; Activity; Focus; Therapeutic alliance; Importance of the first session.

Summary of the subsidiary themes and their place within brief therapy

The subsidiary themes were initially elicited from the clinical work and were subsequently also seen in the literature. These are features which do not so much stand alone as *permeate* the clinical work. As I reflected on the findings from both cases and literature it became clear that a further heading is required as below.

Incisiveness

Incisiveness has not so far been accorded a discrete heading but, from here on I am listing it separately to highlight its importance which has, perhaps, been obscured both in my attempt to be concise and to be faithful to the original themes. Such faithfulness however is erroneous since the nature of the immersion process, within the methodology chosen, anticipates the emergence of new categories, new insights and greater understanding as each cycle of analysis is completed.

Incisiveness is required in challenging, in focusing, in avoiding non-essentials and it enhances other aspects of the approach to accelerate the process. Incisiveness needs to be stressed as an intrinsic and essential aspect of working in the brief method.

A summary of the now more familiar subsidiary themes follows:

the teaching aspect of the therapeutic work;
becoming their own therapists;
intensity;
being attuned; and
experience required of the therapist.

(The more detailed summary of findings is in Chapter 5, Part Two).

The findings as they relate to the latest thinking in the field

This chapter takes account of the literature that has proliferated since the start of my work on this subject. This cycle of analysis strives to ensure that my findings are located within the most up to date thinking about brief therapy.

Throughout the late 1980s to the time of writing in the early 21st century there has been a marked development in public and professional awareness of brief therapy.

In recent years health maintenance organizations (HMOs) have become commonplace and employee assistance programmes (E.A.P's), or outplacement consultancies, as they are often known in Britain, have emerged all around the country. These tend to use the brief approach. Indeed, Austad declares that, "the essence of good HMO therapy is that it is short-term, eclectic and effective" (1995, p. 26). However, this recent interest in brief work has primarily been economic led as opposed to it being a "treatment of choice" as in the empirical material of this book.

Where substantive works about brief therapy were rather few prior to the last decade, there are now, in the early 21st century, a number of volumes about aspects of the approaches. Many of these are updates in the thinking of the key proponents in the field, as identified by my research, such as Davanloo, Mann, Malan and Sifneos. There are also new approaches. There is, for example, Accelerated Empathy proposed by Alpert and the Interpersonal Developmental Existential (I.D.E.) model of Brief Time Sensitive Therapy proposed by Budman and Gurman. There is also Brief Adaptive Psychotherapy (BAP) as developed by Jerome Pollack, Walter Flegenheimer and Arnold Winston in the mid-eighties. H. Strupp and Jeffrey Binder add their approach, called Time Limited Dynamic Psychotherapy (TLDP), to the list for the mid-eighties along with "Short-Term Support Expressive Psychoanalytic Psychotherapy (SE)" as developed by Luborsky. I refer to my own approach as Focal and Short-Term Psychotherapy and Client/ Counselling Education (*FASTPACE*). However, I do not claim this so much as a new approach but rather as a convenient way of expressing what I do within my therapy practice. My examination of the selected cases has shown that, in my practice and in the work of colleagues, the key principles for short-term psychodynamic therapy have been both rediscovered and discovered. "Rediscovered" in that the principles we use are rooted in a psychodynamic tradition and mesh with the developments of the early proponents of brief therapy. "Discovered" in that this is a dynamic process and new dimensions have been emphasized and new techniques incorporated.

A gap in the field

As I studied the latest literature and some of the examples of brief therapy and common features within brief therapy approaches I concluded that there is not, as yet, a clear enough exposition of the key principles. A gap is apparent.

This gap may be seen for example, in the following, supposedly "brief therapy" cases, as described by Hill (1989). These are not the only examples given which I believe demonstrate the lack of understanding of the key principles of the approach. My intention here, however, is not so much to criticize the casework but rather to highlight, from the examples, the need for a clearer exposition of the principles involved in brief therapy. My book aims to provide this. Therefore, in the following extracts where I have italicized the client comments for emphasis, I am drawing attention only to the aspects of the cases that point to this need and I cite the case number only for reference in case the reader wishes to go to the source.

In case (5) there is no clear focus or agreed contract in session one and the time limit is discussed only in the fifth session. When it *is* discussed the reason appears to be that the *therapist* has a deadline, "his wife was having a baby," rather than a clinical decision. Even with regard to the number of sessions it is the therapist's "proposed 18 sessions" that is decided upon rather than the "12" that the client moots (1989, p. 159). The work as one would expect, accelerates in these last sessions but the end is not satisfactorily worked through and ends with the client feeling *"'that Doctor S had not disclosed during the final session about enjoying their working together'"* (p. 170).

The therapist and Hill, in the analysis of the techniques, believed that leaving the control and focus to the client was therapeutic. They perceived the frustration that this caused the client to be part of the process in helping her to become more decisive. However the long-term outcome does not show great change in the client and leaves me wondering if the central issue was ever really addressed. The client reports feeling *"frustrated"* and unfocused. *"Doctor S made her feel responsible for the dialogue"* and by Session 4 the client is suggesting that she ends. This prompted a focusing on *"her feelings for the whole hour"* and subsequently Sessions 5–7 were productive. All credit here to the therapist for allowing the client to supervise him leading to a productive few sessions. The client supervising the therapist is a common feature in therapy recognized by Casement (1985). The analysis shows that the therapist, in brief work, has a responsibility for enabling the client to agree a focus and to relentlessly take control then of maintaining the boundaries and pursuing the agreed issue. In my opinion this did not happen in this example and this concurs with the client's view that "*Doctor S did not focus and structure the therapy enough.*" (p. 170).

In another case example given by Hill, (4), the client also expresses frustration at the "*lack of direction*" by session 4. This is perceived by Hill and the therapist involved to be the client's problem wanting to be told "*what to do*" (1989, p. 138). Could it be that the pace was too slow and the session was lacking in intensity/ activity and direction? This is my view reinforced by Hill's client (5), pejoratively labelled "**rescue me**" and who also felt the sessions lacked focus. There is a lack of flexibility in this example on the part of the therapist about the possibility of renegotiating the contract. In contrast however, in another case (1), "Men on Trial", there is an excellent example of focusing and negotiating the contract. If only one example can be applauded for this aspect of brief work, can the author really have grasped its importance for effective brief work? Another point about her exposition of brief work is that none of these cases are within the definition of "short" that I have described, all being within a range of 12–20 sessions. These examples indicate the need for the exposition of the key principles in brief work that this book hopes to provide. Thus, subsequently, by closer adherence to the principles more speedy results may be possible.

In a more general way Feltham too observes a gap. He points to the need for and lack of, availability of specific training in brief work. He wonders if those without this are working "unethically" (1997, p. 131). McMahon Moughtin also laments this vacuum, observing that "not many counsellors are equipped to offer this approach. This very specific and demanding discipline is not taught in most psychodynamic establishments." (1997, p. 99). Binder and Strupp also refer to the need for "specialized training" (1991, p. 158). Certainly specific training in this area is scarce. Under the auspices of *FASTPACE*, I offer training and supervision to experienced practitioners in the form of short courses, supervision and modular programmes. I see intensive supervision, after the student has understood the key principles, as the most helpful way forward. This coincides with the view of Pollack, Flegenheimer and Winston who also refer to the need for specialist training. Their programme centres in the main on intensive supervision and seminars and discussing and reviewing video sessions. This training targets experienced practitioners and "takes one or two years for the person to become proficient in the technique" (1991, p. 214). I agree with this time scale, since it allows sufficient time for a number of clients to have been seen during this intensive form of training supervision.

Another gap exists in-so-far as, even within some of the latest works about brief therapy, there is a lack of conviction about the method. For example Elton Wilson writes, with reference to the review at the end of a "mini contract of 4–6 sessions": "For the majority of clients, some form of continuation is the optimal choice" (1996, p. 19). Is it? I perceive this attitude as undermining the concept that therapy can be brief even if offered, as in an example of Gilligan's, for "as long as ... needed" (1990, p. ix). As Sifneos observes "What is needed is enthusiasm" (1981, p. 49). Molnos too, stresses the importance of the therapist's attitude. She points out that the "therapist has to be confident and convinced that ... good, productive work can be done within given time limits ... This positive basic attitude towards the task is at least as important as is the therapist's technical ability to perform it" (1995, p. 52).

In the following I attempt to counter some of the modern thinking and on the converse add to and support some of my discoveries by drawing on the latest works with regard to brief therapy. At the same time I do not wish to repeat myself and so will refer the reader back to concepts explored earlier as appropriate. I am following the ordering of the key themes used earlier.

What is understood by short-term?

Many of the modern writers tend to subscribe to Hoyt's statement that "Short-term or brief therapy is often arbitrarily defined as twenty sessions or less" (1995, p. 76). Pollack et al. too, infer that 20 sessions is normal. With reference to a particular group of "patients who all suffer from personality disorders and require a longer course of treatment to alter longstanding characterological patterns", they suggest that their Brief Adaptive Psychotherapy should be longer than the "usual twenty sessions" the mean was "36.27" (1991, pp. 214–5).

These assumptions are in marked contrast to my findings where the empirical studies showed four to six sessions to be the median and 12 sessions to be the maximum.

Speed and ethics

I believe that in therapy speed is of the essence, indeed I wonder with Lazarus and Fay, if the word brief is "redundant" (1990, p. 38). Should not *all* therapy be as brief as possible? Cummings has developed a patient's Bill of Rights which emphasizes this point: "A patient has an inalienable right to relief from pain, anxiety and depression in the shortest time possible and with the least intrusive intervention" (1990, p. 178). Feltham however, in an otherwise excellent, and recent account on brief therapy, issues a strong warning to private practitioners, of the difficulties, in financial terms, of confining themselves to brief work. "Short-term therapy may be seen as anathema to the private and independent practitioner. If you rely for your income on a steady flow of clients who attend regularly, you will not opt for short-term work. If you did, you would find yourself having to constantly find new clients and there would be inevitable gaps in your schedule" (1997, p. 128). Feltham further implies that it is only private practitioners with other sources of income who "engage in short-term work," or those with a particular "clinical interest or training requirements" and others out of "political sympathies" and wanting to provide counselling for a group, whom otherwise might not be a able to have any counselling (p. 129). He warns that even if economic considerations are not enough to dissuade the counsellor from offering brief therapy then there are still further problems to bear in mind: "Anyone considering entering private practice should seriously reflect on the problems to be encountered in offering short-term work or in practising a clinical orientation likely to achieve rapid positive outcomes! ... the costs in terms of stress may be very high" (p. 129). Feltham may, in these statements, have put his finger on one of the reasons why this approach keeps getting lost and that its status tends to be regarded as second best. But are these considerations ethical? Molnos also highlights these difficulties for the therapist, alluding, in addition, to the social pressure on therapists to offer long-term work. Some therapists, she observes, maintain their "status" as long as they agree "with the general opinion that it would be so much better to do long-term work 'if only we had the resources'" (1995, p. 19). McMahon Moughtin, in similar vein, observes: "Few are sufficiently independent minded or financially secure to risk being sent to Coventry" (1997, p. 116). I fully support and endorse Molnos' resounding challenge to these considerations "is it not our ethical responsibility to offer the patient this more cost-, time-, and energy-effective alternative?" (1995, p. 21).

Molnos also saliently points out that "what makes the difference is not the absolute length of time, but what we do with it" (1995, p. 52).

Here and now or cognizant of the past?: Psychodynamic roots

Budman, Friedman and Hoyt list "universal elements" which they claim are shared by all brief therapies (1992, p. 345). Whilst I can endorse some of these, which will be returned to later, here I have to challenge their assumption that there is a: "Here and now orientation, the primary focus being on current life situations and patterns in thinking, feeling, and behaving—and their alterna- tives—rather than extensive reviewing of the 'past' or 'origins' of problems" (p. 346). Here I would remind the reader of Marteau's concept of "reaching through" ... "to the very roots" if any real change is to occur (1986, p. 81). Feltham too, recently refers to brief therapy as having the "same procedures as in long-term work, but much more intensively" (1997, p. 32). This is in part true, as seen from the research in terms of the use of transference, interpretation and the awareness of pattern formation from past events, but the emphasis on focusing, contract making and activity surely differs as has been seen earlier. McMahon Moughtin describes "this concen- trated" form of therapy as "neither an abbreviated nor an inferior form of open ended psychodynamic therapy. It is a different mode of therapy" (1997, p. 98). Certainly it is not inferior if, by the end of therapy, it leaves people more free of their pain or restrictive patterns of behaviour. It is, however, "abbreviated" if this work can be completed in a short number of sessions which the research cases demonstrate. The word *compressed* might be more apt and perhaps leave less room for ambiguity. Is it indeed a different mode? To clarify this one first needs to unravel what it is. This task has been the central focus of this research. The form of therapy referred to in this book is in Sifneos' words a "technique of brief psychotherapy based on psychodynamic theoretical premises" (1992, p. x). Molnos refers to the triangle of conflict as inherent within the brief psychodynamic approach and Malan refers to this concept as "fundamental to dynamic psychotherapy". That is, the interpretation of the client's "defence, anxiety and hidden feeling" (1995, p. 14). He explains that one of the main tasks in therapy is to help the patient to understand the ways in which they avoid pain, and the anxiety caused by the idea of owning up to these hidden emotions and "the nature of the hidden feelings themselves" (p. 16). This triangle relates to what is known as the triangle of the person or triangle of insight, that is "The hidden feeling is directed towards one or more categories of the triangle of person, namely other, transference and parent or sibling" (p. 90). Molnos has developed this concept into four triangles: "A large triangle that is the so called triangle of person, and it contains three triangles of conflict". These reflect "the conflict now, out there; the problem in the past, there and then; and, finally, the problem here and now" (pp. 36–38). She goes on to explain that the task of helping the client to work through the transference involves observing the defensive patterns, allowing these to be expressed and linking them, to both past and current relationships, in order to help the client to change. The empirical casework too, reveals examples of transference, resistance and transference repetitions and is within the psychodynamic frame. However, whilst highlighting the psychoanalytic backcloth, this approach has been shown to go beyond its roots. This is achieved by incorporating a flexible and integrated use of therapeutic skills and assumptions, borrowed from other traditions, to shorten the process. It also shows different ways of dealing with some of the psychoanalytic concepts. Flexibility, activity and the need for a focus, all underpinned with a strong therapeutic alliance, remain to the forefront in the modern thinking about brief therapy.

Flexibility

The use of different techniques requires a certain flexibility on the part of the therapist, who needs to be more concerned with being and keeping in tune with the client, than in remaining loyal to any one school of therapy. The therapist needs to be versatile in embracing important concepts and therapeutic tools from traditions other than the psychoanalytic, in order to inform and speed the process.

The aspect of flexibility also relates to the use of time, that is, in terms of the length of sessions and in the spacing of appointments demonstrated within the analysis. The more recent concept of SST's (the Single Session Therapies) picks up the theme of pacing and spacing in relation to the therapy process. SST's fit well with the concept that emerged in the research, of "intermittent" therapy and the "rites of passage" approach of Kovacs, where clients come into therapy at key times in their lives. Cummings suggests that such therapy would replace the "old fashioned general practitioner ... who had time to listen" and expects to see clients for "intermittent therapy throughout the life cycle" (1990, p. 169). This is akin to the "secular priesthood" referred to by Kovacs as seen in the earlier analysis. One of the features, highlighted by Rosenbaum and Talmon, in the success of the single session approach for example is the need to "take an integrated approach to the psychotherapeutic endeavour" (1995, p. 137). They discovered that where a single school approach was adopted, the results were less successful.

My research emphasizes the integrative approach and like Wolberg and Rosenbaum and Talmon, the flexibility required so that each patient is helped to move on with whatever technique is appropriate. Wolberg aptly used the word "fusion" to describe how the different techniques might be applied and suggested that this requires an "experienced therapist schooled in the widest varieties of techniques" (1965, p. 128). Feltham (1997), Molnos (1995) and McMahon Moughtin (1997), in some of the latest substantive works, also stress flexibility of both technique and the use of time. Several of the writers in the late 1980s to late 1990s emphasize the use of a variety of techniques to provide "novelty" especially in the first session, e.g. , Budman, Friedman and Hoyt (1992, p. 347). The idea is that novelty will stimulate surprise and change. Imagery, gestalt or interpretation can give the client a new perspective on their situation and provide hope. As seen in the earlier analysis, Kovacs stressed that it is important to "make a dent" in the problem quickly. Hoyt et al., demand "an eclectic innovativeness and flexibility that may require clinical experience and seasoning" (1992, p. 77).

Activity

Activity in my findings is seen to be an inherent part of brief work and is a factor in the shortening process. As Wolberg puts it "Anathema to short-term therapy is passivity in the therapist" (1965, p. 135). This energetic engagement in the process is, however, not just for the therapist but is *also expected of the client*. The stress on activity is endorsed by the recent writers. For example where I used the term "sprinter" to highlight the dynamic energy, Budman, Friedman and Hoyt refer to the need for the brief therapist to "hit the ground running" in the first encounter with the client (1992, p. 351).

Focus

My findings show focus to have an intrinsic place within the brief approach. There were differing views in the early literature, however, as to what constitutes a suitable focus. The empirical work shows that the focus can be much wider than was thought by the earlier proponents who held a rather restrictive view. There were also varying opinions as to how the focus is to be found, for example whether this is to be initiated more by the client or therapist. The idea of therapy and finding the focus as a *joint enterprise* is one that I support and the empirical work shows. The importance of *"circumscribing"* the focus, to use the term coined by Sifneos, is emphasized by all. This includes the recent proponents. Indeed, McMahon Moughtin pins the difference between brief and other therapies on the existence of "the focused dimension" (1997, p. 119). Feltham highlights an angle on focus which is important and is at times obscured as authors point to the need to home in on one theme. His useful contribution is to suggest a flexible attitude towards focusing. Balint et al. too, many years ago, had recommended this attitude observing that the "chosen focus (with all the desired flexibility of changing it when required) significantly determines the course of treatment" (1972, p. 158). Feltham points out that the way in which the focus is used may vary and this may be in an "emerging" way (1997, p. 78). In this way the agreed focus might be renegotiated and might equally be used as a backcloth. I would support this and would wish to be wary of the brief therapists being so tied down by the need to have a clear "focus" that they forget to stay in tune with the client. The focus once alluded to, will be there as a backcloth, as in case B, quoted extensively in the analysis, where this can be seen (Chapter 5). In case B the relationship with mother was the key focus agreed and yet, within the sessions, a range of issues were dealt with, all of which were important. This could be interpreted as multi-focus; equally the critic could say that some of the work was not sticking to the agreed circumscribed area. I would counter this by suggesting the process of renegotiation appropriately took place and that each strand of the casework was required to lead to the successful outcome observed. By the final session the relationship with mother had changed radically. I do not believe that this would have been possible, without exploring and dealing with some of the other painful issues covered. Had I insisted on only looking at mother, the agreed focus, the work would have been impoverished. If I reflect further on this case one interpretation is as follows. It would seem in cases like this that the therapist, whilst not ignoring the responsibility of holding the boundaries of the work, needs also to trust the clients to bring the material that they themselves know, relates to the agreed central theme. This may not be instantly apparent to the therapist. It may not be fully apparent to the client either, but once there is an agreed focus it creates a *backcloth* which may enable the unconscious to bring relevant matters to mind. For me this is reminiscent of two classes of children to whom I gave the same piece of Vivaldi and asked them to write a poem inspired by the music. The English class produced secular subject material and the Religious Education class produced prayerful prose. Apart from the groups being different the only other variable was the *backcloth* of the subject normally studied in that period.

Therapeutic alliance

It is the relationship, between the therapist and client, that enables the therapeutic process. Within the brief approach, it is the *rapidity* with which it is established that is of significance. Incisiveness will be covered in greater detail below, but is relevant here as made possible by the relationship. Just as a surgeon cannot generally operate without a painful incision of some kind, neither can therapy be effective without a certain incisiveness. The relentless early challenges and questioning of defences which are cited as short-ening procedures by Molnos take place in the context of a strong therapeutic alliance. Molnos counters the critics of early challenge by highlighting the "deeply caring" attitude of the therapist (1995, p. 50). The challenges may *sound* harsh, but the tone and connectedness of the therapist enables the client to feel *"held"* even and especially at the time of greatest *"incisiveness"*. In today's context of therapist abuse one barely dares to use the word "love", but I would add that the context needs to be one of "love". This intensity of "holding", within the relationship, defies description as one reaches for the inexpressible. Martin Buber refers to this as a "meeting". "The moment of meeting is not an 'experience' that stirs in the receptive soul and grows to perfect blessedness; rather, in that moment something happens to the man. At times it is like a light breath, at times like a wrestling-bout, but always—it *happens*. The man who emerges from the act of pure relation that so involves his being has now in his being something more that has grown in him, of which he did not know before and whose origin he is not rightly able to indicate. However, the source of this new thing is classified in the scientific orientation of the world, with its authorized efforts to establish an unbroken causality, we, whose concern is real consideration of the real, cannot have our purpose served with subconsciousness or any other apparatus of the soul. The reality is that we receive what we did not hitherto have, and receive it in such a way that we know it has been given to us" (1984, p. 109).

Feltham refers to similar concepts as "moments of freedom" and "the healing of the eternal now" ... and suggests that "it may be that heightened presence sometimes acts alongside clinical man-oeuvres," and that it is this presence that achieves the change rather than the therapeutic techniques (1997, p. 26).

Importance of the first session

The first session emerges from the research to be of far greater significance than earlier writers have given it credit for. Every one of the selected cases showed the first session to be significant. Table VII (p. 192) summarizes some of the important aspects which include the testing out process, the giving of clues, touching the pain and the getting started.

Feltham, McMahon Moughtin and Molnos also see the importance of the first session. Feltham refers to getting "to the point" (1997, p. 73). McMahon Moughtin agrees with Molnos who refers to the first session as the "start of the therapy" (1995, p. 86). Cummings examines the idea of doing "something novel in the first session" which he suggests overcomes resistance and "catapults the patient into treatment" (1990, p. 175). I refer to the importance of being alert to the clues the client gives in the first session. Zeig refers to this aspect of clients "giving clues"—or "seeding" in Eriksonian terminology. He gives as an example a client gesturing in a circular fashion prior to talking of "going around in circles" (1990, p. 234).

As the findings showed, it is in this first session that the therapist is tested by the client. Tested for inner strength, for skill and trustworthiness. The process too is tested, both the therapist and the situation are on trial. This is the new emphasis that emerged from the research, rather than the therapist "assessing" the client, "evaluating" the problem or "devising a treatment plan".

The intense therapeutic relationship already referred to needs to happen from the first moments of the first session. Winnicott stresses the importance of this. He noticed that the children he saw would often dream about "the doctor" the night before and this indicated that the first visit was given an added factor that of an intensity of anticipation. Gustafson highlights Winnicott's use of the word "sacred" to describe this. "Either the sacred moment is used or it is wasted" (1986, p. 71). Molnos echoes these sentiments some 25 years after Winnicott, but this time seeing this as a crucial component in the shortening process: "The essential shortening technique consists in using the first hour, the first minutes, of the therapeutic encounter to maximum effect" (1995, p. 45).

The first session and single session therapies

There was a growing acknowledgement in the 1990s, of the value of even one session of therapy, as seen in the emergence of "Single Session Therapies" or "SST's" as they have become known and as Rosenbaum and Talmon observe (1995, p. 105). This is very much in line with my own conclusions that the first session is of paramount importance. McMahon Moughtin too touches on the "initial interview" calling it "the make or break time for establishing the therapeutic alliance" (1997, p. 89). She makes a distinction however, between the initial interview and single session therapy. She stresses that single sessions need to be structured with the end in the mind of both client and therapist, so as not to leave the client "naked" (p. 94). In the single session therapies the time span may be as much as two or more hours as is Davanloo's trial therapy.

Doctor James Thompson, of London's University College Medical School at the 1996 British Psychological Society's annual Conference, spoke out strongly in favour of an "extended single session". This might be of 3 or 4 hours but would be complete in itself rather than a trial therapy.

Although different writers have highlighted different aspects of the first session and many recent works place importance on this, I contend that my research findings go further. They show that the first session needs to be accorded a more significant place in the understanding of brief therapy process. The discoveries about the first session expand awareness of the many facets to be considered *simultaneously*. These go beyond the more narrow perspectives expressed by one or other expert, with regard to the beginning of therapy. They point to the all embracing significance of the first session in all its facets. However, if I am to draw attention to one or other facet in these first moments, it is in terms especially of my understanding of the place of acknowledging the client's pain and in the testing out of the therapist. For full details of the analysis of the first session return to Chapter 5.1.7.

The subsidiary themes

The subsidiary themes will be examined in the following sequence:

The teaching aspect of the therapeutic work;
teaching the clients to be their own therapists;
intensity;
incisiveness;
being attuned; and
experience required of the therapist

The teaching aspect of the therapeutic work

My analysis has shown teaching to be of great significance. Teaching the client about therapy, about the process and about psychological processes is seen as an integral part of the therapy process. Teaching in this way can contribute to the shortening of therapy. It is a way of "melting" the resistance, of facilitating insight and of teaching the client ultimately to be their own therapist. This approach gives control to the client. The therapist is enabling the clients to become their own therapist. The teaching element supports this aim, as does the enlisting of the client's agreement about focus and the time limit in the therapy contract. The use of homework also contributes to this end. As Cummings observes, when the homework is appropriately given in line with the client's own aims the patient will realize: "'Hey, this guy isn't kidding. I'm responsible for my own therapy'" (1990, p. 175).

The teaching aspect emerged from the clinical work with more emphasis than from the early literature, although it was present for some of the key proponents. Teaching was clearly important to Alexander and Sifneos in the 1960s and 1980s. Sifneos for example refers to the therapist as, "a problem solving helper" (1987, p. 196). More recently, Bauer and Kobos stress the fact that the therapist, through teaching, attempts to prepare the patient to become their "own therapist" (1995, p. 253). As a result of this attitude, Hoyt describes clinicians as: "catalysts to ... (the clients) finding ways for more productive and enjoyable living" (1995, p. 204).

Rosenbaum and Talmon impress upon us, that this facilitator role depends upon the therapist believing "that the power is in the client". It is "this therapist attitude" that "encourages client autonomy" (1995, p. 124).

This suggests that the therapist's role is to walk alongside the client in their journey to freedom, flexibly using skills and therapeutic knowledge to enable this process. It proposes "a view of psychotherapy primarily as a learning experience" as Benjamin recommends (1991, p. 249).

These views which give power to the client, which I share and my findings support, run counter to the opinion of Elton Wilson. In looking at the work of Davanloo, Malan and Mann she declares misguidedly "the centrality and the power of the therapist is increased in these briefer versions of psychoanalytic therapy" (1996, p. 9). In seeming contradiction to this comment about the therapies that informed the "time conscious therapy" which she advocates, she does however stress, that therapists should offer "value-free acceptance of clients as experts in their own lives" (1996, p. 178).

Becoming one's own therapist

In respect to the concept of becoming one's own therapist I contend, and Rosenbaum and Talmon observe, that there is a basic assumption in brief therapy that clients have the power to find their own solution. This endorses the non pathologising view of human nature alluded to in the first chapter. The therapist's role is that of a facilitator: as Hoyt points out "The therapist need only facilitate the client's natural tendency to keep changing" ... and to find "his or her own solution" (1995, pp. 121–124).

As Client *I* observed in her commentary on the process it was important that she *"held the brush"*.

The ultimate aim then of brief therapy is that the therapist becomes redundant as soon as possible and that the client goes on alone. As Austad states: "The goal of the HMO therapist is to become unnecessary quickly and to help the patient get "unstuck" and then to move on" (1995, p. 33).

Intensity

Mann and Goldman suggest that time limited therapy is a "treatment experience that rapidly becomes intensely affective for both patient and therapist" (1994, p. 28). Alexander, Davanloo and I see increasing the emotional intensity as a way of decreasing the time required for effective work.

It is increased primarily by our careful *attunement* to the client and especially in relation to the area of "pain".

There is an intensity that exists within every single session. One anticipates a certain "energy" within the interaction that is akin to that required of a sprinter. This is required of both therapist and client. Polster refers to an aspect of this process in terms of "tight sequencing" (1990, p. 379). He explains what he means as follows: "The processes of tightening the sequences may often bank on verbally strong interruptions of the evasive process or on experimental arrangements like the empty chair technique, visualizations, or accentuating sensations" (p. 380).

Attunement

Sensitivity is essential if the therapist is to be in tune with the client. This is evident in all of the cases. This quality is not unique to the brief therapy, but, within this approach, it is seen as an accelerating factor enhancing all of the above principles. This needs to be present from the very first moments of the therapy contract. The stress on sensitivity accords with the latest writings also.

Gustafson refers to it as a "critical element" in brief therapy. It is necessary to stay "close enough to the patient to help him bear his pain. Thus, intuitive mastery is essential to early success, while integration of the relevant concepts of brief therapy is essential to retain this mastery" (1981, p. 83). He recommends, as Havens had before him (1976), staying "with the patient through thick and thin" ... as "the essence of the existential therapeutic relationship" (1981, p. 86).

It is helping the client to bear his "present and *chronically endured pain*" that becomes a central theme in Mann's approach according to Mann and Goldman (1994, p. 23). These authors are reinforcing the discoveries made earlier. Malan also stated that the "aim of every moment of every session is to put the patient in touch with as much of his true feelings as he can bear" (1996, p. 84). The "staying with" the client is indeed of paramount importance and is the essence of what Davanloo is doing in his "relentless healer" approach of "cornering the patient" or in the "hounding" of Sifneos as he demands specifics of his patients or the "nailing one foot to the floor" of Marteau or "sticking like glue" in the term that I tend to use. These descriptions conjure up a harsh picture and critics of the approach are not slow to point to this. Here, I suggest that there is a lack of understanding of the process. This view overlooks the fact that, the context is one of **an agreed contract** with the client and this within a therapeutic alliance. As Molnos highlights "psychic holding" and "relentless challenge" ... "happen simultaneously" (1995, pp. 70–71).

Balint, according to Gustafson, offered a unique contribution to the brief therapy approach that relates especially to "the specific kind of interaction that the patient needs" (1981, p. 121). For Balint the "atmosphere" within the therapy was of overriding significance: "When patient and doctor meet and they embark on the joint venture of psychotherapy, the contribution of each will determine the emotional atmosphere between them and what they will talk about" (Balint et al., 1972, p. 133). Binder and Strupp highlight the need for "sensitivity" in relation to the application of techniques "in ways that are most meaningful to the patient" and the need for the therapist "to be sensitive to the importance of the human element in all therapeutic encounters" (1991, p. 159).

Incisiveness

The concept of incisiveness referred to by Davanloo, Molnos and myself in the 1990s is not new to brief therapy. Hoyt says "make everything count" and I agree with him that many years earlier "Sullivan (1954, p. 224) put it well" advocating an essential psychiatric skill to be "making a rather precise move which has a high probability of achieving what you are attempting to achieve, with a minimum of words" (1995, p. 282). Lazarus and Fay also echo these recommendations "Good therapy is precise ... every intervention" should "tell" (1990, pp. 36–37).

In describing the aspect of incisiveness, Erving Polster uses the metaphor of "slippage" and "meshing". "In mechanics, slippage refers to the loss of motion or power through inadequate connection between gears. When gears mesh properly, the rotation of one gear impels the other; the resulting movement is fluid and powerful" (1990, p. 378). It is the "meshing" that I wish to stress here as therapist and client truly engage. Polster terms this "therapeutic pointedness" and sees it as a "corrective for psychological *slippage*" (ibid). I see this analogy as particularly apt in describing, not just therapeutic interventions, but the therapeutic relationship as well. Polster also sees a certain simplicity as being required in the incisiveness—the "artistry of the therapist rests on creating simplicity" (1990, p. 389). This incisiveness involves the accuracy of a surgeon, as Gustafson puts it: "... finding the best place to give the patient a push. Expertise is knowing where, how and when to push to get the most successful change" (1990, p. 409). This is what I call the "strategic focus". It is "the place of leverage that will bring about movement that has large, benign effects on other fields in the patients's life, creating what Cronen, Johnson and Lannamann (1982) called a 'charmed loop'."—or a "ripple effect" in my terminology (p. 409).

Experience

It is considered that, in order to achieve all of the above, experience is required. Rosenbaum and Talmon in the more recent literature stress the need for experience, a factor which emerged clearly in my study: "Ideally, therapists should be well-trained and skilful with a variety of approaches and techniques so that they can apply what will be best for a client at a particular time" (1995, p. 137).

Mann and Goldman agree with this stating that "Time limited psychotherapy is not for the beginning therapist" (1994, p. 17).

McMahon Moughtin, like Feltham and myself and the earlier writers, sees brief therapy as very demanding on the therapist. "The therapist must be actively involved throughout, fully focused, using the time available to the maximum benefit of the client, fine tuned to each stage of the dynamic process" (1997, p. 100).

These recent writers support the findings from the analysis that experience is required of the therapist for this approach. This factor relates to the other important features of brief work. This includes the limited time available for the therapeutic contract, which means that the therapist needs to be rather **precise** and **incisive** with the interventions made. This requires skill, which assumes training and practice to acquire and inspire confidence.

Summary

This chapter has shown how the latest literature, published since the start of my research for this book, has borne out many of the points that I have drawn from the analysis. However there are some aspects of my discoveries that remain new. This applies in particular to the work on the first session, the teaching element and the stress on the *interweaving* of a number of aspects of therapy in the interests of shortening the process. There are other aspects where my findings raise questions if juxtaposed with the more recent writers. At times these questions have led me to state more clearly my own interpretation of the findings, in others to pose a challenge to the new author. In some instances too, I have become aware of omissions. For example, where a concept has been so taken for granted that it has been subsumed in my summary under one heading, when it would be better accorded a separate heading, this occurred with the positive attitude required of the therapist.

The intensity of the therapeutic encounter and the need to be sensitively in tune, emerged from the empirical work as important principles, not particularly evident in the earlier literature, but endorsed by recent literature. The recent works also pay more attention to the element of mystery, with reference both to the therapeutic relationship and to the process of therapy. Incisiveness is another aspect that was not especially evident in the early work, although it is implicit, but is given a higher profile in my analysis and is reinforced in the later literature. It is a concept that I believe to be a crucial factor within the effective exercise of brief therapy.

The benefits of adopting an integrated approach, as indicated from the findings, are also reinforced by the latest proponents.

This chapter has pointed to some gaps in knowledge about the approach and to some of the areas where my findings can make a particular contribution. The next chapter returns to the literature to examine a number of different broad statements made about essential elements of brief therapy. These too point to a gap which this book fills. It provides an up to date and accessible exposition of the evolution of brief therapy and the key principles in the shortening process and what constitutes brief therapy. The conclusions are drawn from the analysis of the casework and an overview of the field and are presented in concise form as the conceptual framework in the concluding chapter.

CHAPTER EIGHT

Inconsistency in the "universal characteristics" seen in the literature

The last chapter located my findings within the latest literature in respect to the key themes and it pointed to gaps. This chapter returns to the literature, both recent and less recent, to examine a number of different broad statements that Austad refers to as "assumptions that guide most short-term work" that are revealed there (1995, p. 27). These too point to the need for the more comprehensive overview that my findings provide. They also raise a number of questions.

Some of the descriptions, found in particular in the later literature, imply a general consensus as to the key elements of brief therapy but, although there is some overlap, each includes and excludes different features. For example Pollack et al. refer to "the standard techniques of brief dynamic psychotherapy" and include: "the maintenance of a focus, early and repeated work in the transference and a high activity level on the part of the therapist" (1991, p. 203). Christoph, Barber and Kurcias, on the other hand, refer to "a prototypic view of definition" (1991, p. 3). They suggest that if a therapy is to be termed "brief dynamic therapy" it must have the following five criteria: psychoanalytic origins, with regard to both concepts and techniques; a time limit; patient selection; and increased therapist activity in order to maintain a focus. Hoyt in his summary of the "most frequently cited generic components of brief treatment" adds some different facets. He refers to a rapid working alliance, focality, activity and patient participation, stress on patient strength, expectation of change; his "here-and-now (and next) orientation" has already been challenged in the previous chapter (1995, p. 284).

My findings suggest that it is not enough to examine just the present, the current patterns need to be seen as Sifneos recommends, in the light of "therapist–parent connections or past transference link interpretations" (1987, p. 74). Molnos' major ingredients in brief therapy are "early confrontation of the resistance" ... "high activity on the therapist's part" and she introduces "therapist's attitude" (1995, p. 39). Feltham too emphasizes this latter feature recommending an attitude of hope plus a willingness to be flexible and to "adopt degree of eclectism". He adds that the counsellor needs to "be willing to take an active approach, to be focused and realistic (non-perfectionistic)" (1997, p. 59). Goulding is alone amongst the more recent writers in singling out the important aspect of the contract stating that successful "short-term therapy begins with a good contract" (1990, p. 304). In this she echoes Marteau who in his list of principles for short-term work stresses "the therapeutic contract" and ensuring that all techniques "fit the basic contract" he emphasizes that the "contract may have to be spelt out clearly, the client being reminded why he has come and what he agreed to undertake" (1986, pp. 92–93). Marteau's list adds that all the subsequent work with the triangles of conflict and of persons should be "in relation to the crisis" this refers to the "nuclear" crisis "stemming from an emotional crisis in childhood" (1986, p. 80). Wolberg, although he does not talk about contracts does includes the idea of "structuring the therapeutic situation" within his understanding of the establishment of the "rapid working relationship" described in his "flexible" schema for brief therapy. Within this term he also incorporates the following concepts of "communicating understanding, confidence ... reassuring the patient that he is not hopeless" (1965, p. 142). These latter points, that he refers to as sub headings within "relationship", I believe are highly significant factors which appear in some of the later literature and in my own findings but are referred to in different language, for example as "therapist attitude" and "giving hope" and "touching the pain". It is interesting that he refers to a "rapid working relationship" rather than to the "rapid establishment" of the working relationship. This slight shift in language may have been accidental but equally could be indicative of the pace required in brief work. My findings indicate a need for both aspects. Wolberg's list of 14 "ingredients" includes in addition to some of the facets already mentioned some techniques, action planning, diagnosis, dealing with "target symptoms" and "destructive elements in the environment" and "encouraging ... a proper life philosophy", "terminating therapy" and "follow up visits" (1965, p. 142). Overall he promotes a more broad based approach to the work than any of the aforementioned, taking account of the client context outside of the consulting room and some of the aspects that I have studied under the heading of subsidiary themes. I believe he has much to teach us more than 30 years on.

Discovery or rediscovery

Some of the conclusions are shown to be less innovative than claimed and are but rediscoveries of earlier proponents. Laikin, Winston and McCullough for instance, describe the main features of "Intensive Short-Term Dynamic Psychotherapy (ISTDP)" as "therapist activity", "Maintenance of focus" and "Early and extensive analysis of the transference". They also stress the aspect of involvement adding, "Analysis of character defences to achieve a high level of cognitive involvement at all times" and "Extensive linkage of the therapist–patient relationship (transference) with other significant relationships in the patient's life". They describe these as the "major innovations which speed and intensify treatment" (1991, p. 84). It is hard to see how they justify the claim to innovation since these aspects have been referred to for decades previously, as has been shown in earlier sections of the book. Working with the transference is referred to by all the key proponents as seen in Davanloo's summary, for example, where he talks of working "actively on the triangle of defense/anxiety/ impulse–feeling and on the triangle of transference/current/past" and of "relentless confronting the patient with his defences" (1992,

p. 70). Another early proponent, Malan, develops this theme with a colleague Osimo "there are really three *triangles of conflict*, one in relation to each of the corners of the *triangle of person*, thus making four triangles in all" (1992, p. 35). They explain that "the triangle of conflict, which refers to one of the cornerstones of psychodynamic theory, namely that neurosis arises from *defences* against *feelings* or *impulses* which are made intolerable by the *anxiety, guilt* or *pain* with which they are associated, and which therefore become unconscious or 'hidden'" (p. 34). These feelings become transferred onto others in the client's life and onto the therapist in the course of therapy, where they can be examined and worked with, as has been seen earlier when the transference was examined. Molnos develops the triangle concept further as has been seen in the last chapter.

Sifneos' list of important "technical" issues adds the "use of anxiety-provoking questions, confrontations, and clarifications" to the features above and also "Education of the patient" (1987, p. 74). This at the time of his writing he thought might be "a unique feature of STAPP which at times has shocked other workers in the field because it is viewed as being so unorthodox" (1987, p. 167).

Yet again this is a claim to innovation that proves to be a rediscovery. Years earlier Wolberg had referred to "Teaching the patient how to employ insights as a corrective force, how to relate symptoms to inner conflict and how to recognize self defeating mechanisms" as "Ingredients of a short-term system" (1965, pp. 141–3).

Some of the later writers make broad generalizations with little foundation. For example McMahon Moughtin declares that "All practitioners in focused, time limited therapy agree that the mid point in the timescale is a watershed for the client, especially the passing of that point" (1997, p. 110). Do they? Where is her evidence for this statement. It has not been drawn out as a consistent view from the literature that I have studied. Indeed my findings indicate that it is the first session that is of paramount importance.

Lack of consistency

The statements of general principles shown above agree only in respect of the need for a focus and for therapist activity. One or another then cite other important aspects within the approach and between them raise 34 points. Certainly some aspects mentioned separately could be grouped under one heading so that the number of points could be reduced, but if we are talking about general principles should we not expect to find more consistency? How can statements of *essential ingredients* embrace such diversity? My findings go beyond some of the "commonly agreed" ingredients of brief therapy and some conflict with the "universal elements" that one or other proponent, old or new, state.

Why such disparity in "common ingredients"?

It seems appropriate to consider possible reasons for this lack of unanimity for "common ingredients" and Sifneos gives us one possibility as to why this might be. He observes that "All short-term dynamic psychotherapies are based on psychoanalytic principles, but the technical issues used by various workers in the field may vary considerably" (1987, p. 74). In the above generalizations both principles and techniques are referred to. Certainly principles require techniques in order to be effective but herein may lie the confusion and the variations in the above descriptions.

Another possible source of the variations is the number of new schools of thought espousing different approaches that have emerged and the particular point each wants to emphasize. As Gustafson observes "... when you make a discovery of your own. You want to generalize your glory ... You propose your own school, like Jung, Adler or Reich, or your own method of brief therapy, like Malan, Mann, Sifneos and so forth" (1986, p. 341). "All were ambitious ... to define a standard technique of their own". In a sense he suggests, these then became "defenders of their own dogma" (p. 44). Malan as we have previously observed is perhaps an exception when he stands down and, with almost evangelical zeal, promotes the approach of Davanloo who came after him. He calls Davanloo's approach "the 20th Century miracle" (1992, p. 18). Malan and Osimo state that Davanloo's method is a technique that makes use of interpretation and systematically "challenges the patient's resistance" (1992, p. 326). As seen from video taped demonstrations they declare that "the effectiveness of this method can be in no doubt; it is of a different order of magnitude from that of methods that rely on interpretation alone; and in time all other methods of psychotherapy are likely to be supplanted by it" (p. 326). Whilst this may be so, the idea that Davanloo's is the last word on the subject is unlikely. As one observes the discoveries and rediscoveries in the different forms of the brief approach it is hard to see how they can be defended as "dogma" one against another. The integrative approach already referred to is more defensible. This is especially so, if the best of new and old discoveries can be fused in the interests of the client. As Levey says "The therapist needs to be versatile, innovative and pragmatic" a sentiment that echoes Wolberg's of many years earlier (1995, p. 142).

I puzzle as to why Wolberg, who is often quoted in works on brief therapy, does not so often figure when more modern writers refer to the key proponents. In my view his exposition of brief therapy of 1965 is excellent. He is a very key proponent and his work is as pertinent in the late 1990s and indeed for the 21st century as it was in the 1960s. There is little reference to Balint either, with his exploration of the importance of the "Focal aim" in the early 1950s and the term "focal therapy" that derived from his work, although Gustafson does commend Balint to us referring to his "intuitive brilliance" with regard to "the specific kind of interaction that the patient needs" (1981, p. 121). Could it be that if a proponent *does not* "become a defender of their own dogma", which Gustafson criticizes, that the work lacks an advocate and therefore fades into the background? (1986, p. 341). No doubt such work will be rediscovered at a later date!

Why does the secret of brief therapy keep getting lost?

I wonder with Gustafson "Why is it that the secret of brief psycho-therapy keeps getting lost?" and I would add "and rediscovered" (1981, p. 83). Perhaps Coltart has one of the answers. She reminds us that no matter how accurate our interpretations might be, insight needs to come from the patient. She observes that often they will tell the analyst a "piece of insight as if it is completely new, and has never been alluded to before, and furthermore is the patient's own discovery. And in a sense it *is* all those things". She goes on to say the "practice of analytic therapy, far more than most professions—and more than any lay-person could believe—requires a real worked through capacity to be humble and self effacing. What matters is that the patient has truly grasped the insight. Not whether one was bright enough to have seen it long since" (1996, p. 59). Perhaps therefore each theorist, like the client, needs to find the answers for themselves.

Another possible answer is that there is not, as yet, a clear enough exposition of the principles involved. This book goes some way towards remedying this in attempting to present my findings in a clear and accessible way. The next step towards this is to examine my overall findings in the context of the research process which begins the next chapter leads to my statement of key principles within a conceptual framework.

CHAPTER NINE

Concluding chapter:
Brief psychodynamic psychotherapy:
A contextual framework and key principles

The previous chapter examined a variety of broad statements, which are to be found in the literature, with regard to the essential ingredients of brief therapy, but there is not a consistent view. This chapter gives a brief overall picture of the process leading to my conclusions and issues arising from these.

In order to try and avoid some of the pitfalls observed with the aforementioned generalizations I need to find a way of articulating my findings in a concise and accessible way. My conclusions also need to be set in the context of the research process and certain limitations of the study clarified. However I do not plan to reiterate the limitations that have already been pointed out in the methodology section such as the limited number of cases in the empirical work or bias in view of these coming from my colleagues clinical practices and my own, but rather draw attention to some more general limitations. These limitations are of a broader nature and wider application but are none the less relevant. I point to some of the strengths of the process also. Then follows a final formulation of my findings. This takes into account the whole process of the investigation, from the empirical work undertaken and the work of the key early proponents, to setting these findings against the views of the newer proponents and more recent revisions of the pioneers. Following this concise and clear exposition of the key principles and shortening factors in brief therapy, which answered my initial questions, a new insight as to this shortening process unexpectedly emerged. I share with the reader some reflections on the process that led to the final conjecture.

Firstly however a brief resumé of the research context and some reflections on it. In this study I set out to answer the questions: **"What is brief psychodynamic therapy and what makes it brief?"** I set the parameters within which I would explore and I defined my terms. The project was to be based on empirical work with clinical cases and a small sample of these were chosen and put under the microscope. These, as outlined in my methodology, were to be studied first before attending to the past and present literature.

One of the reasons for embarking on the study was my inability to explain what brief therapy is—a question which I was so often asked. So much was *implicitly* understood, I knew I practised it and it seemed to help the clients. I needed to be able to make *explicit* those features that were involved and that I had assimilated through training and experience, and taken for granted within the clinical practice. At the end of several years of research and detailed analysis of cases and the literature I am now in a better position to articulate an answer to the above questions.

As I near the conclusion of the book and am looking at the process of the analysis I wish to be quite explicit about what I am going to call some overarching considerations.

In this study I have undertaken a detailed analysis of brief psychodynamic therapy to contribute to the body of knowledge available and hopefully to make this approach more accessible. Part of that process is to make the *implicit, explicit*. Here I want to make explicit that my conclusions need to be viewed against a backcloth of understanding so well expressed by Guntrip: "I cannot think of psychotherapy as a technique but only as the provision of the possibility of a genuine, reliable, understanding, and respecting, caring personal relationship in which a human being whose true self has been crushed ... can begin at last to feel his own true feelings, and think his own spontaneous thoughts, and find himself to be real" (1991, p. 182). .... "psychotherapy is simply the application of the fundamental importance of personal relationships, in the sense of using good relationships to undo the harm done by bad ones, follows automatically" (p. 194).

It is the early writers, Wolberg, Balint and Malan, who lay the greatest stress on the *relationship*. Strupp observes that "the quality of patient–therapist interaction represents the fulcrum upon which therapeutic progress turns" (1986, p. 229).

Regardless of our methodological expertise or theoretical constructs Feltham adds rightly I think, that the therapist should "always be concerned with the overarching ethical question of how best to relieve suffering" (1997, p. 59).

However, against this backcloth my findings show that there are definite principles that need to be applied in the brief work.

Limitations/strengths

Before I can move to a final summary there is a need to look at some limiting and qualifying factors with regard to this research and also to any research within a similar area.

Reflexivity is one aspect of the exploration that I highlight as a strength. It is this participant–observer, subjective–objective stance that has enabled some of the subsidiary themes to surface for analysis and which also informs my conclusions as I strive to make the *implicit*, *explicit*. It is perhaps this aspect linked with the immersion process that has enabled me to provide a new perspective on the subject. Clearly I approached the study from a particular stance and in the early chapters I came "clean" about this as expected within the methodology I chose (1995, p. 280). Polanyi sees this as an advantage, he states "that into every act of knowing there enters a passionate contribution of the person knowing what is being known, and that this coefficient is no mere imperfection but a vital component of his knowledge" (1974, p. viii). There may be other interpretations of my case material by other therapists or researchers, but that possibility does not invalidate my particular perspective and conclusions that have the weight of a systematic research process to back them. They are as Marshall would describe them "my translation, what I have found and interpreted from the data" (1981, p. 399). Polanyi says that such "personal participation of the knower in all acts of understanding ... does not make our understanding subjective ... Such knowing is indeed objective in the sense of establishing contact with a hidden reality" (1974, p. vii).

Another strength is the small number of cases. This is despite the fact that the number has been referred to earlier as a limitation. Here I draw attention to the limited number as a strength since, in line with my stated methodology, by "immersing" myself in these 11 cases I have been able to do so "thoroughly". This process would not have been possible with a larger sample in the given time.

No universal method

As I come near to stating my particular perspective one of the limitations of the research must be acknowledged that Gustafson puts very well: "I say there is no universal method of brief psychotherapy. Every observing position has its advantages, its successes and its dangers. Every position has a periphery where important phenomena will occur and be missed, because of the centre of interest of that position" (1986, p. 7).

This idea was amply illustrated at a gathering I attended some years ago where Marteau spoke of a group seminar where a group of his students presented him with the following scenario for interpretation. He recalled that:

> In the middle of the circle was a somewhat large chair with a woman's jacket across the top of it. There was a tubular chair next door to it and in front of these was a wastepaper basket with a book on top, closed, there was an umbrella half opened, a woman's handbag and there was one woman's shoe more or less forming a circle around the bucket with the book on top and I sat down and one member of the group said: "*Analyse that then.*" and I said: "*Would you like a Freudian analysis, a Jungian analysis, a Gestalt or a Behavioural?*"

Marteau proceeded to interpret the scene in the terms and language of each theoretical construction. He pointed out that the exercise demonstrated that theoretical constructions can be useful but were not necessarily talking truth or absolutes but each one might have a validity for a particular individual.

The considerations that I have drawn attention to above, resulting from my reflections on the research process, are in parallel with the views expressed by Clarkson who encapsulates them in the term after "schoolism". This refers "to a situation in psychotherapy where "schools" or "orientations" or "approaches" will be acknowledged as less important than the therapeutic relationship itself" (1998, p. 15).

Jung too warns of the danger of fitting people into frameworks rather than adapting frameworks to people: "I must confess that experience has taught me to keep away from the therapeutic 'method' as much as from diagnoses. The enormous variation among individuals and their neurosis set before me the ideal of approaching each case with a minimum of prior assumptions. The ideal would naturally be to have no assumptions at all" (1993, p. 329).

Thus, no matter how clearly conclusions can be drawn from a carefully worked out study such as this, the results are influenced by the perspective of the researcher and should not be seen as either the last word nor as something to be applied with a rigidity that overlooks the individual need.

Magic

Although I have attempted a rigorous study within the methodology outlined earlier it must be acknowledged that in this study as in any examination of therapy there is an aspect that simply defies analysis. I will refer to this aspect as "magic" and it is a limitation of any study in this field. In my approach to this study reflexivity is an important element and it is with reference to the more intangible aspects that defy analysis that reflexivity becomes of greater importance and could be considered a strength. Here metaphors and analogies are perhaps the only way of outlining the desired concepts. Such aspects lie in what Polanyi would term the "ineffable domain" of personal knowledge "where the tacit predominates to the extent that articulation is virtually impossible" (1974, p. 87).

This mystery or magic element is a limiting factor in the academic context as de Shazer admirably expresses it: "Well, no matter how scientifically rigorous and philosophically elegant any description of brief therapy is, there is still magic" (1990, p. 90).

It is with these aforementioned qualifying statements in mind that I provide a final summary of my analysis of key principles.

Reflections leading to the final statement

This section returns to the task of providing a clear and concise statement as to what constitutes brief therapy. A summary that not only complies with my stated aim that I should be able to articulate an answer to the initial questions but also, a statement could go beyond the academic environment and be of service to the community it serves. It might for example be a useful teaching tool for those promoting the brief approach and in this way, in line with Lincoln's view of the "communitarian" aspect of research, can "link itself" with "social action" recognizing that "research is first and foremost a community project, not a project of the academic discipline alone (or even primarily)" (1995, p. 282).

It's clarity, accessibility and brevity may well also contribute to the "secret" of brief therapy remaining in the public domain. It can then serve as a starting point for further research and development.

To avoid the confusion noted in the generalizations studied earlier, for example where some made no distinction between techniques and principles, I have considered carefully the best way of describing my findings. Some of the confusion in the previous descriptions may have contributed to the "secret of brief therapy" so often being lost. To achieve clarity I have tried to be very explicit about the *status* of each aspect of the findings, rather than simply referring to them generically as key principles. This exercise has brought the essential elements of the approach clearly into focus, not all of these can be designated **"principles"**. Some, on examination, are **"prerequisites"** that need to be in place for the work to be effective, others are **"hoped for consequences"** either within or subsequent to the therapy. Making these distinctions has enabled me to provide a new understanding of brief therapy within this concise and accessible summary of my findings.

Since I am now able to formulate a clear description of brief therapy I have also achieved a personal aim in embarking on this study. That is, that I would be able to articulate an answer to the questions I have so often been asked and which the research sought to respond to:

"What is brief therapy? and: What makes it brief?"

Brief psychodynamic psychotherapy: a conceptual framework

THE CONTRACT

The contract, which has been shown to be of importance in this approach, is being placed at the start of this *conceptual* framework to set the *context* for what follows. The contract described here is that of a therapeutic alliance within a psychodynamic framework for a brief period of time.

Pre-requisites for best results

EXPERIENCE REQUIRED OF THE THERAPIST

The experience seen to be required of the therapist for this approach relates especially to *the limited time* available for the therapeutic contract, which means that the therapist needs to be rather *precise with the interventions made*. This *requires skill*, which assumes training and practice to acquire and *inspire confidence*.

MOTIVATION ON THE PART OF THE CLIENT

Client *motivation* has been shown to be an important facet of the brief approach. This includes both the wish *to understand* themselves and *the desire to change*. I see motivation as a *prerequisite for brief therapy*. This highlights the importance of the client *choosing* to enter into therapy.

Key principles of brief psychodynamic psychotherapy

1. UNDERSTANDING OF PSYCHODYNAMIC PRINCIPLES

As seen above, the contextual framework for the brief therapy, which is under scrutiny, is psychodynamic and therefore an understanding of psychodynamic principles such as transference, resistance and transference repetitions is seen to be essential. However, whilst highlighting the psychodynamic roots, this approach goes beyond its roots and shows different ways of dealing with some of the psychoanalytic concepts, such as the use of a teaching approach to circumvent the resistance. It also includes a flexible and integrated use of therapeutic skills and assumptions adopted from other traditions to shorten the process.

2. IMPORTANCE OF THE FIRST SESSION

The first session is of paramount importance in the *early appropriate application of all the principles and appropriate techniques*. It is the *early use* of appropriate techniques that contributes to the shortening process. The use of challenge/confrontation, clarification, transference and teaching are shown to be particularly useful in brief therapy. A great deal needs to happen from the first moments of the first encounter and the findings bring to light many interesting aspects.

The first session in brief therapy emerges from the research to be of far greater *all embracing significance* than the early writers gave it. The more recent literature supports this too with some emphasis also on single session therapies. Every one of the research cases showed the first session to be significant. The *first session sets the scene* in terms of agreeing the contract for example with regard to focus, realistic goals, time scale and cost; *the temperature* in terms both of the rapid formation of the therapeutic alliance and the active involvement of both client and therapist with its resulting intensity; and the *pace* in that it "begins the therapy process". The therapist being in tune and sensitive to the client's pain and communicating this to the client in the first session was seen to be especially relevant in helping the therapy to proceed rapidly. The first session is a time to assess the client's suitability but my research emphasizes that the first session is especially the *testing ground for the client*. That is the client tests *the therapy situation* and *the therapist's strength and skill in picking up and "running" with their clues*.

Table VII on page 192 summarizes some of the important aspects which are present in the first session and which deserve a prominent place in the thinking about what short-term therapy is and what shortens it.

3. THERAPY AS SHORT AS CLIENT NEED ALLOWS

Short-term or *brief therapy* here refers to a therapy that is to be *as short as possible*. In the approach studied the terms allows for the therapy *time scale to be negotiated for each individual* providing for a flexible approach *according to need*. The anticipated median is four–six sessions. The *"dynamics of the deadline"* is seen to be a way of concentrating the mind and energy and contributing to the shortening effect. The spacing of sessions is flexible and negotiated with the client.

The empirical study relates to a small number of cases where the *median was four–six sessions* and the average number of sessions was 6.6. The brevity of the empirical examples suggests that within the clinical work there exists clues as to the shortening of therapy. This concept of short-term differs from the key proponents who expect to have considerably more sessions many from 15–25 sessions. There is no consensus as to the number of sessions in the literature and in view of this terms such as "time sensitive" or "cost–effective" have been suggested to describe short-term therapy. My own view is that the terms "brief" or "short-term" are sufficiently descriptive for this treatment of choice.

4. EARLY ESTABLISHMENT OF THE THERAPEUTIC ALLIANCE

The *therapeutic alliance* is both a *form of contract and a form of relationship*. As for any form of therapy it is the relationship between the therapist and client that enables and gives power to the therapeutic process. Within the brief approach it is the *rapidity with which the therapeutic alliance is established* that is of significance. The therapeutic alliance also has a key place in coming to an agreement as to the focal area to be explored. The client's motivation will influence this. A teaching process is often used to help motivate the client to undertake sometimes painful work and to agree to the therapeutic contract. Therapist sensitivity to the client's pain and generally being in tune with the client, contributes both to finding the focal area and in forming the therapeutic alliance.

5. THERAPIST ATTITUDE

The therapist's attitude needs to be one that shows that *every minute counts*. The therapist's *expectation that change* can occur and that the *therapy can be completed in a short time*, possibly in only one session, more usually between four and six sessions, conveys a confidence that inspires hope. This attitude should be seen as a permeating feature in this approach. Its existence makes a fast outcome more likely!

6. TEACHING

This analysis has shown *teaching* to be of great significance in the brief therapy described. It is one of the permeating features that I have referred to since it has its influence on all the other principles and holds a key place in the all important first session. It can be used as a way of *circumventing resistance*. Teaching is the key to *making the therapist redundant* and in enhancing the client's autonomy for example by teaching the client about their own emotions and patterns of behaviour and how to observe and find ways of changing them.

7. ENABLING CLIENTS TO BECOME THEIR OWN THERAPISTS

The therapist enables the client to become their own therapist and gives control to the client. The teaching element supports this as does the use of the client's "at home work" and the enlisting of the client's agreement about focus and time limit in the therapy contract. The *therapist's role is to walk alongside the client in their journey to freedom* using skills and therapeutic knowledge flexibly in this enabling process. It is *the role of a facilitator* and requires a certain "humility" on the part of the therapist and a willingness to "let go" of the client.

8. ACTIVITY

Activity is seen to be an inherent part of brief work and is a factor in the shortening process. As Wolberg puts it "Anathema to short-term therapy is passivity in the therapist" (1965, p. 135). *Activity* however, is *not just for the therapist* but is *also expected of the client*. The client is expected to take an active part in the therapy process, for example undertaking "homework tasks" better described as "at home work" or "own work" to move away from schoolroom connotations. I often say to clients *"This is your trip. I'll be alongside you but you have to do the work."* In being alongside the client the therapist needs sensitivity and needs to be in tune with the client in order to be able to utilize the appropriate skills to move the client on. The activity contributes to the intensity of the process.

9. FOCUS

The focus occupies an intrinsic place in the brief approach. Its establishment is contingent upon a good therapeutic alliance having been formed. There were differing views however as to what constitutes a suitable focus. The empirical work shows that the focus can be much wider than was thought by the earlier, rather restrictive view as to what was appropriate for brief work. There were also varying opinions as to how the focus was to be found and whether this initiated more from the client or therapist or both. The idea of therapy and finding the focus being a *joint enterprise* is one that I support and the empirical work shows. The possibility of *renegotiating the focus* and the importance of finding the "**strategic focus**" is brought to light. The importance of "*circumscribing*" the focus, to use the term coined by Sifneos, is emphasized by all.

10. FLEXIBILITY AND FUSION

The brief therapist uses *a number of different techniques as* and when they are *appropriate*. This *requires a certain flexibility* on the part of the therapist, who needs to be more concerned with *keeping in tune with the client*, than in remaining loyal to any one school of therapy. Flexibility is required of the therapist in *embracing important concepts and therapeutic tools from traditions other than the psychoanalytic to inform and speed the process*.

Flexibility is also required in terms of *renegotiating the contract vis-à-vis both time and focus*.

Wolberg aptly uses the word "*fusion*" to describe how the different techniques might be integrated and suggests that this requires an "experienced therapist schooled in the widest varieties of techniques" (1965, p. 128). I too, consider that flexibility takes for granted the experience and substantial training needed. This is required in order for the therapist to work with the *range of skills and to creatively adapt these to the needs of each client*.

In his recommendations to use a variety of techniques Wolberg might be considered to be pioneering and perhaps prophetic when one looks at the recent debate about integration or eclecticism. This is summed up neatly by Norcross and Grencavage who observe that therapists are integrating "everything". They are "mixing and mingling" technique, theories and formats from every theory ever promulgated" (1989, p. 106). In this there is a return to the concept of rediscovery discussed in the history of brief therapy!

This flexibility is seen as a key *factor in shortening therapy*.

11. INCISIVENESS

Incisiveness needs to be stressed as *an intrinsic and essential aspect of working in the brief method*. Incisiveness with the use of appropriate interventions is something acquired with experience. *Incisiveness is required in challenging, in focusing, in avoiding non-essentials* and it enhances other aspects of the approach *to accelerate the process*.

Principle of principles and key permeating feature

12. THE SENSITIVITY OF THE THERAPIST IN ORDER TO BE IN TUNE WITH THE CLIENT

The most important of the facets that I have referred to as "permeating features" is sensitivity. In order to achieve the effective operation of the key principles sensitivity is required to enable the therapist to be *in tune with the client* or as it has been put in the earlier analysis more colloquially "sticking like glue" to where the client "is". This involves being attentive to every nuance of the client spoken and unspoken and every aspect of what is happening within the therapy. Sensitivity is not unique to brief therapy but, within this approach, it is seen as an *accelerating factor enhancing all* of the above principles. This attentive awareness needs to be present from the very first moments of the therapeutic encounter and enables the rapid establishment of the therapeutic alliance, the intensity of the experiences referred to above and the possibility of appropriate incisive interventions.

Hoped for consequences within sessions

HOPE

Hope is inspired by a number of the above principles. The expectation of change in a short time, the confidence of the therapist stemming usually from experience and training, the feeling of being understood, because of the careful attunement of the therapist and the getting on with it from the first moment all contribute to this. This leads the clients to becoming actively involved in the process.

INVOLVEMENT

Involvement is seen to be a very important aspect of brief therapy. Although it could almost be subsumed under the heading therapeutic alliance I have separated it out to draw attention to it. Like "mystery" and "intensity" it is recognized by the clients and therapists but hard to analyse. It belongs to the realm of personal knowledge Polanyi refers to as "ineffable" (1974, p. 87). This involvement of both client and therapist speeds the process as Goulding says: "Working quickly means being involved every minute of the therapy hour" (1990, p. 317). It is described by Malan as a *"special variety of ... involvement"* (1963, p. 275).

It leads to an intensity within the therapy.

INTENSITY

Intensity is often referred to in the analysis. As a participant observer in some of the clinical work I am able to comment from an inside perspective. The case commentaries and case examples can give the reader a more objective, outside view. It is also evident however as I analysed the content of the cases of colleagues and appears in the literature also. It is not an easy aspect to quantify and relates to some degree to the mystery element discussed earlier. This applies both to the therapeutic relationship and to the process of therapy. It is an aspect of the process that *is recognized by clients and therapists*. It is enhanced by the *limited number of sessions* for the encounter. This makes for a more *compressed process*. The *circumscribed focal area* that helps to concentrate the minds of both therapists and clients also has its impact on the intensity. The *rapid establishment of the therapeutic alliance* and the *immediate and active start of the therapy* even from the first moments of the first session all contribute to this *particularly intense form of therapy*. Whilst I suspect it is necessary for all successful therapy, I believe that in brief therapy it is present in a more concentrated way and from the first moments of the first session. That quality is to do with the intensity of the encounter, where two individuals meet and which is enabling of change. I have referred to the quality of such a "meeting" earlier.

MAGIC

Both involvement and the intensity it leads to seem to open the way for the possibility of a certain *"magic"* in the process of therapy such as described by BN, one of the independent assessors, when looking at Case J. This is not unique to brief therapy, as de Shazer says: "It is magic. I do not know how clients do it. Well, all therapy involves some sort of magic" (1990, p. 90). Yalom too, as he reflects on what makes up successful therapy, finds that there always seems to be something more required that cannot be explained or taught. The reader may recall his analogy about the cooking class referred to in an earlier section, it is the "surreptitious throw-ins" that makes the difference ..."these elusive, 'off the record' extras" (1980, pp. 3–4).

Feltham refers to the concept of "miracle": "we do well to allow for them as an ever-present possibility" (1997, p. 73).

Groves touches on this *mystery element* too as he reflects on the work of Winnicott who frequently makes comments such as *"I knew what I must say."* Groves refers to this as "an uncanny moment of pure intuition, one representing the summit of the therapist's art" (1992, p. 55). These concepts relate also to the mystery of the relationship referred to earlier.

Enid Balint, Michael Balint's wife and part of Balint's research team in the Focal Therapy Workshops of the 1950s completed some of Balint's work from his notes. She raises an interesting question about how a focus is chosen and acknowledges that there may be more than one focus. She alludes to the "possibility of what we call 'ten minute psychotherapy' " which demands a "very high intensity of interaction between patient and doctor" which helps the doctor "to 'tune in' to the patient". When this is sufficiently accurate there is a " *'flash' of understanding* which usually unites patient and doctor and is felt by both ... 'the meeting of minds' ... 'the moment of truth'." (Balint et al., 1972, pp. 151–2). She goes on to point out the research teams experience to show that "in focal therapy this experience must be expressed by the therapist ... translating the flash experience into concise words". This must be achieved in a way that is in tune with and meaningful to the patient and not in "well-worn psychoanalytic phrases" (p. 152). She struggles for words in describing this and is aware of another way in which the research team reached a chosen focus since Malan describes it as "a crystallization of a focus. This means not a flash but a gradual emergence in the give and take between patient and therapist" (p. 153). The flash experience referred to above *seems linked to the mystery or magic element referred to here.*

Hoped for consequences as a result of therapy

1. CLIENT IS CAPABLE OF BEING OWN THERAPIST

It is hoped that the client will as a result of the therapy have *learned sufficient* about themselves, their patterns of behaviour and some techniques in dealing with maladaptive aspects of these to be able to *continue applying these skills* subsequent to the therapy contract. For many, what they have learned will be sufficient and they may never return to therapy, while others, the findings suggest, may decide to check in at important times in their lives for a further contract and another period of personal learning.

2. CLIENT IS FREE FROM PAST TO COPE WITH PRESENT

It is hoped that the *past emotional encumbrances* that have been causing the clients pain, difficulty or confusion and preventing them from successfully dealing with their present day lives *will be "unhooked"* as a result of the brief therapy contract. Marteau observes that "releasing the client from the past so that he is free to face the present is the final goal" within the therapy (1986, p. 42).

A new slant

In looking for the key principles of brief therapy and in examining what shortens it I have "rediscovered" many elements that are prevalent in the history of brief therapy. Some aspects such as activity, focus, flexibility and therapeutic alliance reinforce and extend the earlier discoveries.

I have also uncovered key elements that are not so much a new revelation but a further and deeper analysis of elements that only one or two of even the later writers have emphasized. I have, I believe, also brought to light some new aspects. The brevity in being chosen, individually agreed and well below the number of sesssons often cited by the early proponents and by many of my contemporaries.

The pervading influence of the teaching element is a new perspective as is the discovery that the first session is of overriding importance. These depend heavily on the therapist's attitude and expectations.

The term "permeating features" relates to facets of brief therapy, that were studied initially under the heading "subsidiary themes" and were elicited primarily from the clinical research work. They emerge as **important features which do not so much stand alone as permeate the fabric of the sessions in the clinical work**. The clinical work indicates that these aspects merit more significance than is allotted by the key proponents. It is not so much that these are new or different features within the brief approach, or indeed one could argue within therapy as a whole, as that highlighting their importance brings a new dimension of short-term work into the foreground. I suggest that it is the *early application of an appropriate combination* of these aspects, in addition to the principles emerging from the key themes, *that is a contributing factor in the shortening of therapy*.

My findings also highlight *the need to hold all of the key facets in mind simultaneously*.

This reformulation of the findings into the above Conceptual Framework contributes both new insights and a new perspective to the existing body of knowledge and concludes my analysis—almost.

Further reflections

Something more

As I reflected on this final formulation of my conclusions I *sensed* that there was something more to be unravelled. Was it in the comparison with longer-term work? It has not been the task of this book to do a comparative study with longer-term work and others have addressed this. Sifneos for example points to focus as "taboo in psychoanalysis" (1987, p. 195) and Wolberg highlights activity and the time limit as against a passivity and sense of timelessness that would "let the patient pick his way through the lush jungles of his psyche" (1965, p. 135). In contrast to the fusion of skills advocated above Wolberg observes that "psychoanalysts are particularly fearful of therapeutic contaminants" and then there's the joint and interactive nature of the therapeutic alliance versus the non involvement of the analyst. Sifneos also observes that for the "therapist to show his interest" is again "(taboo in psychoanalysis)" (1987, p. 138). Wolberg finds this to be "one of the most difficult things to teach a student aspiring to become a short-term therapist ..." that ... "involvement of oneself as a real person, and open expressions of ... encouragement are permissible" (1965, p. 135).

This kind of comparison was not the answer, I still *felt* that there was something more to uncover. Polanyi believes that we should "acknowledge our capacity both to sense the accessibility of a hidden inference from given premises, and to invent transformations of the premises which increase the accessibility of the hidden inference" (1974, p. 129). I therefore returned to the conclusions above, now in the satisfying clear form that the conceptual framework provides, in search of what the material itself could tell me and I began to see some hints of an answer. This is in keeping with the "immersion process" inherent in my research methodology and is again in tune with Polanyi who observes's that "we should look at the known data, but not in themselves, rather as clues to the unknown; as pointers to it and parts of it" (1974, pp. 127–8).

What makes the difference?

In looking at the data I was wondering what it is about these key principles that affects the length? Is there some critical factor that makes the difference?

Earlier writers have pinpointed client motivation in this regard, a concept addressed particularly by Sifneos and this includes the idea of commitment to the process, but as seen above I have defined this as a *precondition* for embarking on short-term therapy. So the answer did not lie here. The findings show that some proponents stress the place of focus in the approach and others again, point to activity.

Is there something more that my findings can suggest in this regard? All the factors above are important and, in being inherent in the brief approach, all clearly contribute to the shortening effect. I have stressed particularly the need to hold all in mind simultaneously, if indeed such a task is humanly possible, and I have placed emphasis on some facets.

The clarity provided by looking at the status of each important facet of brief therapy as shown in the conceptual framework began to give me a clue in this regard. Could it be what these features do to the client?

Here I return again to the ideas of Polanyi who seems to describe the process of reflection that occurred here. He refers to "our premonition of the solutions's proximity" and that the "last stage of the solution may therefore be frequently achieved in a self-accelerating manner and the final discovery may be upon us in a flash" (1974, p. 129).

So what do these key features, seen to be inherent in the brief approach, do to the client? Returning to the principles, the "dynamics of the deadline" puts pressure on the client to *dive in* and to get on with it, there is *involvement* of the client in jointly *choosing the focus* and in actively doing their *"own work"* on themselves outside of the therapy sessions. The active techniques that may be employed perhaps drawn from gestalt or psychosynthesis or art all *actively involve* the client.

Is it that the *critical factor* is the client's personal *involvement* and that the key principles above contribute to this? As van Kaam puts it "to be *there* means that I gather together all my thoughts, feelings and memories. I am wholly with what I am doing, creating, perceiving" (1970, p. 14). He goes on to point out that "no involvement is possible without detachment: no detachment is meaningful without a deepening of involvement" (p. 70). So is it possible that, as the client becomes involved in the process of self discovery, their detachment from what has been becomes easier and this is a self perpetuating process enhanced by the facets of brief therapy referred to above. Van Kaam says "one way of looking at the necessity of detachment and new involvement ... is to reflect on my potentiality as a human person. Human potentiality is not something inert; rather it is a dynamic tendency towards self actualization which permeates my life" (p. 92).

This leads me to a theory or as Morse would call it, a "conjecture" for consideration (1992, p. 260).

MY CONJECTURE

My conjecture is that *client involvement* is *central to the shortening process*.

For me there was a sense of rightness about this conclusion and I again call upon Polanyi's thought in support of this nebulous aspect of reflexivity: "Therefore, as it emerges in response to our search for something we believe to be there, discovery, or supposed discovery, will always come to us with the conviction of its being true. It arrives accredited in advance by the heuristic craving which evoked it" (1974, p. 130).

However Polanyi goes on the "most daring feats of originality are still subject to this law; they must be performed on the assumption that they originate nothing, but merely reveal what is there. And their triumph confirms this assumption, for what has been found bears the mark of reality in being pregnant with yet unforeseeable implications ... Such a flash of triumph usually offers no final solution, but only the envisagement of a solution which has yet to be tested" (1974, p. 130).

The "testing" of this conjecture is for others, who may find both the final formulation of my findings, in the conceptual framework above and this conjecture a useful starting point.

Selected reviews, substantive early works and status of authors

MALAN, David (1963) (1976)
> FRC Psych. formerly Consultant Psychiatrist, Tavistock Clinic (1992, p. iii).

WOLBERG, Lewis (1965) (1980)
> Clinical Professor of Psychiatry. New York University School of Medicine. Founder and Emeritus Dean, Postgraduate Center for Mental Health, New York (1980, p. i).

MARMOR, Judd (1980)
> Franz Alexander Professor of Psychiatry, University of Southern California School of Medicine, Los Angeles, California (1979, p. 149).

ROGAWSKI, Alexander (1982)
> Clinical Professor, Department of Psychiatry and Biobehavioural Science, School of Medicine, University of California at Los Angeles; Professor of Psychiatry (Emeritus), School of Medicine, University of Southern California, Los Angeles, California (1982, p. 331).

KOVACS, Arthur (1982)

Ph.D ... California School of Professional Psychology, Los Angeles (1982, p. 142).

BUDMAN, Simon (1983)

Director of Mental Health Research at the Harvard Community Mental Health Plan and a faculty member in the department of Psychiatry at the Harvard Medical School. Boston Massachusetts (1983, p. 939).

STONE, Jennifer (1983)

Research Assistant at the Harvard Community Mental Health Plan and a doctoral candidate in clinical psychology at Boston University (1983, p. 939).

BAUER, Gregory (1984)

Distinguished Psychologist, University of Winsconsin—Stevens Point Counselling Center (1995, p. ii).

KOBOS, Joseph (1984)

Director of the Counselling Service, Office of Student Services, and Professor, Department of Psychiatry, University of Texas Health Centre at San Antonio (1995, p. ii).

SIFNEOS, Peter (1984)

Professor of Psychiatry, Harvard Medical School; Associate Director, Psychiatry Department, Beth Israel Hospital, MA (1984, p. 472).

MIGONE, Paolo (1985)

Presented a paper "at the meeting of the Society of Medical Psychoanalysts, New York, November 10, 1982" (1985, p. 615).

REICH, James (1986)

Assistant Professor of Psychiatry, University of Iowa College of Medicine (1986, p. 62).

NEENAN, P (1986)

Research Assistant, University of Iowa College of Medicine, Dept of Psychiatry (1986, p. 62).

BIBLIOGRAPHY

Alexander, F. (1965). Psychoanalytic contributions to short-term psychotherapy. In: L. Wolberg (Ed.), *Short-Term Psychotherapy*. New York: Grune and Stratton.

Alexander, F., Selesnick, S. (1967). *The History of Psychiatry: An Evaluation of Psychiatric Thought and Practice from Pre-historic Times to the Present*. Woking: George Allen and Unwin.

Alexander, F., Eisenstein, S., & Grotjahn, M. (Eds.) (1966). *Psychoanalytic Pioneers*. New York: Basic Books.

Alpert, M. (1992). Accelerated empathic therapy: a new short-term dynamic psychotherapy. *International Journal of Short-term Psychotherapy*, 7: 133–156.

Anon Counsellor London F.E. College. (1991). True story. *Association of Student Counselling (ASC) Newsletter*, 2: 11.

Assagioli, R. (1985). *The Act of Will, A Guide to Self Actualisation and Self Realisation*. Kent: Whitstable Litho.

Austad, C. (1995). Psychotherapy in a staff-model HMO: providing and assuring quality care in the future. In: M. Hoyt (Ed.), *Brief Therapy and Managed Care, Readings for Contemporary Practice*. San Francisco: Jossey-Bass Publishers.

Balint, M., Ornstein, P., & Balint, E. (1972). *Focal Psychotherapy—An Example of Applied Psychoanalysis*. London: Tavistock Publications.

Barber, J. (1994). Efficacy of short-term dynamic psychotherapy, past, present, and future. *Journal of Psychotherapy Practice and Research*, 3(2): 108–121.

Bauer, G., & Kobos, J. (1984). Short-term psychodynamic psychotherapy, reflections on the past and current practice. *Psychotherapy*, 21(2): 153–169.

Bauer, G., & Mills, J. (1989). Use of transference in short-term dynamic psychotherapy. *Psychotherapy*, 26(3): 338–343.

Bauer, G., & Kobos, J. (1995). *Brief Therapy: Short-term Psychodynamic Intervention*. Northvale, New Jersey: Jason Aronson.

Benjamin, L. S. (1991). Brief SASB (Structural Analysis of Social Behaviour) directed reconstructive learning therapy. In: P. Crits-Christoph & J. Barber (Eds), *Handbook of Short-Term Dynamic Psychotherapy*. USA: Basic Books.

Bennett, M. (1984). Brief psychotherapy and adult development. *Psychotherapy*, 21(2): 171–177.

Binder, J., & Strupp, H. (1991). The Vanderbilt approach to time limited dynamic psychotherapy. In: P. Crits-Christoph & J. Barber (Eds), *Handbook of Short-Term Dynamic Psychotherapy*. USA: Basic Books.

Bittle, C. (1950). *The Science of Correct Thinking*. Milwaukee: The Bruce Publishing Company.

Bond, T. (1994). *Standards and Ethics for Counselling in Action*. London: Sage Publications.

Brodaty, H. (1983). Techniques of brief psychotherapy. *Australian and New Zealand Journal of Psychiatry*, 17: 109–115.

Bromley, D. B. (1986). *The Case Study Method in Psychology and Related Disciplines*. Chichester: John Wiley and Sons.

Buber, M. (1984). *I and Thou* (Translated by Ronald S. Smith). Edinburgh: T & T Clark.

Budman, S. (Ed.) (1981). *Forms of Brief Therapy*. New York: The Guilford Press.

Budman, S., & Gurman, A. (1983). The practice of brief psychotherapy. *Professional Psychology*, 14: 277–292.

Budman, S., & Stone, J. (1983). Advances in brief psychotherapy—a review of recent literature. *Hospital and Community Psychiatry*, 34(10): 939–946.

Budman, S., Friedman, S., & Hoyt, M. (1992). Last words on first sessions. In: S. Budman, M. Hoyt & S. Friedman (Eds), *The First Session in Brief Therapy. New York: The Guilford Press*.

Budman, S., Hoyt, M., & Friedman, S. (Eds.) (1992). *The First Session in Brief Therapy*. New York: The Guilford Press.

Butler, S., Strupp, H., & Binder, J. (1992). Time limited dynamic psychotherapy. In: S. Budman, M. Hoyt & S. Friedman (Eds), *The First Session in Brief Therapy*. New York: The Guilford Press.

Cade, B., & Hudson O'Hanlon, W. (1993). *A Brief Guide to Brief Therapy*. New York: W. W. Norton & Co.

Calloway, H. (1981). Women's perspectives: research as revision. In: P. Reason & J. Rowan (Eds), *Human Inquiry—A Source Book of New Paradigm Research*. Chichester: John Wiley & Sons.

Campbell, A. (Ed.) (1987). *A Dictionary of Pastoral Care*. Oxford: SPCK.

Casement, P. (1985). *On Learning from the Patient*. London: Tavistock.

Clarkson, P. (1998). Beyond 'Schoolism'. The implications of psychotherapy outcome research for counselling and psychotherapy trainees. *Counsellor and Psychotherapist Dialogue*, 1(2): 13–19.

Coltart, N. (1996). *The Baby and the Bath Water*. London: Karnac Books.

Crits-Christoph, P., & Barber, J. (Eds.) (1991). *Handbook of Short-term Dynamic Psychotherapy*. USA: Basic Books.

Crits-Christoph, P., Barber, J., & Kurcias, J. (1991). Introduction and historical background. In: P. Crits-Christoph & J. Barber (Eds), *Handbook of Short-Term Dynamic Psychotherapy*. USA: Basic Books.

Cummings, N. (1990). Brief intermittent psychotherapy throughout the life cycle. In: J. Zeig & S. Gilligan (Eds), *Brief Therapy, Myths, Methods and Metaphors*. New York: Brunner/Mazel.

Dasberg, H., & Winokur, M. (1984). Teaching and learning short-term dynamic psychotherapy: parallel processes. *Psychotherapy*, 21(2): 184–188.

Davanloo, H. (1980). A method of short-term dynamic psychotherapy. In: H. Davanloo (Ed.), *Short-Term Dynamic Psychotherapy*. Northvale, New Jersey: Jason Aronson.

Davanloo, H. (Ed.) (1992, 1980). *Short-Term Dynamic Psychotherapy*. Northvale, New Jersey: Jason Aronson.

Demos, V., & Prout, M. (1993). A comparison of seven approaches to brief psychotherapy. *International Journal of Short-Term Psychotherapy*, 8(1): 3–22.

De Shazer, S. (1990). What is it about brief therapy that works? In: J. Zeig & S. Gilligan (Eds), *Brief Therapy, Myths, Methods and Metaphors*. New York: Brunner/Mazel.

Dey, I. (1993). *Qualitative Data Analysis—A User-friendly Guide for Social Scientists*. London: Routledge.

Dryden, W. (Ed.) (1994). *Individual Therapy—a Handbook*. Milton Keynes: The Open University Press.

Dryden, W., & Feltham, C. (1992). *Brief Counselling—A Practical Guide for Beginning Practitioners*. Milton Keynes: Open University Press.

EAPA (Employee Assistance Professionals Association). (1995). EAPA Britannic Chapter, *Employee Assistance Programmes in the UK Information Sheet*, April 1995 E/1060.

Egan, G. (1998). *The Skilled Helper—a Problem Management Approach to Helping*. USA: Brooks/Cole Publishing Co.

Eisenstein, S. (1992). *The Contributions of Franz Alexander in Short-term Dynamic Psychotherapy*, H. Davanloo (Ed.). Northvale, New Jersey: Jason Aronson Inc.

Elton Wilson, J. (1996). *Time Conscious Psychological Therapy, A Life Stage to Go Through*. London: Routledge.

Feldman, M. (1994). *Strategies for Interpreting Qualitative Data, Qualitative Research Methods Series 33* (October). London: Sage Publications.

Feltham, C. (1997a). Challenging the core theoretical model. *Counselling*, 5: 121–125.

Feltham, C. (1997). *Time Limited Counselling*. London: Sage Publications.

Feltham, C., & Dryden, W. (1993). *Dictionary of Counselling*. London: Whurr Publishers.

Ferenczi, S. (1919, 1920). The further development of an active therapy in psychoanalysis. In: *Further Contributions to the Theory and Technique of Psychoanalysis*. London: Hogarth Press, 1950.

Ferrucci, P. (1982). *What We May Be, The Visions and Techniques of Psychosynthesis*. Northamptonshire: Turnstone Press.

Fowler, H. W., & Fowler, F. G. (1964). *The Concise Oxford Dictionary of Current English*. Oxford: Clarendon Press.

Frankl, V. (1982). *Man's Search for Meaning—an Introduction to Logotherapy*. London: Hodder and Stoughton.

Freud, S. (1991, 1955). Case history II from the history of an infantile neurosis (the 'wolf man'), (1918,(1914)). In: A. Richards (Ed.), *Vol XVII in Case Histories II*. London: Penguin Books.

Garfield, S. (1989). *The Practice of Brief Psychotherapy*. New York: Pergamon Press.

George, E., Iveson, C., & Ratner, H. (1970). *Problem to Solutions, Brief Therapy with Individuals and Families*. London: B.T. Press.

Gilligan, S. (1990). Preface, brief therapy, myths and metaphors. In: J. Zeig & S. Gilligan (Eds), *Brief Therapy, Myths, Methods and Metaphors*. New York: Brunner/Mazel.

Goffman, E. (1991). *Asylums*. London: Penguin Books.

Goulding McClure, M. (1990). Getting the important work done fast. Contract plus redecision. In: J. Zeig & S. Gilligan (Eds), *Brief Therapy, Myths, Methods and Metaphors*. New York: Brunner/Mazel.

Greenberg, L. (1994). The investigation of change; its measurement and explanation. In: R. Russell (Ed.), *Reassessing Psychotherapy Research*. New York: The Guilford Press.

Groves, J. (1992). *The Short-Term Dynamic Psychotherapies: An Overview in Psychotherapy for the 1990s*, J. S. Rutan (Ed.). London: The Guilford Press.

Guntrip, H. (1991, 1971). *Psychoanalytic Theory, Therapy and the Self*. London: Karnac.

Gustafson, J. P. (1981). The complex secret of brief psychotherapy in the words of Malan and Balint. In: S. Budman (Ed.), *Forms of Brief Psychotherapy*. New York: The Guilford Press.

Gustafson, J. P. (1984). An integration of brief dynamic psychotherapy. *American Journal of Psychiatry*, 141(8): 935–944.

Gustafson, J. P. (1986). *The Complex Secret of Brief Psychotherapy*. New York: Norton, W. & Company.

Gustafson, J. P. (1990). The great simplifying conventions of brief individual psychotherapy. In: J. Zeig and S. Gilligan (Eds), *Brief Therapy, Myths, Methods and Metaphors*. New York: Brunner/Mazel.

Havens, L. (1976). *Participant Observation*. New Jersey: Jason Aronson.

Held, B. (1984). Towards a strategic eclecticism: a proposal. *Psychotherapy*, 21(2): 232–241.

Henry, W., Strupp, H., Butler, S., Scacht, T., & Binder, J. (1993). Effects of training in time—limited dynamic psychotherapy: changes in therapist behaviour. *Journal of Consulting and Clinical Psychology*, 61(3): 434–440.

Heron, J. (1981). Philosophical basis for a new paradigm. In: P. Reason & J. Rowan (Eds), *Human Inquiry—A Source Book of New Paradigm Research*. Chichester: John Wiley & Sons.

Hill, C. (1989). *Therapist Techniques and Client Outcomes. Eight cases of Brief Psychotherapy*. Newbury Park, California: Sage Publications.

Hoch, P. (1965). Short-term versus long-term therapy. In: L. Wolberg (Ed.), *Short-Term Psychotherapy*. New York: Grune and Stratton.

Hoyt, M. (Ed.) (1995). *Brief Therapy and Managed Care. Readings for Contemporary Practice*. San Francisco: Jossey-Bass Publishers.

Hoyt, M., Rosenbaum, R., & Talmon, M. (1992). Planned single session psychotherapy. In: S. Budman, M. Hoyt & S. Friedman

(Eds), *The First Session in Brief Therapy*. New York: The Guilford Press.

Jones, D. (Ed.) (1994). *Innovative Therapy. A Handbook*. Buckingham: Open University Press.

Jung, C. G. (1993, 1937). *The Practice of Psychotherapy, Volume 16, Essays on the Psychology of the Transference and Other Subjects*. London: Routledge.

Kalpin, A. (1993). The use of time in intensive short-term dynamic psychotherapy. *International Journal of Short-Term Psychotherapy*, 8/ 2(4): 75–91.

Kalpin, A. (1994). Effective use of Davanloo's head-on collision. *International Journal of Short-Term Psychotherapy*, 9(1): 19–36.

Klagsbrun, J., & Brown, D. (1984). Getting the picture: the use of imagery to clarify therapeutic impasses. *Psychotherapy*, 21(2): 254–259.

Konzelmann, C. (1995). Head-on collision with resistance against emotional closeness in intensive short-term dynamic psychotherapy. *International Journal of Short-term Psychotherapy*, 10: 35–51.

Kovacs, A. (1982). Survival in the 1980s. On the theory and practice of brief psychotherapy. *Psychotherapy: Theory, Research and Practice*, 19(2): 142–159.

Laikin, M., Winston, A., & McCullough, L. (1991). Intensive short-term dynamic psychotherapy. In: P. Crits-Christoph & J. Barber (Eds), *Handbook of Short-Term Dynamic Psychotherapy*. USA: Basic Books.

Lazurus, A., & Fay, A. (1990). Brief psychotherapy: tautology or oxymoron. In: J. Zeig & S. Gilligan (Eds), *Brief Therapy, Myths, Methods and Metaphors*. New York: Brunner/Mazel.

Levey, K. (1995). Single session solutions. In: M. Hoyt (Ed.), *Brief Therapy and Managed Care, Readings for Contemporary Practice*. San Francisco: Jossey-Bass Publishers.

Lincoln, Y. (1995). Emerging criteria for qualitative and interpretative research. In: *Qualitative Inquiry* (I, No 3: 275–289). London: Sage Publications.

Luborsky, L., & Mark, D. (1991). Short-term support expressive psychoanalytic psychotherapy. In: P. Crits-Christoph & J. Barber (Eds), *Handbook of Short-Term Dynamic Psychotherapy*. USA: Basic Books.

Lynch, G. (1996). What is truth? A philosophical introduction to counselling research. *Counselling*, May: 144–148.

Macnab, F. (1993). *Brief Psychotherapy, An Integrative Approach to Clinical Practice*. Chichester: John Wiley & Sons.

Magnavita, J. (1993). The evolution of short-term dynamic psychother-apy: treatment of the future? *Professional Psychology: Research and Practice*, 24(3): 360–365.

Magnavita, J. (1994). Premature termination of short-term dynamic psychotherapy. *International Journal of Short-term Psychotherapy*, 9: 213–228.

Malan, D. (1963). *A Study of Brief Psychotherapy*. London: Tavistock Publications, Charles Thomas, Publisher.

Malan, D. (1976) *The Frontier of Brief Psychotherapy, An Example of the Convergence of Research and Practice*. New York: Plenum Publishing Corporation, Plenum Medical Book Company.

Malan, D. (1979). *Individual Psychotherapy and the Science of Psychody-namics*. Oxford: Butterworth-Heinemann, 1995.

Malan, D. (1992). The most important development in psychotherapy since the discovery of the unconscious. In: H. Davanloo (Ed.), *Short-Term Dynamic Psychotherapy*. Northvale, New Jersey: Jason Aronson.

Malan, D., & Osimo, F. (1992). *Psychodynamics Training and Outcome in Brief Psychotherapy*. Oxford: Butterworth Heinemann.

Mann, J. (1973). *Time Limited Psychotherapy*. Massachusetts: Harvard University Press.

Mann, J. (1981). The case of time limited psychotherapy: time and the central issue. In: S. Budman (Ed.), *Forms of Brief Therapy*. New York: The Guilford Press.

Mann, J. (1991). Time limited psychotherapy. In: P. Crits-Christoph & J. Barber (Eds), *Handbook of Short-Term Dynamic Psychotherapy*. USA: Basic Books.

Mann, J., & Goldman, R. (1994). *A Casebook in Time Limited Psychotherapy*. Northvale, New Jersey: Jason Aronson.

Marmor, J. (1979). Short-term dynamic psychotherapy. *The American Journal of Psychiatry*, 136(2): 149–155.

Marmor, J. (1980). Historical roots. In: H. Davanloo (Ed.), *Short-Term Dynamic Psychotherapy*. Northvale, New Jersey: Jason Aronson.

Marshall, J. (1981). Making sense as a personal process. In: P. Reason & J. Rowan (Eds), *Human Inquiry—A Source Book of New Paradigm Research*. Chichester: John Wiley & Sons.

Marteau, L. (1986). *Existential Short-Term Therapy*. London: The Dympna Centre.

Maslow, A. (1981). The psychology of science: editorial appreciation. In: P. Reason & J. Rowan (Eds), *Human Inquiry—A Source Book of New Paradigm Research*. Chichester: John Wiley & Sons.

McCall, R. (1983). *Phenomenological Psychology*. USA: The University of Wisconsin Press.

McLeod, J. (1994). *Doing Counselling Research*. London: Sage Publications.

McMahon Moughtin, K. (1997). *Focused Therapy for Organisations and Individuals*. London: Minerva Press.

Migone, P. (1985). Short-term dynamic psychotherapy from a psycho-analytic viewpoint. Paper presented at a Meeting of the Society of Medical Psychoanalysts, New York, Nov 10, (1982), *Psychoanalytic Review*, 72(4): 615–633.

Mitroff, I. (1981). The subjective side of science; editorial appreciation. In: P. Reason & J. Rowan (Eds), *Human Inquiry—A Source Book of New Paradigm Research*. Chichester: John Wiley & Sons.

Molnos, A. (1986). Anger that destroys and anger that heals: handling hostility in group analysis and in dynamic brief psychotherapy. *Group Analysis* (Volume 19, pp. 207–221). London: Sage Publications.

Molnos, A. (1995). *A Question of Time, Essentials of Brief Psychotherapy*. London: Karnac Books.

Morse, J. (Ed.) (1992). If you believe in theories. In: *Qualitative Health Research*, 2, No. 3 (Volume 8, pp. 257–261). London: Sage Publications.

Moustakas, C. (1981). Heuristic research. In: P. Reason & J. Rowan (Eds), *Human Inquiry—A Source Book of New Paradigm Research*. Chichester: John Wiley and Sons.

Murphy, J., John, M., & Brown, H. (Eds.) (1984). *Dialogues and Debates in Social Psychology*. London: Lawrence Erlbaum Associates, The Open University.

Nelson-Jones, R. (1994). *The Theory and Practice of Counselling Psychology*. London: Cassell.

Norcross, J., & Grencavage, L. (1989). Eclecticism and integration in counselling and psychotherapy: major themes and obstacles. *British Journal of Guidance and Counselling*, 17/3(8): 97–124.

Orlinsky, D., & Russell, R. (1994). Tradition and change in psychother-apy research, notes on the fourth generation. In: R. Russell (Ed.), *Reassessing Psychotherapy Research*. New York: The Guilford Press.

Osimo, F. (1994). Method, personality and training in short-term psychotherapy. *International Journal of Short-term Psychotherapy*, 9: 173–187.

Polanyi, M. (1974). *Personal Knowledge. Towards a Post-Critical Philosophy*. USA: The Universisty of Chicago Press.

Pollack, J., Flegheimer, W., & and Winston, A. (1991). Brief adaptive psychotherapy. In: P. Crits-Christoph & J. Barber (Eds), *Handbook of Short-Term Dynamic Psychotherapy*. USA: Basic Books.

Polster, E. (1990). Tight therapeutic sequences. In: J. Zeig & S. Gilligan (Eds), *Brief Therapy, Myths, Methods and Metaphors*. New York: Brunner/Mazel.

Rabkin, R. (1977). *Strategic Psychotherapy—Brief and Symptomatic Treatment*. New York: Basic Books.

Rasmussen, A., & Messer, S. (1986). A comparison and critique of Mann's time limited psychotherapy and Davanloo's short-term dynamic psychotherapy. *Bulletin of the Menninger Clinic*, 50(2): 163–184.

Rawson, P. (1990). *Parables*. London: FASTPACE.

Rawson, P. (1992). Focal and short-term therapy is a treatment of choice. *Counselling*, (5): 106–107.

Rawson, P. (1995). By mutual arrangement. *Counselling News*, (6): 8–9.

Rawson, P. (1996). *FASTPACE Training Manual*. London: FASTPACE.

Reason, P., & Rowan, J. (1981). *Human Inquiry—A Source Book of New Paradigm Research*. Chichester: John Wiley and Sons.

Reich, J., & Neenan, P. (1986). Principles common to different short-term psychotherapies. *American Journal of Psychotherapy*, XL/1(1): 62–69.

Rennie, D., Phillips, J., & Quartaro, G. (1988). Grounded theory: a promising approach to conceptualisation in psychology. *Canadian Psychology*, 29: 2.

Roberts, J. (1992). Time limited counselling. *Psychodynamic Counselling*, 1.1.(10): 93–105.

Rogawski, A. (1982). Current status of brief psychotherapy. Taken from a paper at the 3rd Annual Vail Psychiatry Conference: *The Art of Psychotherapy*, The Menninger Foundation Vail, Colorado, (1981). *Bulletin of the Menninger Clinic*, 1982, 46(4): 331–351.

Rosenbaum, R., & Talmon, M. (1995). The challenge of single session therapies creating pivotal movements. In: M. Hoyt (Ed.), *Brief Therapy and Managed Care, Readings for Contemporary Practice*. San Francisco: Jossey-Bass Publishers.

Rowan, J., & Reason, P. (Eds) (1981). *Human Inquiry—A Source Book of New Paradigm Research*. Chichester: John Wiley and Sons.

Russell, R. (Ed.) (1994). *Reassessing Psychotherapy Research*. New York: The Guilford Press.

Rutan, J. S. (Ed.) (1992). *Psychotherapy for the 1990s*. New York: The Guilford Press.

Ryle, A., with contributions from Poynton, A., & Brockman, B. (1990). *Cognitive—Analytic Therapy: Active Participation in Change A new Integration in Brief Psychotherapy*. Chichester: John Wiley and Sons.

Said, T. (1990). The process of working through in intensive short-term dynamic psychotherapy. *International Journal of Short-term Dynamic Psychotherapy*, 5: 247–276.

Sandler, J. (Ed.) (1989). *Projection, Identification, Projective Identification*. London: Karnac Books.

Sapsford, R., Dallos, R., & Proctor, H. (1984) *Creating a Social World*. London: The Open University Press.

Selvini-Palazzoli, M., Boscolo, L., Cecchin, G. *et al.* (1978). *Paradox and Counterparadox*. New Jersey: Jason Aronson.

Shefler, G. (1988) Application of basic psychoanalytic clinical concepts in short-term dynamic psychotherapy. *1st J. Psychiatry Relat. Sci*, 25(3–4): 203–211.

Sifneos, P. (1979). *Short-Term Dynamic Psychotherapy Evaluation and Technique*. New York: Plenum Medical Book Company.

Sifneos, P. (1981). Short-term anxiety provoking psychotherapy. Its history, technique, outcome and instruction. In: S. Budman (Ed.), *Forms of Brief Therapy*. New York: The Guilford Press.

Sifneos, P. (1984). The current status of individual short-term dynamic psychotherapy and its future: an overview. *American Journal of Psychotherapy*, 38/(10): 472–483.

Sifneos, P. (1992). *Short-term Anxiety—Provoking Psychotherapy: A Treatment Manual*. USA: Basic Books, Harper Collins.

Sifneos, P., Apfel, R., Bassuk, E., Fishman, G., & Gill, A. (1980). Ongoing outcome research on short-term dynamic psychotherapy, *Psychotherapy and Psychosomatics*, 33: 233–241.

Sperry, L. (1987) ERIC: A cognitive map for guiding brief therapy and health care counselling. *Individual Psychology*, 43/2(6): 237–241.

Spinelli, E. (1989). *The Interpreted World—An Introduction to Phenomenological Psychology*. London: Sage Publications.

Stevens, R. (1983). *Freud and Psychoanalysis, An Exhibition and Appraisal*. Milton Keynes: The Open University Press.

Stevens, R. (1984). *Social Psychology: Development, Experience and Behaviour in a Social World*. Milton Keynes: The Open University Press.

Storr, A. (1979). *The Art of Psychotherapy*. London: M. Secker and Warburg Ltd., & William Heineman Medical Books.

Storr, A. (1988). *Jung's Selected Writings*. London: Fontana Books.

Strupp, H. (1980). Success and failure in time limited psychotherapy. Further evidence. *Archives of General Psychiatry*, 37(8): 947–954.

Strupp, H. (1986). Toward the refinement of time limited dynamic psychotherapy. In: S. Budman (Ed.), *Forms of Brief Therapy*. New York: The Guilford Press.

Strupp, H., & Hadley, S. W. (1979). Specific and non-specific factors in psychotherapy. A controlled study of outcome. *Archives of General Psychiatry*, 36(10): 1125–1136.

Strupp, H., & Binder, J. (1983). Time Limited Dynamic Psychotherapy (TLDP), a treatment manual. In: Recent Developments in the Care, Treatment and Rehabilitation of the Mentally Ill in Italy, Mosler. *Hospital & Community Psychiatry*, 34(10): 941.

Svartberg, M., & Stiles, T. (1992). Predicting patient change from therapist competence and patient therapist complementarity in short-term anxiety-provoking psychotherapy: a pilot study. *Journal of Consulting and Clinical Psychology*, 60(2): 304–307.

Svartberg, M., & Stiles, T. (1994). Therapeutic alliance, therapist competence, and client change in short-term anxiety-provoking psychotherapy. *Psychotherapy Research*, 4(1): 20–33.

Toukmanian, S., & Rennie, D. (Eds.) (1992). *Psychotherapy Process Research—Paradigmatic and Narrative Approaches*. California, USA: Sage Publications.

Van Deurzen-Smith, E. (1988). *Existential Counselling in Practice*. London: Sage Publications.

Van Kaam, A. (1970). *On Being Involved, The Rythm of Involvement and Detachment in Daily Life*. Denville, New Jersey: Dimension Books.

Van Londen, J, (1981). Short-term psychotherapy, a major development for patients and psychotherapy. *Psychotherapy and Psychosomatics*, 35: 221–223.

Wells, R., & Gianetti, V. (Eds.) (1993). *Casebook of the Brief Psychotherapies*. New York: Plenum Press.

Westen, D. (1986). What changes in short-term psychodynamic psychotherapy? *Psychotherapy*, 23(4) Winter: 501–512.

Whitmore, D. (1995). *New Directions in Counselling, a Round Table*, I. Horton, R. Bayne & J. Bimrose (Eds), *Counselling*, 6(1) Feb: 34–40.

Winokur, M., & Dasberg, H. (1983). Teaching and learning short-term psychotherapy: techniques and resistances. *Bulletin of the Menninger Clinic*, 47(1): 36–52.

Wolberg, L. (Ed.) (1965). *The Technique of Short-Term Psychotherapy*. New York: Grune and Stratton.

Wolberg, L. (1980). *Handbook of Short-Term Psychotherapy.* New York: Thieme—Stratton.

Wolcott, H. (1990). *Qualitative Research Methods,* Series 20. California: Sage Publications.

Woolfe, R. (1995). *New Directions in Counselling, a Round Table,* I. Horton, R. Bayne & J. Bimrose (Eds), *Counselling,* 6(1) Feb: 34–40.

Yalom, I. (1980, 1931). *Existential Psychotherapy,* USA: Basic Books, & Harper Collins.

Yin, R. (1994). *Case Study Research—Design and Methods.* California: Sage Publications.

Zeig, J. (1990). Seeding. In: J. Zeig & S. Gilligan (Eds), *Brief Therapy, Myths, Methods and Metaphors.* New York: Brunner/Mazel.

INDEX

293